STORMING THE MILLENNIUM
THE NEW POLITICS OF CHANGE

Lawrence & Wishart Limited
99a Wallis Road
London E9 5LN

First published 1999

British Library Cataloguing in Publication data.
A catalogue record for this book is available from the
British Library.

ISBN 0 85315 873 8

Photoset in North Wales by
Derek Doyle & Associates, Mold, Flintshire.
Printed and bound in Great Britain by
Redwood Books Limited, Trowbridge

STORMING THE MILLENNIUM
THE NEW POLITICS OF CHANGE

Edited by
Tim Jordan and Adam Lent

Lawrence & Wishart
LONDON

Notes on contributors

Pam Alldred researches identity and political rhetoric in relation to parents. She currently divides her energy between teaching women's and psychosocial studies and eco/anarcho/feminist activism.

Peter Beresford has written extensively on welfare policy and on the rights of disabled people and survivors of the psychiatric system. He is an active campaigner within these areas.

Tessa Bird is an activist with Reclaim the Streets.

Patrick Field has written extensively on environmental issues and movements and campaigns actively in these areas.

Tony Fitzpatrick is Lecturer in Social Policy at the University of Luton. He is currently writing a book on welfare policy entitled *Freedom and Security* which is due for publication in 1999.

Shirin Housee is presently senior lecturer in the Sociology Department at the University of Wolverhampton. She has published in the areas of 'race', racism, gender inequalities and 'identity'.

Rupa Huq has researched youth culture at the University of East London Cultural Studies Department. Her publications include book chapters and articles on the politics of pop and second generation Asian youth cultural process.

Tim Jordan works in the Sociology Department at the University of East London and is a co-director of the New Politics Research Group, He is the author of *Cyberpower: The Culture of Politics and Cyberspace and the Internet* (Routledge, 1998) and *Reinventing Revolution: Value and Difference in New Social Movements and the Left* (Avebury, 1994).

Adam Lent is currently writing *Sex, Colour, Peace and Power: Movements of Rebellion in Britain Since the 1960s* to be published by Macmillan in 2000. He recently edited *New Political Thought: An Introduction,* published by Lawrence and Wishart in 1998.

Sanjay Sharma works in the Department of Media and Cultural studies at the University of Staffordshire. He is a co-editor of the book *Dis-Orienting Rhythms: The politics of the New Asian Dance Music* (Zed Books, 1996).

Merl Storr lectures in Sociology at the University of East London. She has published a number of articles on sexual politics and sexual identity. She is co-editor of *The Bisexual Imaginary* (Cassell, 1997) and editor of *Bisexuality: A Critical Reader* (Routledge, forthcoming 1999).

Contents

THE HARDEST QUESTION: AN INTRODUCTION TO THE NEW POLITICS OF CHANGE

Tim Jordan

> *Hope is what you say and do.*
> M.Oil

A NEW POLITICS OF CHANGE

The times are always right for change: new radicalism, new hopes, new politics of change are with us now. Neither the nostalgia of the left, those old bearers of hope, for the times when it knew the correct line, nor the arrogant insecurity of a right that simultaneously declares the grass roots dead while fearing its demands, can alter the fact that new forces for change have coalesced into a new politics. This did not begin yesterday: our roots are in civil rights movements, anti-colonial movements, the New Left and feminist movements. And, although it has taken some time to be certain it would not evaporate, a new politics of change is here. We might tip our hats to ideas and organisations past but we know we are our own politics now. A new politics of change is the only effective force for grabbing social structures and transforming them so that the vast majority of people can one day be liberated and unexploited. 'Now' is always a good time to stand up and fight for your life: *Storming the Millennium* tries to show that many are doing just that, and tries to understand what it means.

What do ravers, the disabled, bisexuals, anti-roads campaigners, cyberactivists, and anti-racists have in common? And what do these six movements, all studied in this book, have in common with women struggling to redistribute society's resources, with people saving animals, with those resisting downsizing, flexible work practices, part-timeism, redundancy, rejection and decay? And where do all of these fit with those, cited in the final chapter, who still make a good case for worrying about the word 'socialism'? We argue that they all fit together as part of the new politics of change.

1

Yet these hopes, these renewed desires – backed by action – for a different world, also pose many questions. Has politics changed? Have the words, organisations, actions, signs and passions that have fuelled and informed the many desires to remake our world changed? And if they have changed, as indicated by, for example, the end of the cold war, a resurgence of non-violent direct action, the revision of political history, then we are left with more hard questions. Whatever relief comes from realising that radical, grass-roots social action is more vibrant than ever, it is immediately accompanied by questions about the meaning of this action. Take the word 'radical' itself. Once it might have been assumed that talking about radical politics meant talking about 'harder' left politics, perhaps the extra-parliamentary or anarchist left, but in the last twenty years most radical change in Western societies has been driven by the right. The left, paradoxically, has found itself defending and conserving gains it once thought untouchable. Then, when we had only just become used to 'radical' being the 'right', the prime minister of the United Kingdom and the President of the United States stood together in 1997 and declared themselves for the 'radical centre'. It is no longer clear at all what being a radical means.

This is the hardest question that new politics poses. Not, 'is there radical politics?', but, 'what would it mean to storm the millennium?' Here is the challenge of new politics in its transformatory sense: the field of radical, emancipatory political action has been torn apart and remade in the last thirty years. The emphasis of this collection is not on the emergence of 'social movements' – as if social movements have not always dotted the political landscape from the Levellers and Diggers in the seventeenth century to the Chiapas in the late twentieth – but on a configuration of the political field that is different from the one that dominated the post-Second World War period. This is not a total break. A reinvigorated non-violent direct action movement carries with it a history that reaches back at least to many post-war anti-colonial struggles and to the United States civil rights movement, both of the 1950s. In addition, the feminist movement that began in the 1960s, second wave feminism, and the emergence of the New Left in the late 1950s are crucial to the development of new politics. The fracturing of a certain way of conducting politics began with these four struggles. The old way of negotiating political solutions had become dominant after World War Two and had at its heart negotiations between capital and labour. The Keynesian (corporate) state of the post-Second World War period in the overdeveloped nations ensured that politics was ordered between these two great antagonists: capital and labour. This arrangement was fought for not only by liberal capitalists such as Keynes and his followers, but also by labour movements bargaining for higher wages and better conditions. This is no doubt something of a caricature, with enough complexities to be argued over in great detail, but it is also accurate enough to define the typical political conflicts that new politics has disturbed.[1]

What followed the 1960s and 1970s was not only the intensification of the four political movements already mentioned, but also a prolonged crisis and restructuring of socio-economies on a global scale that is only now beginning to look as if it may have settled into recurring patterns. From the oil shocks of the 1970s, when hyper-inflation and economic chaos beckoned the West, to the collapse of the Soviet Union and the end of the Cold War, world-wide human society changed. Always at work, within many other changes, were changes within the field of radical politics. A different politics should not be read solely as the result (or epiphenomenon) of a great capitalist restructuring – even though that may be partly true – but also as a cause of change. Tianamen Square and the collapse of the Soviet Union posed almost unanswerable questions to Marxist radicals who have consistently sought either to lead new political movements or to integrate them within what they hoped would be a newly radicalised labour movement. As argued in many places, the Marxist, or more broadly the class or labour-centred, paradigm for radical politics has been broken.[2] Settled ways of understanding and negotiating politics have changed not only between left and right, but within left and right.

The result of these changes has been the emergence of a new paradigm of radical politics which this collection attempts to outline and develop. Looking over our shoulder to the struggles of the 1950s that were refusing to bury all politics except the negotiations between capital and labour, we can see where this new paradigm began. We can see prophets such as Frantz Fanon or Simone de Beauvoir, who couldn't know that their work would ultimately help to undermine a framework for politics which they also helped establish. It is only now that we can for certain see a new paradigm for liberation and can feel, as much as know, that a new politics of change is here. *Storming the Millennium* sets out to chronicle this new politics, its practices and its theories, and to contribute to it by helping to explore its nature. However, even if we know that this politics has arrived, we are less certain what it means. We are less certain what it is to liberate and be liberated. The hardest question new politics poses is not if it exists or if it will succeed or fail, but what it means. Here, just after the dawn of a new paradigm of radical political emancipation, we are drawing breath to ask this hardest question and to name the new politics of change.

THE FIELD OF NEW POLITICAL THOUGHT

No thought exists in a vacuum; it is always connected to other ideas and to concrete manifestations in organisations and books, journals and libraries. The thoughts that have just been outlined, that inform this collection, exist within a three-fold field of intellectual endeavour and a wider field of ongoing political activism. The field of political activism is indicated by the empirical accounts of movements contained in chapters two to six; in the remainder of this chapter the intellectual context will be briefly outlined. Intellectual efforts have been underway for some time to come to grips with new politics, though it is often not called this, and these efforts can be characterised in three ways: rethinking politics and difference, rethinking collective action and new social movements, and historical studies. These three areas can be seen as separate but interrelated and consist of two mainly theoretical and one mainly empirical approach that, taken together, constitute studies of new politics. For clarity and convenience they will be treated in turn.[3]

A number of intellectuals have discussed questions of difference and its effects on radical liberatory politics. As the assumption – if never the actuality – of a single framework within which different radical politics would be reconciled faded, some theorists became devoted to working out the consequences of such a change. Stuart Hall notes that this poses 'a different kind of political problem from the one that you would have if you imagined it [oppression] all came from one place, because if it all comes from one place then your politics is to blast that one place out of existence and everything else will change.'[4] A number of thinkers have approached this different kind of problem. Each has tried to develop an understanding of what politics means when a unified framework is not assumed. Three distinct areas of work have emerged, creating a connected though uncoordinated set of ideas. These are: political theories, post-structural theories, and theories of a new democracy. Of course, the thinkers do not work in isolation from each other or from activism, but for the purposes of a brief summary they can be categorised in this way.

A number of theorists have confronted classical political theory with the problem of a multiplicity of politics. Most prominent here have been Iris Marion Young and William Connolly. Young's work has diligently explored the relationship between injustice and oppression, without assuming that either of these terms is singular.[5] Connolly's work is littered with the history of political theory: even (or perhaps especially) Augustine, Bishop of Hippo plays a role. Again, there is scrupulous attention to questions of good and evil and to the negotiation of political paradox, within a framework that takes the problem of difference as a foundation.[6] In addition to these two, numerous other intellectuals have attempted to reinterpret political theory in relation to radical politics on the assumption that difference is a constitutive element.[7]

From another direction, a number of thinkers have developed a politics of difference from within the intellectual movement that can broadly be labelled post-structuralist, including the related set of debates called postmodernism. Many could be mentioned in this context but the work of Deleuze and Guattari and the debates around postmodern feminism are emblematic. Deleuze and Guattari have elaborated an explicitly political theory of difference, in which the opposition between the one and the many is replaced with the assumption that everything is multiple. Highly allusive and elusive, intoxicated by language but also scrupulously realising all the consequences of beginning from the multiple, their theories make clear what a radical politics of difference might be.[8] The debate around the meaning of postmodernism within feminism provides a rethinking within one movement of the meaning of difference for political change. Here the more abstract forms of thought that have often been generated from within post-structuralism and postmodernism are subject to an inquisition for their political meaning in the context of the subordination of women.[9] Numerous other texts, thinkers and ideas could be introduced, for example the debate over the relevance of Michel Foucault's work to feminism would provide another avenue for this more general discussion.[10]

Finally, there is the debate around radical democracy. Undoubtedly the seminal work is Ernesto Laclau and Chantal Mouffe's, both together and separately.[11] Here the premise that the social and the political are fields that can never be closed or totalised within one understanding is related to the necessity of radicalising democracy. The shifts between political movements that are particular or specific, but that come to believe they are universal and then re-recognise their particularity, are understood as a field of politics that must be guaranteed by a radical democracy. The opportunity for all movements to participate in the political, and so the opportunity for all movements to realise their claims, is secured by new forms of democracy. These claims make democracy into something like the guarantor that the idea of difference is essential to any new form of politics.[12]

The various strands of thought that take up difference as a central problem in rethinking the nature of politics tend to coalesce around reconceptualisations of democracy and/or around developing the political consequences of post-structural and postmodern thought. Ideas that begin from a basis in classical political theory tend towards analyses of democracy, and Laclau and Mouffe's work relies heavily upon analyses from the post-structural tradition. Clear conclusions from this developing tradition of thought are not available, which is one reason why it continues to deserve attention. However new social and political theories, constituted at fundamental levels around concepts of difference and radicalised notions of democracy, are one result from this theoretical work. The consequences of new politics are, on the one hand, a range of theoretical resources with which the meaning of particular movements can be explored and, on the other, some admittedly abstract ideas about the nature of a field of politics within which no one movement or ideology is dominant or can encompass all other movements.

Another major area of work consists of theories of new politics developed out of ongoing empirical analyses of new social movements. Rather than beginning with difficult and abstract – though important – theoretical questions, this strand engages with the movements that have appeared, studies them empirically and tries to develop relevant concepts. In this context studies of anti-nuclear movements, of Solidarity in Poland, of youth movements in Italy, and more, have been developed.[13] Two key areas of this work have emerged: new politics as middle-class radicalism and new understandings of collective action.

One of these areas has been around the influence which members of the middle class have on new political movements. It has been argued that most movements have a proportion of members who, being middle-class, have significant financial and intellectual resources to bring to politics. New political movements are here re-interpreted within a class framework and deradicalised when they are understood as attempts by the middle-class to attain its goals irrespective of the effect on others. A number of theorists, in particular Eder and

Inglehart, have developed general theories of new movements which emphasise middle-class radicalism.[14] Undoubtedly the middle class and the resources its members command have been important to a number of new political movements. Newspaper reports often note, in a tone of hurt surprise, that protests are created not only by anarchist outcasts but by respectable professionals as well. However the reduction of new politics to middle class radicalism seems both an attempt to rescue class as the dominant framework for understanding political action and a narrow interpretation of social movements. The breadth and commitment of new political movements, and the importance of a new paradigm of politics, seem simply too strong to be reduced to a dismissal as middle-class.[15] This does not mean that much of this work is invalid, only that its strongest claim (that new politics is solely about middle-class radicalism) seems unsupportable.

The second area of work has been to develop theories of collective action that see new political movements not as single actors on a new political stage but as diverse networks of individuals, organisations and ideologies. These theories develop plural understandings of social movements by analysing the ways individuals coalesce their actions into collective action. This approach has generated fascinating and complex theoretical structures that, by taking the actions which movements themselves generate as the starting point, do not reduce new politics to existing political or sociological theories. The work of Alain Touraine, both empirically and theoretically, opened a path here that Alberto Melucci has particularly developed.[16] Other work in this area has come from a number of sources, perhaps most notably Michel Maffesoli's development of a theory of 'tribes' within a polycultural politics and Barry Barnes's theory of collective action as the fundamental structuring force in society.[17] The common theme is the development of perspectives that begin from actions that members of movements take and then refuse to reify as collective action. Rather, actions and individuals exist in networks that spread throughout society, but may not be easily visible. Spectacular protests and mobilisations here become the public side of the commitments which new politics' activists are giving to dissident ways of life. In this way reductive understandings of new politics are avoided, as are over-enthusiastic readings which only seem to notice sensational actions and which ignore the social networks that make such actions possible.

The final major area of work on new politics is the generation of empirical studies of new politics. The chronicling, recording and archiving of movements is important for the role it plays in establishing the traditions of movements that often present themselves as entirely new. This work acts as a collective memory allowing, for example, Outrage activists to know what the Stonewall riots meant. Spectacular events that have a powerful grip on the imagination are here placed within historical contexts. The clearest example of this is a tendency among some theorists to see new politics as the result of the events of 1968 and, even more narrowly, the events in France of May 1968. By establishing connections to anti-colonial or civil rights struggles of the 1950s, it is possible to grasp exactly what is changing, and when it changed. Exemplary here is George McKay's study of British resistance and protest since the 1960s. His work makes particularly clear the importance of post-1960s festivals to ongoing radical protest.[18] Apart from McKay there seems to be no single author or tradition that is dominant, simply an ongoing accumulation of studies.[19]

The three key areas that have been outlined do not, of course, constitute the only contributors to this new political paradigm. Theories and organisations that have always been plural and that have refused to reduce radical politics to class politics need particular mention. Anarchism especially has been a major influence on much new politics.[20] Anarchism's long and honourable resistance to the more totalitarian tendencies of Leninism, and some anarchists' commitment to a politics that has many centres, only one of which is the labour movement, has provided both models and inspiration for new political activists. Along with the living traditions that have flowed into new politics, these three areas of difference and political theory, new social movement studies, and histories of political movements, have convincingly established that a new paradigm of politics has emerged and have provided first explorations of what might constitute that paradigm. This collection takes these developments forward, not by focusing specifically on these contributions but by developing case studies and theoretical conclusions that assist in our understandings of this new politics.

THE BOOK'S CONTENTS

Whatever anyone believes to be the 'real nature' of new politics, the fact that liberatory politics has undergone a transformation in the last thirty years is undeniable. To focus on developing new politics thus seems undoubtedly the right step. If the majority who have moved into new political forms, even unthinkingly, must continually fight for the legitimacy of their political paradigm, then they will never develop new politics but will remain prisoners of the past. There is value in further discussion and confrontation with the class-centred paradigm of radical liberatory politics, but this collection attempts to put any such discussion – for example the one with the editors of *Soundings* in chapter twelve – within a framework that centres on the meaning of new politics (and not the meaning of new politics for socialism). Further, this volume does not try to summarise the work, described in the previous section, that has helped to establish the intellectual context of new politics. The areas mentioned all appear in the following chapters, but there are no explicit attempts to, for example, summarise new social movement studies or define the current state of political theories of difference. *Storming the Millennium* aims to develop new politics by engaging directly with current movements and by elaborating theories in relation to specific questions. The aim is to build directly on top of present understandings of new politics and to outline the current situation, putting aside the interesting but long and complex task of defining how this situation came about. *Storming the Millennium* does this with two interrelated parts: accounts of new movements and reflections on new movements. Part 1 offers five case studies of five new political movements. Part 2 takes up a number of general reflections on the meaning of new politics.

In relation to movements we try to see how some of them have worked and what they have fought for. As reflections of new politics, the movements are a disparate group: ravers against repressive legislation; the United Kingdom disability movement; campaigns to turn society away from cars; the bisexual movement; and United States Internet civil rights activists. In Part 1 we will find party-goers whose distinctive style of celebration – the techno-based, ecstasy-driven rave – has been criminalised and attacked by the state, alongside a history of the increasing dominance of roads in London and the current tactics of direct action to prevent more roads being built. While ravers offer a familiar issue (protest against repressive legislation), they are not typical actors in radical politics (who could have foreseen a government that would name and criminalise a style of music – techno – and so recognise and attempt to repress a carnivalesque politics of pleasure and freedom?); and while ecological and anti-roads campaigners now seem familiar political actors, the tactics and actions they have developed mark them as a new phase in the history of non-violent direct action. As with ravers, the disabled and bisexuals appear as part of new political movements, while the subject of Internet activists' concerns, the Internet, has only existed since the early 1970s. Examining these five movements does not, however, lead to an easy definition of 'new politics' because difference as well as sameness can be found. The analysis of Internet activists leads to an ambiguity in that this movement is simultaneously arguing for grassroots or user interests but is also participating in the development of a new power élite. Such a combination need not be surprising, as élites sometimes develop social patterns that then become part of mass society. For example, many forms of consumption now taken for granted by most people in the over-developed countries were developed in the nineteenth century by the aristocracy and upper classes. However such a comparison raises questions about the meaning of Internet activism and its significance to new politics. Ravers might also be thought of as having been forcibly politicised rather than engaging in politics. If the UK government had simply left ravers to develop their pleasures, would any recognisable politics ever have emerged? Finally, if all five are taken together, the obvious question might not be what are the similarities and differences; rather, the question might be, are there any similarities?

That last question might lead to a common (mis)understanding of new politics. If the movements that make up new politics reflect a series of separate, disconnected and different concerns, then the only unity in the field of new politics is that it is single-issue politics. The broad understanding of new politics would then be very simple: radical politics would consist of separate issues, each with its associated political actors, and no further general theory would be needed. The simple response is that each of these politics affects everyone because they all concern not solely the disabled, bisexuals or Internet users, but everyone, because we are all abled, all have sexualities and all communicate. New political movements may all be single-issue movements, usually taken to mean relevant only to a minority, but they all address universal issues. Here questions arise that are explored in Part 2, where the broader implications of new political or social movements are examined.

Part 2 begins by extending the range of movements looked at through a case study of anti-racist politics in the context of a community's response to racist murders. The implications drawn from the organisation and negotiation of political identities such as black or Asian clearly have a broad significance beyond their importance to the particular struggle described by Sanjay Sharma and Shirin Housee.

An interview with Nancy Fraser follows, that explores the relationship between a politics of recognition or identity and a politics of redistribution. Fraser stresses the need to explore the distribution of material resources in addition to maintaining the gains of a general cultural politics that focuses on the generation of different political identities. Tim Jordan explores one of the questions posed by new politics – how we understand a political field in which a number of different but universal politics co-exist. Disability and sexuality are universals because we all have relationships based upon our varying abilities and sexuality. Tim takes up the problem of 'too many universals' and explores new definitions of liberation and exploitation that might help towards an understanding of new politics. The question of social policy in relation to new politics, of what demands on the state are relevant to new political movements, is a field too rarely explored. Tony Fitzpatrick begins to address this problem by examining the challenge which local, autonomous, wealth-creating intiatives (such as LET Schemes and Credit Unions) pose for traditional notions of welfare promoted, historically, by the left. Adam Lent looks more closely at the disputes within new politics, identifying a three-way division that has dogged campaigns for change throughout history and which, he argues, current movements will have difficulty avoiding. *Storming the Millennium* closes with an interview with the editors of the journal *Soundings*, founded to develop the legacy of the left and liberatory politics. Stuart Hall, Doreen Massey and Michael Rustin are long-standing activists and outstanding intellectuals and they explore how they see new politics. They discuss what is 'new' about new social movements and analyse the nature of activism, relations between intellectuals and activists within movements, what currency 'socialism' has or should have, and the difficulties facing new political movements.

New politics, in all its contradictory and glorious guises, can be found throughout these pages. Broad theoretical pictures are painted and specific empirical analyses are established. All of these contribute to the developing field of new politics. If radical forms of liberation are to survive the collapse of an old way of doing politics, then a new way of doing politics has to be recognised, explored and developed. Ways of being political that previously seemed of little importance now hold central lessons.

It now seems naïve to hope for a single cataclysmic struggle that will finally rid the world of exploitation. But hope has appeared for many cataclysms, each of which will, in its own way, re-order social relations that affect us all. Perhaps these several cataclysms will be less dramatic than the machismo of storming the barricades, and perhaps, even taken together, they won't constitute an entirely emancipated world, and perhaps there is no one utopia, only many utopias. But the time to change the world is now. It always will be, and the radicalism of the new millennium is in your hands.

NOTES

1. But not such a caricature as to be unsupported by many analyses. See M. Castells, *The Rise of the Network Society: The Information Age Volume 1*, Blackwell, Oxford 1996; S. Hall and M. Jaques (eds), *New Times: the changing face of politics in the 1990s*, Lawrence and Wishart, London 1989; D. Harvey, *The Condition of Postmodernity*, Blackwell, Oxford 1989.

2. See J. Pakulski, 'Social Movements and Class: the decline of the Marxist paradigm', in L. Maheu (ed), *Social Movements and Social Classes*, Sage, London 1995, pp55-86; E. Laclau, *New Reflections on the Revolution of Our Time*, Verso, London 1990; T. Jordan, *Reinventing Revolution: value and difference in new social movements and the left*, Avebury, Aldershot, 1994.

3. Of course the following summary cannot hope to be comprehensive, nor does it imply approval of those discussed.

4. Stuart Hall in chapter 12 of this volume.

5. I.M. Young, *Justice and the Politics of Difference*, Princeton University Press, Princeton, New Jersey 1990.

6. W. Connolly, *Identity\Difference: democratic negotiations of political paradox*, Cornell University Press, Ithaca, 1991.

7. See, for example, contributions in J. Squires (ed), *Principled Positions: postmodernism and the rediscovery of value*, Lawrence and Wishart, London 1993; and M. Perryman (ed), *Altered States: postmodernism, politics, culture*, Lawrence and Wishart, London 1994.

8. G. Deleuze, and F. Guattari, *Anti-Oedipus: capitalism and schizophrenia*, Viking, New York City 1972; *A Thousand Plateaus: capitalism and schizophrenia*, Athlone Press, London 1982; see T. Jordan, 'Collective Bodies: raving and the politics of Gilles Deleuze and Felix Guattari', *Body and Society*, 1 (1), 1995, pp125-44, for an analysis of the political consequences of Deleuze and Guattari's commitment to difference.

9. There are too many texts to name here; the seminal beginning point is L. Nicholson (ed), *Feminism/Postmodernism*, Routledge, London 1990.

10. L. McNay (ed), *Foucault and Feminism*, Polity, Cambridge 1992; C. Ramazanoglu (ed), *Up Against Foucault*, Routledge, London 1993.

11. E. Laclau, and C. Mouffe, *Hegemony and Socialist Strategy: towards a radical democratic politics*, Verso, London 1985; E. Laclau, *New Reflections on the Revolution of Our Time*, Verso, London 1990; E. Laclau, *Emancipation(s)*, Verso, London 1996; C. Mouffe, *The Return of the Political*, Verso, London 1993.

12. Jean-Francois Lyotard develops similar conclusions from within one of the most influential analyses of postmodernism. He argues that the incommensurability of different language games means that the only common political principle that can be justified within postmodernity is the right to participate in politics, and democracy appears to be the only clear means of ensuring that right. See T. Jordan, 'The Philosophical Politics of Jean-Francois Lyotard', *Philosophy of the Social Sciences*, 25(3), 1995, pp267-85.

13. The best introduction is M. Diani, 'The Concept of Social Movements', *Sociological Review*, 40(1), 1992, pp1-25; or L. Maheu (ed), *op.cit.*.

14. K. Eder, 'Does Social Class Matter in the Study of Social Movements?: a theory of middle class radicalism', in L. Maheu, *op.cit.*, pp55-86; R. Inglehart, *The Silent Revolution*, Princeton University Press, Princeton, New Jersey 1977.

15. See especially J. Pakulski, *op.cit.*, and any case study of a movement, including the case studies in this volume, for evidence of greater political significance than simply middle-class demands.

16. A. Touraine, *The Voice and the Eye: an analysis of social movements*, Cambridge University Press, Cambridge 1981; A. Touraine, F. Dubet, Z. Hegedus, and M.Wieviorka, *Anti-nuclear Protest: the opposition to nuclear energy in France*, Cambridge University Press, Cambridge 1983; A. Touraine, F. Dubet, M. Wieviorka, and J. Strzlecki, *Solidarity: Poland 1980-1981*, Cambridge University Press, Cambridge 1983; A. Melucci, *Challenging Codes: collective action in the information age*, Cambridge University Press, Cambridge 1996; *The Playing Self: person and meaning in the planetary society*, Cambridge University Press, Cambridge 1996. See also L. Maheu (ed), *op.cit.*

17. M. Maffesoli, *The Time of the Tribes: the decline of individualism in mass society*, Sage, London 1996; B. Barnes, *The Elements of Social Theory*, UCL Press, London 1995.

18. G. McKay, *Senseless Acts of Beauty: cultures of resistance since the sixties*, Verso, London 1996.

19. For example, see P. Bagguley, 'Protest, Power and Poverty: a case study of the anti-poll tax movement', *Sociological Review*, 43(4), 1995, pp693-719; or S.

Evans, *Personal Politics: the roots of women's liberation in the civil rights movement and the new left*, Vintage, New York 1980.
20. For example, see G.McKay, *op.cit.*, chapter 3.

THE RIGHT TO RAVE: OPPOSITION TO THE CRIMINAL JUSTICE AND PUBLIC ORDER ACT 1994

Rupa Huq

INTRODUCTION[1]

The Criminal Justice and Public Order Act 1994, after numerous false starts, finally became law on 3 November of the same year to a chorus of disapproval from various sections of British society. This chapter examines the legislation's impact on one such group, the 'rave community', and draws on my own involvement throughout 1994 with Advance Party, a group of rave-goers and free party organisers formed in opposition to the contents of the Act in its earlier form as the Criminal Justice Bill. Will the events have lasting results or will they fade from memory as quickly as they seemed to occur?

RAVE VS THE CRIMINAL JUSTICE AND PUBLIC ORDER ACT 1994

The mass mobilisations of ravers, against the introduction of laws that threatened to criminalise their lifestyle, played an important part in the wave of mid-1990s non violent direct action, which was on a scale unseen in the UK for some years, and raises important questions about changing notions of politics, youth culture, new alliances and ideology in the 1990s. In order to examine these further an understanding of the roots of rave is important.

Numerous clichés have attached themselves to 1990s youth. The cohort variously labelled as the 'slackers' or 'Generation X' in the US and 'Thatcher's children' in the UK were born too late for the golden years of the subcultural explosion of the 1960s and 1970s, and also missed out on the 1980s boom. Consistently suffering the consequences of the Conservative 'rolling back' of the welfare state – social policy from a party whose leader had claimed that there is no such thing as society[2] – by the mid-1990s popular wisdom dictated that this was a dispossessed and alienated generation. Even the usual healthy characteristic of risk-taking that we have come to accept as part of being young seemed to be in disconcertingly short supply. AIDS signalled constraints on free love given that casual sex now carries a potential death sentence. That one-time barometer of youth consciousness, the political demonstration, was conspicuous by its absence; the 1990s meagre efforts (eg mobilisations over the naked self-interest of student grants) underline the passing of the 1968 spirit. Vietnam is over and Bosnia is too complex an issue to grapple with compared to the computer games in which today's young find solace, such as the appropriately titled 'Doom'.

For their addition to the great British youth culture collection, the 1980s and early 1990s bequeathed us 'rave', which has been interpreted by some as entirely appropriate for this so-called ideologically void generation. Unlike some of its spectacular subcultural antecedents, rave's 'come as you are' dress code carries no strongly identifiable subcultural style. Rejecting idealist chants of subcultural antecedents, such as 'all you need is love' (hippie), or 'anarchy in the UK' (punk), the nearest rave has to a slogan is simply 'on one' – the affirmation of having taken an Ecstasy tablet. E, as it is more commonly called, is the subculture's drug of choice. E shapes many of the subculture's rituals (baggy clothing as the uniform and bottled water as the raver's drink are both necessitated by ecstasy's dehydrating properties). Rave's ideology rejects idealism for hedonism in the clouds. 'Techno', its electronically processed music, has a name that appears to suggest the value of technical expertise over all the other qualities that we have come to recognise as essential to music and the song in the twentieth century: passion, authenticity and soul. Interestingly the term 'rave', used here for reasons of convenience, is disliked by many involved who prefer the expression 'party'. Yet techno's alleged impersonality is belied by the sociability of the dance and of sound systems (teams of DJs that play together). The square root of rave was always the pleasure of the dance. Perhaps this can be seen as a realistic response to 1990s harsh circumstances. Steve Redhead calls it 'hedonism in hard times'.[3] Rave had never in its wildest E-induced dreams dabbled in what we have come conventionally to recognise as politics,[4] until the Criminal Justice Bill.

By the mid-1990s rave was still central to UK youth culture, demonstrating an impressive lasting power dating from at least acid house and the 'second summer of love' of 1988. However, noticeable changes had occurred throughout this period and, far from existing as a single entity, two separate scenes had evolved, broadly classifiable as the illegal (underground) and the legal (overground, official), each with its own multifarious facets and myriad of different musical soundtracks for which 'rave' serviced the event. Before outlining the Bill's contents, it is important here to distinguish the illegal (free entry) rave parties implicated in the legislation from the legal raves (of the pay-scene) which are largely unchanged as a result. While entry to a commercial rave comes at a price, the lack of an entrance charge at donation-financed illegal raves (often collected in a bucket passed around for participants to 'give what they can') should theoretically ensure a wider mix of people in free rather than pay events. However, conversely, the exclusivity demanded by this form of clandestine clubbing can never really make illegal raves a truly all-embracing democratic force. Calling one of several underground rave phonelines accesses immediate events unlisted by the listings magazines. Such leads may be no more than a junction number of a motorway, since the final venue is still secret, a precaution to counter the police. However not everyone will know how to find an illegal rave, indeed their existence is founded on this very mystique.

The rave departs from many constraints of the 'conventional' rock concert, bending and at times breaking the usual rules of the game. The DJ-centred culture is the antithesis of the spectacle. Within this premise itself, the free party goes even further. The illegal rave is non-linear; it will not only possibly change place throughout its course but its time will also be unfixed. While the legal rave will have a defined start time and an end, its illegal counterpart will be of potentially infinite duration. Participants dance like there's no tomorrow because literally tomorrow just isn't going to happen; no one will hurry you out because there is no terminus, no curfew when the licence ends. The public will dance for perhaps ten hours on end at a legal rave. The illegal rave may sometimes last for several days, pushing this boundary even further. The legal rave will be sited at a premises which has the requisite number of fire exits and toilets whereas the illegal rave will often be in a squatted building, either a boarded-up former domestic dwelling or church, or a deserted warehouse on the edge of town: a new type of urban regeneration in the failed industrial estates where the traditional manufacturing industry has collapsed. Lighting will often be basic at an illegal event due to the use of hot-wired electricity. For this reason the free rave will also be unable to boast a mind-boggling number of kilowatts-powered sound system in the way a club such as the world-reputed Ministry of Sound in London does. The legal and illegal rave will also draw two differently- constituted publics, with some overlap.

The target of the CJA was not then just the stereotype of the ecstasy-guzzling raver that had been forming in the public imagination as a result of negative coverage since the late 1980s, but the illegal-rave goer, an even more extreme version. This character – an amalgam of raver, squatter and traveller, with roots in paganism and technology, punk and hippy – quickly became known as the 'crusty'. According to Press: 'in reality there is no generic squatter or traveller; instead there is a multitude of "tribes".'[5] Lowe and Shaw's interviewee, Jeremy, claims: 'People called us crusties and that label's stuck and become a sort of fashion thing which is ridiculous really because it was the opposite of that ... It was anti-fashion, anti-image. It was supposed to be a viable alternative way of life'.[6] The crusty rapidly became a new folk devil fuelling moral panic. By Autumn 1992 the music press were in time honoured tradition running 'how to dress crusty' items for their youthful readership. Simultaneously the hysterical and alarmist right-wing press were fuelling the ire of the 'disgusted of deep suburbia' of the nation with scare stories. Admittedly the free party scene is inescapably elitist. However those encompassed by it, crusties and their dogs on strings, are the very people excluded from 'straight society' and do not fit with our usual perceptions of the selectivity that defines a clique. The state had already practised its attempts to rein in rave in the earlier Entertainments (Increased Penalties) Act 1989 which was introduced as a private member's bill sponsored by the backbench Conservative Graham Bright MP to put restrictions on the licensing of legal raves. Now with the Criminal Justice Bill it was the turn of the illegal scene.

Few pieces of legislation have generated as much debate and disagreement as the Criminal Justice and Public Order Act of 1994.[7] At the time of the legislation's passage through Parliament in Bill form, Channel 4 Television's satirical programme *Drop the Dead Donkey* joked that the CJA contained implications for 'every living organism'. The allegation was in reality not as far removed from the truth as it sounds given the Criminal Justice Act's wide scope. Young offenders, the prevention of terrorism, football ticket touts and the lowering of the age of consent for homosexual acts are also among its sprawling contents. Part three includes the abolition of the Right of Silence. Part four increases police stop and search powers considerably. It is for part five however – public order – that the CJB and subsequently CJA became best known. Many of the provisions relating to raves and festivals are nothing short of Draconian. Police are given powers to end outdoor happenings. It becomes a criminal offence to disobey a direction to leave a rave event. If a police officer 'reasonably believes' ten or more people are waiting for or setting up a rave, they can be ordered to disperse and a refusal to do so carries the liability of three months' imprisonment or a £2500 fine, even if the event has the permission of the landowner. The police can also turn away anyone who comes within five miles of a potential rave, and they can enter land and seize vehicles and sound equipment which the courts then have forfeiture powers over.

Most bizarre of all is the state definition of rave as 'music wholly or predominantly characterised by the emission of a succession of repetitive beats.' The definition is ridiculous because all music is organised sound.[8] As Debby Staunton of ravers' pressure group Advance Party has pointed out: 'I guess that's goodbye to Ravel's Bolero then.' This is state intervention on grounds of musical taste with censure for those who do not conform to the state's chosen view of society. Andrew Blake sees it as a return to an eighteenth century concept of privatised land. He claims, 'It is the mobility, the mixability, of club culture that conservative "essential England" wishes to banish with the Criminal Justice Bill'. Home Secretary Michael Howard claimed that the legislation was directed to 'tackle crime, punish criminals and protect people'. George McKay calls it 'the criminalisation of diversity'. As Robertson has pointed out: 'The traditional liberties are easy to erode when times call for financial sacrifices or action against terrorism'.[9] Accordingly the Criminal Justice Bill was introduced to regulate lifestyles by the self-styled non-interventionist Conservative Party under the pretext of a crime-prevention measure. Exploiting fears of rising criminality and placing the accent on law and order was key to this strategy.

ANTI-CJA CAMPAIGNING
In July 1993 I was given a telephone number for Spiral Tribe, a sound system playing and organising free parties around London. By January 1994, when I actually rang, it had become the contact number

for Advance Party, a civil liberties collective formed to protect the rights of festivals and free parties. My call's interceptor told me, 'The proposed legislation is disgusting. It abuses people's rights to choose their own lifestyle'. Thus began my own involvement with the anti-CJB campaign. Over the next year I attended meetings at venues ranging from derelict launderettes to Squatland Yard (a disused mansion block in central London) and alternative community centres in an ex-dole office and a former church. Gatherings were comprised of a fluid composition of DJs and sound system teams sitting round in a circle, smoking dope and discussing non-violent action as if it had never gone out of fashion. Despite being 'new' the scene had historical landmarks. Certain pre-Act festivals and parties stood out as key flashpoints in the anti-CJB legacy. The Castlemorton Free Festival, an open air gathering which took place in 1992, is seen by party-goers as foreshadowing the gloomy way ahead following the Bill's enactment. Suing the organisers for constituting a public nuisance resulted in the expenditure of £4 million of taxpayers' money. All were eventually acquitted. Gradually other raves added themselves to the legendary list, including the ill-fated '7th of the 7th' Festival to have been held in July 1995 as the first large-scale party after the Bill's enactment, but which was prevented by the police.

Advance Party was structured as a loose-knit, decentralised, leaderless (dis)organisation. Its two main speakers always seemed unlikely pied pipers of rave: Michelle Poole, a former teacher, veteran anti-abortion, IMG, SWP and CND campaigner, aged around the half century mark, and Debby Staunton, ex-CPSA (civil service trade union) representative mother of two who reached suffrage in 1979. Michelle told me in January 1995, 'I say you're never too old to dance'. Early aims emphasised rights awareness, training people in police negotiation and legal observation, plus organising rallies, fundraising and media functions. The proposed legal rights card became a booklet due to the sheer volume of contents. The voguish word 'network' – or several co-existing networks – has often been employed to describe the CJB campaign, rather than calling it a social movement. Advance Party's logo was, appropriately, a spider web. However, much social movement writing argues that movements are networks anyway, therefore a false dichotomy between network and movement is suggested. 'Bottom up' is equally unhelpful in describing the structure because the top and bottom were indistinguishable. In any case, the contrast with old-style political parties and traditional pressure groups was marked in aims and means. Anti-CJBism avoided, for example, the London-centrism of other political campaigns, such as much of the anti-racist movement which had been concentrated largely in and on East London.[10] Ad hoc groups were often launched as the result of localised issues. FINs – Free Information Networks – sprouted in such ostensibly reactionary locations as Guildford and Dorset.

The legislation was quickly dubbed the 'Criminal In-Justice Bill', emphasising an acute sense of the Government publicly selecting scapegoats to compensate for its own failures. At various press conferences and rallies held throughout 1994, a careful balance of those affected was assembled, representing squatters, ravers, road protesters and travellers under a backdrop reading 'Defending Diversity, Defending Dissent' – Home Secretary Michael Howard's worst nightmare, an assortment of social undesirables. Continuity was underlined, with the right to rave presented as part of a traditional cultural heritage. Ward writes, 'Dance reinforces community ... For society to continue operating effectively (it can be argued) it is necessary for individuals to have some release from their daily routines and pressures'.[11] Debby Staunton's speeches similarly refer to 'our inalienable right to hold parties and dance as our ancestors have done for hundreds of years'. It is an alternative 'back to basics', a bastardisation of the philosophy espoused by the then-current Conservative Party, selecting different antecedents than Victorian Values. Much of the legitimacy laid claim to by the road protesters at Twyford Down and Solsbury Hill is rooted in their status as ancient festival sites. Rights can then be claimed by all sides, not just the 1990s complaining culture of consumers rights. Freedom Network, a loose alliance of grassroots protesters used the phrase 'CJA: together we'll crack it,' directly subverting the government's 'Crime: together we'll crack it' slogan. Lord Justice Hoffman's affirmation of 'an ancient and honourable tradition of peaceful public protest' adorned a campaign postcard.

Strategies to oppose the Bill drew other groups. Liberty (civil liberties organisation), Shelter (homeless charity), the Green Party (ecologists) and Charter '88 (constitutional reform group) took up the cause from the more organised and more respectable end of the organised pressure group spectrum. The joint Charter 88/Advance Party January 1994 lobby of Parliament resulted in a turnout of 300 (very) odd DJs, squatters, ravers and conscience-stricken middle/chattering class card-carrying Charter '88 members. 1994 saw three marches between Hyde Park and Trafalgar Square in London, each larger than the last in numbers, media attention and entryism from other factions determined to climb aboard the Criminal Justice bandwagon.

The first one, which occurred on 1 May, probably represented the movement at its most 'pure'. The turnout was probably somewhere between the police estimates of 10,000 and the organisers' reckoning of 30,000: an impressive number given that it received no (mainstream) advance publicity, and instead relied solely on underground mobilisation. Unlike traditional antagonistic demonstrations, a good humoured crowd raved down the streets of Monopoly board fame, let loose in the city in the blazing sunshine. Present were playful elements of spectacle: jugglers, stilt-walkers and a bicycle-powered rave which engendered a carnival-like spirit and countered the 'faceless techno' image of rave. Striking a sinister note, however, was the absence of media coverage, despite the fact that the march cannot have escaped the attention of anyone present in Central London on the day.

In August the route was altered to pass Whitehall, where an altercation at the gates of Downing Street followed: the Socialist Workers Party (SWP) were blamed for their supposedly inflammatory slogan 'Kill the Bill' that could be interpreted as an incitement to anti-police violence.[12] In October, after another re-routing, the looting of shops in Oxford Street completed the proceedings, which triggered far-fetched media comparisons with the poll tax riot of 1989. In November a meeting at Westminster Central Hall, on the eve of the Bill's enactment, was due to have been followed by a lobby of Parliament. However Parliament itself was sealed off and scenes of bloody violence perpetrated against the police made it onto the evening news bulletins, ignoring the role that police provocation played.[13]

DIY culture, denoting 'Do It Yourself', is also a key concept in the anti-Criminal Justice Bill's theory and practice. With such tools as desktop publishing and camcorders, the mastery of media manipulation and new technology has been an important part of the strategy to (re)claim ancient rights. After Advance Party meetings people were urged to leave with one copy of each leaflet, go forth and photocopy, jam radio phone-in switchboards and flood newspaper postbags. Marchers were encouraged to carry hand-held cameras on actions, as evidence in the event of police aggravation, and to serve as symbolic and material counterpoints to big brother police surveillance. Campaigner George Monbiot of the Centre for Environmental Studies, Green College, Oxford, told me in January 1995 that 'creating great spectacles and harnessing the power of the media to make really grand alliances right across the spectrum' was a pivotal priority. Television pictures of a June 1994 protest were helped by the irresistible imagery of campaigners dressed as suffragettes chained to the railings outside Parliament, demanding not the right to vote but the right to protest. The BBC *Open Space* documentary of June 1994, in which final editorial control rested with Advance Party, was an example of open access media exemplifying the DIY principle.

It is interesting to note parallel developments, across the divide, which involved the legal rave scene in the anti-CJB campaigns. Regular pay venues unaffected by the legislation have, depending on your interpretation, either cynically cashed in on the campaign or shown solidarity to the cause by collecting petitions and hosting benefit nights. Megatripolis in Central London represents the greatest blurring of boundaries with its hi-tech counterculture new-age festival-like format including fortune-tellers, internet terminals, alcohol-free energy drinks, subversive leaflets stall and 'parallel university' talks and music in a legal setting. The club was run by ex-free party personnel who often name-checked illegal events on the PA. 'It's for people who want to take a walk towards the wild side but don't want to go over the edge', Blue, the organiser, told me in November 1993. Less admirable was the commercial three-day legal outdoor festival in Oxfordshire, improbably titled 'Tribal Gathering', organised by club giants Universe Promotions in 1995 and advertising itself as 'the first legal rave'. Its publicity strongly attached itself to the language of resistance, yet such use of the language of resistance sat somewhat incongruously with its £25 ticket price.

THE 'NEW POLITICS' AND THE RIGHT TO RAVE

Just as rave departs from the traditional conventions of pop music and spectacle, the politics of its defence in the face of the Criminal Justice Bill breaks with what we recognise as traditional politics, in theory and practice. The Labour Party, Her Majesty's loyal opposition, abstained rather than opposing the CJB in Parliament, leaving it as detested as the Government. Debby consistently mocked 'the members of the opposition who are no longer performing their rightful role in moderating the excesses of their colleagues.' Extraparliamentary parties were less slow to take up the cause. The Revolutionary Communist Party (RCP) launched a CJB telephone hotline and clothing range. The Socialist Workers Party (SWP) formed the offshoot, The Coalition Against the Criminal Justice Bill, to draw political profit in terms of recruiting new members. Their CJB poster confusingly urged 'Defend Britain's Hospitals. Fight the Criminal Justice Bill,' lumping the two valid yet unconnected causes uncomfortably together. It would appear that the two are not connected anywhere, except in the SWP's fetid imagination. Paul Foot explains the SWP position in classic class terms: 'The world we live in is controlled by an oligarchy whose only interest is to preserve for themselves inordinate wealth and power which they filch from what other people produce. They know their enemy: trade unions the one day, travellers and ravers the next. They seek to crush us all with equal ruthlessness'.[14] Its validity is, however, limited; whether most ravers are aware that they are fighting the class war is doubtful. That large numbers of people were involved in CJA protests, and in the wave of non-violent actions which followed, seems to underline the fact that society is changing faster than the traditional political parties, constrained by totalising rigid dogma, can.

Paradoxically, the Criminal Justice Bill, by attempting to crush a legion of diverse, disparate and desperate groups, has succeeded in uniting them with a single purpose and a common enemy. Rick, a despatch rider and occasional DJ, told me his message for the Government: 'Cheers, thanks a lot for bringing us all together. We're a lot more networked now than we ever were.' The right to rave protests, along with road campaigns and animal rights demonstrations, form a new wave of non-violent direct action (NVDA) operating outside existing political structures; a new politics serving a different type of constituency. Definitions vary. C.J. Stone identifies 'justice, peace and natural goodness' as key ingredients.[15] Michelle Poole has called it 'the process of radicalisation on people's own terms.' The new politics is issue-based and extra-parliamentary, bypassing the Westminster system because those involved do not feel they have to seek their MP's permission to participate. Old-style deference is no longer the compelling force that it once was, with the collapse of traditional institutions such as the royal family and the escalation of corruption in old politics, termed 'sleaze' in 1990s-speak. As a result, MPs quite simply cannot be trusted. Rave has often been seen as primarily hedonistic, and this is reflected in its politics. 'We might prefer putting on parties to angry marches but that's because it's what we do best', Debby explained at the Left Forum '95 Conference at SOAS in March 1995 to a heckler who had difficulties with such unalloyed pleasure-seeking as politics. The point is that in the face of the Bill/Act the continuation of free parties has become highly charged political rhetoric in itself. C.J. Stone writes: 'People don't go on demos these days, they celebrate. They don't protest, they party.'

The question of 'right(s)' forms the philosophical common ground of the alliance of groups opposing the Criminal Justice Act. Non-violent action is, in the eyes of its perpetrators, carried out in a moral dimension with a higher value than the simple administrative mechanisms of the Law. A slogan on a leaflet from the M11 Link Road protesters in East London urges: 'Resist the roadbuilders, they are strong but we are right.' Liberty's Andrew Puddephatt claimed at the 1 May march: 'When tyranny is at home you have a duty to resist.' Here the principle of the Rule of Law, central in the UK's constitutionless constitutional apparatus, is under threat because it relies on respect for the Law as its basis, raising the question of justification. Hart wrote of this in relation to state action over the citizen: 'In asking it [justification] we are committed to at least the general critical principle that the use of coercion in any society calls for justification as something prima facie objectionable to be only tolerated for the sake of some countervailing good.' Even Card and Ward in their dispassionate guide to the Criminal Justice Act express doubts regarding section 5: 'Whether these new offences and police powers are necessary and can be justified – and any extension of the criminal law should be justified up to the hilt – is open to doubt'.[16]

Replacing a straightforward class analysis, postmodernist tendencies can be seen in The Criminal Justice protests' general characteristics. Identity politics has assumed major significance and has institutionalised pluralism and variety. DIY culture, with its assembly of new forms of culture from fragments, brings to mind the favourite postmodern principle of bricolage. Practitioners and theorists are sometimes the same. Oxford academic George Monbiot is, for example, often seen as the leading intellectual of the NVDA. Manchester Freedom Network organiser Ally Fogg, 26, a psychology researcher at Salford University, told me in June 1995: 'Our post-modern generation is very self-conscious. We know what we are doing, we know who we are. We know that the way we are portrayed in the media is different to what we are. The text and representation are two intrinsically different things. Whether people have read sociology textbooks and understand the jargon or not they still have a sense of postmodernism.'

However postmoderism itself can mean everything and nothing. Anti-CJBism is postmodern by Bauman's contention that 'incoherence is the most distinctive among the attributes of postmodernity (arguably its most defining feature).'[17]

Post-war French post-structural sociology also has a number of points in common with the general thrust of the CJA campaigning in some of its theories. The echoes of the past used by the campaigners as reference points (ancient festivals, suffragettes) are pertinent to Foucault and his interdisciplinary discourse theory which maps out a history of the present through archaeological analyses of past discourse. Foucault's work also displays a deep distrust of all institutional power, inspired by the authorities' response to the 1968 *évenèments*. The same period also influenced Lyotard, who argued that universal theories should be dismissed out of hand and that the 'grand narrative' should be replaced by the 'little narratives' of individual human beings. The Criminal Justice protesters likewise are drawn from a wide spectrum of society (travellers, ravers, hunt saboteurs), each with different individual experiences to bring. The totality of influences is consequently heterogeneous. In turn we can invoke the name of the deconstructionist Derrida, who influenced Lyotard and theorised the shifting and interdeterminate nature of meaning. Bordieu's theory of practice based on the analysis of the practical intelligibility governing action can also be applied. Other philosophers who have been associated with rave include post-structuralists Deleuze and Guattari and Baudrillard, which seems to suggest that, at a theoretical level anyway, for contemporary chroniclers of rave the dictum 'each to their own frog' (*chacun a sa grenouille* in French), could be coined.[18]

It is interesting here to draw comparisons with social movement theorists of the late twentieth century. According to Diani and Melucci, social movements are founded on diversity through networks, and unity through creative identity.[19] They are composed of a plurality of individuals and organisations who have a collective identity that draws these various elements into a single entity. Diani identifies the twin forces of politics (challenging uneven distribution of power and social structures) and social conflict (challenging the shared meanings and ways of defining and interpreting reality). Here are echoes of the anti-CJB networks. Tourraine also reinterprets the past in a process of what he calls 'historicity'. For him the élite of the social order must be countered by initiating lines of protest which generate new social movements. Examples given are the 1960s student movement and 1980s environmentalists.[20] As with the 1990s non-violent direct action and the Criminal Justice movement, these new struggles will be quite different from old forms of class conflict. Mafessoli's theory of neo-tribes holds that these are formed as concepts rather than integrated social bodies, self-constructed with an inevitable inconclusiveness. He writes 'there will be more coming and going between the tribe and the mass ... at the defined interior of a matrix crystallise a magnitude of poles of attraction ... we find there vagueness, mobility, experience, emotional life'.[21] However it is not easy to categorise CJAism. As Jordan points out: 'If it is easy to see women's liberation as a new left political actor, it is not so easy to see animal liberation or raving in this way'.[22] In a way, the campaign has rested on its internal (ir)rationale rather than on imposed political concepts from outside movements, although this has not stopped such external forces from trying to use the momentum of the protests for their own ends.

CONCLUSION: RAVE'S OPPOSITION TO THE CRIMINAL JUSTICE AND PUBLIC ORDER ACT 1994, NET RESULTS

The anti-Criminal Justice Bill campaign, by definition, has failed.[23] The Bill is now an Act of Parliament, with little chance of repeal under a Labour government, given that Tony Blair was the architect of many of its provisions while he was Shadow Home Secretary. However the legislation's smooth Parliamentary passage was always inevitable given the majority Conservative government. Outside Parliament however, what impact has the experience had on youth and politics?

'Thatcher's children are revolting', SWP coalition spokesman Weyman Bennett ebulliently told an audience at the party summer school in 1995, a perfect soundbite for the perfect moment. Jeremy Gilbert similarly claimed that the Criminal Justice Bill unleashed 'an intense and rapid repoliticisation of youth culture'. However, despite all the excitement of new politics, the old politics has undeniably also been present at every level of the Criminal Justice Bill campaign.[24] For the old left, battered by Thatcherism, betrayed by Blair, the Criminal Justice Bill represented a new version of the 1960s dream of politically conscious youth. However the spectre of false left optimism is ever important here. Jordan sees the rise of the protests corresponding with a prolonged crisis of the left. The criminal justice issue by 1994 was simply the latest leftist political cause to champion. I would claim that many ravers, of legal and illegal scenes, even at the height of the actions remained blissfully unaware of the CJA.[25] Perhaps the most accurate answer to the question of whether the CJA has resulted in a radicalising of youth is 'yes and no'.

Concentrating on section five of the Act to portray it as 'the anti-rave bill' has also deflected from other key provisions. Youth are addressed in provisions to lengthen custodial sentences for the detention of young offenders, the contracting out of secure training centres and the lowering of the minimum age at which young offenders can be detained by the police from fifteen to twelve. Increased police powers, such as the 'sus' laws (arrest on suspicion), are bound disproportionately to affect young black people. Hutnyk has written of its impact on Asians. Bhattacharyra has contrasted the sentimental attention focused by animal rights campaigners on calves in veal crates, to the human suffering of (similarly doe-eyed and brown) deportation victims who are just as roughly treated at the hands of the immigration authorities, claiming that the latter surely carries a higher price. Furthermore the imagery invoked by many (e.g. Rietveld) of rave as hypnotic, tribal, even primal, carries dangerous suppositions of western supremacy over a caricatured valorisation of savages in grass skirts banging tom-tom drums, and is deeply offensive to those of contemporary tribal communities. Paradoxically the campaign at times comes close to treading a little Englander, parochial path, yearning for an idealised imagined past that never was.[26]

Redhead sees the Act, along with the Entertainments (Increased Penalties) Act 1990 and the Football Spectators and Football Offence Acts of 1989 and 1991 respectively, as part of a pattern of the regulation of youth culture. He writes: 'These regulatory regimes all exhibit familiar features of the relationships between law, market and state in the 1990s and illustrate contemporary attempts to regulate, discipline and police popular culture in the late twentieth century'.[27] This example of attempted social control by Law is rooted in precedent, stemming from crowd fear and the idea of intoxicated dance. Plato saw the mob as 'the beast' and Shakespeare called the crowd 'the many headed hydra'. Some claim that within rational industrial/post industrial societies dance will be peripheral to the main forms of activity and social relationships. Furthermore, those for whom dance does play an important role are definitely marginal and almost always suspect. However the Government's determination to legislate rave away, to the extent of devising a statutory definition of it, has been unheard of in any youth culture. McKay claims that 'rave culture has been subject to a sustained assault by legislative forces ... far more sustained than on earlier subcultures of resistance'.[28] The Bill itself emerged against a backdrop of moral panic surrounding youth, fuelled by media uproar over joyriding, the murder of toddler Jamie Bulger by two juveniles, estate riots in Blackbird Leys, Oxford, and the murder of headteacher Philip Lawrence.

However the moral absolutism of the new right's 'back to basics' may have been a political misjudgment. The Criminal Justice Bill and New Politics issues have spread beyond a 'youth' campaign. If its purpose was to appease the electorate of the Tory shires, the consequence of the politicisation of middle-aged, middle-class, respectable England by the anti-CJB cause or animal rights and road campaigns was surely unintended. John Stewart of road-protesting group Alarm UK told me in 1995, 'Protesting is becoming almost respectable for the middle class. The middle classes are experiencing the same uncertainties the working class always had. No job is safe anymore. People are much more critical and more prepared to take on the establishment'.

Furthermore 'crusty' lifestyles are having an increasing impact on mainstream culture. With the growth in alternative lifestyles – vegetarianism, availability of herbal alternative medicines – the crusty may not any longer be so much of a bogey-man. Much has been made of the facile selection of societal scapegoats in the legislation. The government's targeting of ravers and crusties can also be read as fulfilling a need now that the Eastern bloc threat (arguably always dubious) has receded. This time however the perceived threat to stability is from the enemy within.

The question of who exactly is scapegoating whom is also important. The Government can be seen to be using the police. On asking officers in a parked police car outside an unlicensed party in Uxbridge in July 1995 what action they would take, I was told: 'Look love. If you saw 400 kids in a warehouse having a good time what would you do about it?': the officers made it clear that as far as they were concerned, providing that health and safety were not compromised, no action was needed.

In the short term there have been some tangible effects of the Criminal Justice mobilisations. Recent years have seen a cut-down of the government's road building programme, generated by cost considerations and the anti-roads lobby's ire. Summer 1995 saw a climbdown by Shell over the Brent Spar oil platform. On the eve of the Act's first anniversary Liberty released the results of their twelve month public order monitoring project, which encouragingly showed that only three people had been arrested under the section five provisions. Of these three arrests only one had involved the Act's power to seize vehicles and sound equipment (effectively impounding sound systems). It was reported that there had only been two large-scale events in the twelve months following enactment but that smaller events with less than 500 attending had continued largely unhindered, indicating that the more Draconian sections of the CJA were not yet being enforced.

Nonetheless the provisions are enshrined in law if the state ever needs them. The disequilibrium of local variations in the law's application, depending on the extent of the local constabulary's individual zealousness, is also a cause for concern, in that it is effectively an unequal and arbitrary application of justice. Liberty's report claimed, 'The possibility that legislation enacted in this country could have produced a new group of cultural refugees would have been almost unthinkable until recently'. On the one hand, it seems that yesterday's power networks are no longer as assured as they once were now that issue-based politics and direct action are increasingly making their presence felt. On the other, unless the momentum is maintained, there is a perpetual danger that the movement could easily go into a sense of drift. With the Criminal Justice Act on the statute book, the movement has by definition lost its *raison d'etre*. George Monbiot told me: 'So far we're lacking a sense of what we're for, as opposed to what we're against'.

Other less tangible results, such as a change in generational consciousness, are not yet apparent. They may come to light only if and when the anti-CJA protestors reach positions of influence. One thing however seems certain, the free party movement, in spite of the Law, is defiantly following the spirit of the Happy Monday's hit of 1989: *Rave on*.

NOTES

1. All the quotations with no reference are taken from interviews conducted by the author.
2. This of course was the famous utterance of Mrs Thatcher in 1988.
3. S. Redhead, *The End of the Century Party*, MUP, Manchester 1989.
4. 'Politics' of course is a much contested term, subject to various definitions. This statement is used here as 'scene-setting'. Rave can be read as a politics of

the body and pleasure. For more discussion around these themes see T. Jordan, 'Raving and the Future of Revolution: cultural and political social movements', paper given at the *Shouts from the Street* Conference, Manchester Metropolitan University Institute for Popular Culture, September 1995.

5. J. Press, 'The Killing of Crusty' in J. Savage and H. Kureishi (eds), *The Faber Book of Pop*, Faber, London 1995, pp797-806.

6. R. Lowe and W. Shaw, *Travellers: Voices of the New Age Nomads*, Fourth Estate, London 1993.

7. R. Card and R. Ward, *The Criminal Justice and Public Order Act 1994*, Jordans, London 1996.

8. The Oxford English Dictionary describes music as 'the art of arranging the sound of voice(s) or instrument(s) or both in a pleasing combination'.

9. A. Blake, 'Village Green, Urban Jungle' in *New Statesman and Society*, 12.8.94; G. McKay, *Senseless Acts of Beauty: Cultures of Resistance since the Sixties*, Verso, London 1996; G. Robertson, *Freedom, The Individual and the Law*, Pelican, London 1989.

10. The UK anti-racism pressure groups have always been very East London-centred, e.g. Anti-Racist Action, Anti-Nazi League and others all have London premises and concentrate their activity in large degree on the London Borough of Tower Hamlets, in recent years a site of far-right political activity.

11. Card and Ward, *op.cit.*

12. 'The Bill' being British slang for police.

13. Media reactions to the marches ranged from a trite picture story on the back cover of the *Guardian*, 2 May 1995, following the May march, to the exposé of *News at Ten*, following the October lobby, which outlined the structure and workings of various anarchist groups, such as the anachronistic, numerically insignificant if well-meaning anarchists, Class War. The *Guardian* item was the May 1994 event's sole mention in the national newspapers. Vicky Hutchins' article in the *New Statesman* took much the same tone, marvelling at the weirdos. V. Hutchins, 'Fight for Your Right to Party', *New Statesman and Society*, 6 May 1994. Of course the marchers included people other than ravers. Groups such as Football Fans Against the Bill and the motorcyclists, Bikers Against the Bill also had banners at the demonstrations.

14. P. Foot, 'In the Vanguard', *Red Pepper*, No. 6, 1995, pp34-36.

15. C. J. Stone, 'Let's Have a Revolution for Fun', *New Statesman and Society*, 29 July 1994.

16. H. Hart, *Law, Liberty and Morality*, OUP, Oxford 1963, Card and Ward, *op.cit.*

17. Z. Bauman, *Intimations of Postmodernity*, Routledge, London 1992.

18. M. Foucault, *Les Mots et Les Choses: une archaeologie des sciences*, Gallimard, Paris 1968; JF Lyotard, *La Condition Postmodern*, Minuit, Paris 1968; S. Redhead (ed), *Rave Off*, Avebury, Aldershot 1993; T. Jordan, 'Collective Bodies: raving and the politics of Gilles Deleuze and Felix Guattari', *The Body and Society*, 1(1), 1995, pp125-144.

19. M. Diani, 'The Concept of Social Movements', *Sociological Review*, 40(1), 1992, pp1-25; A. Melucci, *Nomads of the Present*, Century Hutchinson, London 1989.

20. A. Tourraine, *Le Retour a l'Acteur*, Denoels, Paris 1984.

21. M. Maffesoli, *Les Temps des Tribus: le declin de l'invididualisme dans les societes de masse*, Meridiens Klincksieck, Paris 1988, p182.

22. T. Jordan, 1995, *op.cit.*

23. At the time of writing (second half of 1997) it seems that the old CJB campaigners have diversified into a number of different directions. The 'Green Field' of the 1997 three-day Glastonbury festival (largest open-air arts festival in Europe), usually a good gauge of these things, included speeches from Swampy, new media-friendly eco-warrior who had made a name opposing the Manchester Airport expansion, and the McLibel pair, two anti-McDonalds activists who had won a moral and partial legal victory over the hamburger giants after their DIY literature raised the multi-national's corporate ire. In 1994, the last time that I attended the festival, Debby Staunton's speech resulted in an anti-CJB protest march inside the ramparts of the festival, which struck me as the ultimate preaching to the converted.

24. The intersections of the two are numerous. A group known as Labour Campaign For Travellers' Rights even emerged. In March 1995 the GMB, the boilermakers union, began a tour of raves up and down the country to spread the word on the joys of collective action and to enlist some more youthful members. Charter 88's youth wing, Active 88, organised a travelling roadshow of student towns to raise awareness and shake people out of apathy, using film, DJs, live music, and drama, in the form of a short sketch rather crudely representing police brutality against ravers as a sign of things to come under the impending draconian legislation.

25. Mckay, *op.cit.*; J. Hutnyk, 'Repetitive Beatings or Criminal Justice?' in *Dis-Orienting Rhythms: the Politics of the New Asian Dance Music*, Zed, London 1996; Jordan, 'Collective Bodies', *op.cit.*

26. P. Cavadino, 'The Criminal Justice Act 1994 and Young Offenders', *Youth And Policy, the Journal of Critical Analysis*, 48, 1995; Hutnyk, *op.cit.*; G. Bhattacharya, 'White Angst', paper delivered at Race, Ethnicity, Politics seminar, Birkbeck College 20 January 1996; H. Rietveld, 'Living the Dream', in Redhead (ed), 1993, *op.cit.*, pp41-78.

27. S. Redhead, *Unpopular Cultures*, MUP, Manchester 1995.
28. McKay, *op.cit.*, p165.

MAKING PARTICIPATION POSSIBLE: MOVEMENTS OF DISABLED PEOPLE AND PSYCHIATRIC SURVIVORS

Peter Beresford

> Nutters
> Get
> Compulsory sunsets.
> Wall to wall landscaping of the soul.
> Always a rugged coast, Salt-flecked but liveable.
> Always a hero looking west,
> Going on about
> The forward march of science.
>
> Peter Campbell, *Drug Time Cowboy*[1]

This chapter explores both the pioneering new politics developed by disabled people and psychiatric survivors, and the challenge they make to discrimination as experienced by the two groups. It also suggests that these principles and ways of working have important implications for transforming politics more generally.

For a long time the roles and imagery of disability and distress have been fixed in politics. Disabled people and psychiatric survivors have been cast as the subjects of public policy, which many of them experience as unpleasant and oppressive. At election times the homes and institutions in which they are segregated become photo-opportunities to demonstrate politicians' altruism and good works. Words such as 'loony' are used to condemn political extremists (left *or* right), and failed administrations are written off as 'spineless', 'crippled' or 'lame duck'.

But these attitudes and labels are now being challenged and the challenge is coming from disabled people, mental health service users and people with learning difficulties. I have started with a poem because the politics of these groups is a holistic one which grows out of the self, the personal and the heart, as well as the intellect and collective action. It is a politics of experience and this makes it different to many of the politics we know and have known, including oppositional politics.

THE EMERGENCE OF DISABILITY MOVEMENTS

In recent years, separate movements of disabled people, psychiatric survivors, older people, those with learning difficulties and other groups of health and welfare service users have emerged in the UK, North America, Europe and the South. There are now local, regional, national, European and world-wide organisations, democratically constituted and controlled by these various groups. The UK umbrella organisation of the disabled is the British Council of Disabled People (BCODP), which is a founder member of the Disabled People's International. There are six national organisations of mental health service users: the United Kingdom Advocacy Network, MINDLink, Survivors Speak Out, the Scottish Users Network, Afro-Caribbean Users' Forum and the Hearing Voices Network. These movements and organisations have grown in numbers, confidence and power since their origins in the 1970s.

So far the most visible of these movements is that of the disabled. BCODP now has more than 100 member organisations representing over 400,000 disabled people. The disabled people's movement has drawn a key distinction between organisations and agencies for disabled people which are controlled by the non-disabled, and organisations of disabled people which they themselves control. In this way the movement has been able to make explicit where power, control and resources lie in the disability field and has also made plain the need for a positive redistribution of these to disabled people.

There are differences as well as similarities between these movements. Some psychiatric survivors include themselves as disabled, while others reject this identity because they see their experience and perceptions as different rather than as an impairment.[2] There are also overlaps between those involved in the different movements. For example, some disabled people are also psychiatric survivors and some survivors are disabled. There has also been a growing pattern of collaboration and joint activity between the two movements.

CHALLENGING MEDICINE AND WELFARE

The development of these movements has meant that disabled people and survivors have challenged traditional roles imposed upon them.

Particularly important, there has been a fundamental shift from being passive recipients of policies and services, to asserting themselves as active participants, critiquing (and possibly rejecting) dominant analyses and responses to them and their needs. Such traditional responses have generally been framed in health and welfare terms, with disabled people, those with learning difficulties and psychiatric system survivors being primarily perceived as having individual deficiencies which demand welfare solutions that will provide income maintenance, occupation, rehabilitation, treatment and support.

All the movements have challenged this assumption, but this has perhaps been most clearly expressed by the disabled people's movement with its development of the social model of disability. This draws a distinction between a disabled person's individual impairment, that is to say the loss or defect of a limb or a sense, or of intellectual ability, an organ or physical mechanism of the body, and 'disability', which means:

> all the things which impose restrictions on disabled people, ranging from individual prejudice to institutional discrimination; from inaccessible public buildings to unusable transport systems; from segregated education to excluding work arrangements and so on ... This falls systematically upon disabled people as a group who experience this failure as discrimination institutionalised throughout society.[3]

By making this distinction the movements have been much more than a reaction to welfare arrangements, which is why they are important for a new politics. But so far outside attention has mainly focused on the challenge they make to traditional public policy and ideology, particularly in health and welfare. The service system has also tended to conceive of them in its own terms as social care or service users' organisations and movements. This has been reinforced by the parallel shift to the market in welfare with a new emphasis on consumerism and the 'consumer' and associated ideas of 'user involvement' and 'user-centred' services.[4] But the movements have generally not perceived themselves in this way. Instead one of their key objectives has been to transcend the conceptualisation of their constituencies in narrow welfare terms.

They have conceived of themselves more broadly in political terms. Thus while they have important things to say about social care and welfare and have made a major impact on both, this arises from their broader political agendas and preoccupations. This is particularly true of the disabled people's movement, which of all these movements is perhaps the one which is most explicitly political.[5] Its emphasis is on disabled people's civil rights and citizenship, rather than welfare needs. The movements also represent a challenge to traditional politics and embody a new politics of their own. They have insights to offer about both old and new politics. This begins to emerge on closer examination of their nature.

THE NEW MOVEMENTS

The movements of disabled people and survivors are much more than collections of individuals, groups and organisations. Each has its own history, goals, values, culture, analysis and ways of doing things. As Jane Campbell of the British Council of Disabled People has said:

> Disabled people's organisations have clear objectives and their own philosophy. There is now a disabled people's culture and disability arts. The movement is multi-faceted. There is direct action campaigning on the street. There is letter writing and political work in parliament. There is intellectual work and arts. The movement involves all of these and people cross over. People who write the books are also on the picket line. This has given us a much fuller representation because we have a much more holistic approach and understanding.[6]

The same is true of the psychiatric survivors' movement. In the 1960s and early 1970s there were important challenges to the medicalisation of distress, such as 'anti-psychiatry', in which some mental health service users were involved. But these were relatively narrowly based, dominated by professionals and certainly not led by survivors themselves. In a short space of time, however, survivors have developed their own organisations, networks, knowledge and alternatives.

In America, this is something which survivors have done very much On Our Own – the title of a key text by Judi Chamberlin, one of the US movement's leaders.[7] In the UK, the movement grew with the involvement and help of allies and supporters who were not survivors themselves. One consequence of this was that the movement was more closely bound up with the service system and efforts to reform it. Louise Pembroke, then Secretary of Survivors Speak Out, spoke of some of the dilemmas and contradictions that this posed:

I want to make things better for people in the psychiatric system but I also want to demolish it. There are dangers in collaboration, but there are positive things too, like patients' councils where we can at least help people gain their voice before leaving the bin. I feel one of the dangers with collaboration is that we can change the icing on the cake but we don't change the cake. To get separatist initiatives going we need money. We need to channel our energies more to fighting for that money.[8]

As Anne Plumb says, survivors see themselves variously as survivors of the psychiatric system, of social structures and institutions, and of cultural practices and values.[9] Peter Campbell, a founding member of Survivors Speak Out, wrote:

One great challenge for survivors is the establishment of our own identities. We are not only survivors of a mental health system that regularly fails to meet our wants and needs. We are also survivors of social attitudes and practices that exclude us and discount our experience ... Survivors are not incompetent. Nor are we devoid of insight. Many of the problems we share with other disadvantaged minorities – unemployment, poverty, isolation – are the results of discrimination rather than incapacity.[10]

Members of the survivors and disabled people's movements make connections and identify with other movements such as the women's, black people's, gay men and lesbians' movements. They see themselves as sharing a number of key characteristics with them. They: 'come out' about, and take a pride in, who they are and the validity of their experience and understanding; value their history and culture; experience social oppression; frame their activities in political terms. There has been some discussion among disabled commentators about whether the disabled people's movement is a liberation or new kind of social action.[11] While there is no agreement about this, what is not in doubt among activist survivors and disabled people is that both have now established their own movements. The development of these movements clearly relates to the desire of survivors and disabled people to develop their own identities, collectivities and agendas. But it is also linked with their relation to existing politics and their inability to achieve these objectives within them.

RELATIONS WITH EXISTING POLITICS

The relationship of survivors and disabled people to broader politics has essentially been one of exclusion. They have been marginalised by traditional mainstream politics, 'mass' politics and movements for change. This is reflected in four key political areas: parliamentary, pressure group, oppositional and alternative.

Parliamentary politics

There are many obstacles to the equal participation of survivors and disabled people.[12] A 1987 study found that many disabled people and those with learning difficulties did not even appear on the electoral register.[13] A study of fifty-two people in their twenties with Down's syndrome found that if their mental condition was entered on the household electoral form they tended not to get issued with a polling card.[14] People living in mental handicap hospitals who want to vote have had to fill in a complex 'patient's declaration', which amounts to a test of competence.[15] The citizen's and political rights of compulsorily detained patients are restricted and institutionalised mental health service users have received little support when they have wanted to take part in the political process. Also the stigma associated with mental distress is a strong barrier to the selection of survivors as political candidates. Disability writers have characterised Labour and Conservative parties as sharing the same 'benevolent paternalism'.[16]

Pressure group politics

The disabled people's movement has generally viewed conventional pressure group politics as an additional problem, reinforcing their political exclusion rather than challenging it. Pressure group politics has been dominated by organisations controlled by non-disabled people and is based on a model of 'public education' and parliamentary lobbying by non-disabled 'experts'. It has reinforced dominant models and images of disability, dependence and charity and has attracted the lion's share of state and public funding. While the attitude of the psychiatric survivors' movement to traditional mental health voluntary organisations has been more mixed, it has, in the same way as the disabled people's movement, sought to challenge the tradition of non-survivors speaking on behalf of survivors.

Left and oppositional politics

Left and oppositional politics and their organisations have generally failed to include disabled people or their issues. The trade union movement has reflected the interests of its non-disabled workforce and health and welfare workers rather than users.[17] Jenny Morris, the disability issues writer and activist, has written positively about her political involvement before she was disabled:

> I'd been political since I was 16 in terms of being involved in trade unions and the Labour Party ... Although I wasn't properly aware of disability as an issue, it was around, and so non-disabled people in the Labour Party knew that it was a political issue.[18]

But other disabled people report a less positive experience. Chris Harrison, for example, active in both the survivors and disabled people's movements, says:

> I was one of those disabled people who got involved in left-wing politics. It seemed the obvious place to turn. But there wasn't really any interest in my issues. You kept at it, but it didn't get anywhere. It wasn't on their agenda. They were touched that I was interested in their struggle and had a vague idea I was part of it. If I over-compensated by selling more papers or whatever, that was a way of gaining their approval. In their own organisation, they weren't interested in access or support so disabled people could be properly involved. We weren't really part of the struggle; just a welfare issue that more should be done for.[19]

Alternative politics

While psychiatric survivors and disabled people have undoubtedly had a presence in other movements and alternative politics, generally their struggles 'barely get a mention'.[20] They have largely been marginalised in modern counterculture and alternative politics.[21] The Real World Coalition, for example, was set up in 1996 to push the issues of social justice, anti-poverty and the environment onto the electoral agenda. It was narrowly based, its signatories predominantly coming from large non-governmental organisations, pressure groups and organisations for groups facing disadvantage and oppression.[22] Not one represented an organisation of disabled people or mental health service users.

While anti-roads and environmental campaigns have emphasised participation and inclusion, neither their tactics nor processes have necessarily extended these to disabled people or survivors. The 1996 Wandsworth Guinness site occupation by The Land Is Ours to create 'a sustainable village, with gardens and public amenities' highlights the problems.[23] Examining its failure in the *Guardian*, John Vidal identified one of the causes as the 'mentally disturbed' and others who lived on the site because of 'the gaping holes in council social services'.[24] George Monbiot, its highest profile organiser, writing alongside this, argued for the future '… we must persuade other communities of interest to clear off and find their own spatial and political commons'.[25] This version of the occupation not only reflects dominant perceptions and exclusions of disabled people and survivors, but also ignores the way in which the organisers themselves parachuted into an inner city multi-racial area with high levels of poverty and powerlessness, without local involvement, consultation or consent.

A POLITICS OF PARTICIPATION

The lives of survivors and disabled people have long been shaped and dominated by economic, social, cultural and political exclusion. They have been kept apart in welfare institutions and service systems as well as being restricted to the margins of society by discrimination, poverty and stigma.[26] This exclusion has defined their experience and identity. It helps explain the central priority which their movements give to participation. Participation is at the heart of their objectives as well as their processes. While neither movement claims to involve the mass of its constituency, both seek to involve members as fully as possible. There is a commitment to 'mass action rather than elite action';[27] to participatory rather than representative democracy. 'They are part of the underlying struggle for genuinely participatory democracy, social equality and justice'.[28] Outside these movements, interest in direct democracy is currently focused on the role of new technology[29] and more consensual activities.[30] The survivors' and disabled people's movements instead stress self-advocacy; people acting and speaking on their own behalf. Great value is attached to each individual articulating her or his own experience, feelings and demands, challenging a long history of other people speaking for them.

Inclusion

There has also been a concern to involve people on equal terms and to acknowledge diversity; for example, to include people who communicate differently: non-verbally, in deaf sign language, using braille and audio-tape and in minority ethnic languages. There is a strong sense in both the survivors' and disabled people's movements that the full and equal involvement of black people, women, older people and gay men and lesbians remains an objective rather than an achievement, but there is growing public debate and determination to make it possible.[31]

Self-organisation

Another expression of the commitment of these movements to participation is their emphasis on the idea of 'self-organisation'. By this, psychiatric survivors and the disabled mean establishing independent organisations and initiatives which they themselves control and which are democratically constituted. They have also developed different forms of action and organisation. The disabled people's movement has pioneered new forms of direct action which are accessible to disabled people. These protests, demonstrations, boycotts and sit-downs have been effective, empowering and have challenged stereotypes.[32] Because survivors may have times when they feel wobbly or stressed, their organisations have developed forms of working and collective action sympathetic to their participation; for example, providing quiet rooms and time-out at meetings; providing supporters for speakers and representatives; including ground rules, safety measures and facilitation for people who find being in groups or talking in public difficult; and running social as well as business meetings. Self-organisation also extends to disabled people and survivors developing their own arts, culture, media, theories, knowledge and discussions.

Reuniting the self and society

This relates to a broader point. Both movements have recognised that support is a pre-requisite for political participation. There is a conscious linking of personal support and self-help with political change. Instead of seeing the two as polarised, mutual aid being associated with the status quo and collective action with political change, as traditionally has tended to be the case, there is an appreciation that the two are inextricable. This connection is made in different ways. Mike Oliver argues that personal empowerment in the disabled people's movement has come from people's involvement in collective action.[33] Terry Simpson, a survivor, on the other hand, has written about how his involvement in a support group empowered him to take action to change the mental health system.[34] As Peter Campbell says:

While user/survivor action is often significantly different from main-stream self-help work because of its concentration on social, structural and political change rather than individual change, every action group will spend energy and time supporting members through distress. Self-help principles lie close to the heart of most user/survivor enterprises. The public acceptance of the value of self-help, the valid therapeutic contribution of the non-expert, and the centrality of personal experience as a powerful tool for change have helped create a climate in which it is increasingly possible to tolerate and respect the positive activity of madpersons.[35]

This desire to reunify support and action has many expressions in the politics of these movements. It is reflected in their programmes. In the disabled people's movement this is embodied in the concern to change both the individual disabled person's life and broader society. The aim of the movement is 'to promote change; to improve the quality of our lives and promote our full inclusion in society'.[36] At the core of this goal lies the idea of independent living. This turns on its head the traditional political interpretation of independence as 'standing on your own two feet'. Instead it means ensuring that disabled people have appropriate and adequate support and personal assistance in order for them to have the same rights, choices and opportunities as non-disabled people. It rejects the traditional welfare approach imposed on disabled people and survivors, which restricts them to a separate segre-gating service system, and demands instead a social and political structure which enables them to contribute and participate culturally and socially, in relationships and in work. It was 'the idea of indepen-dent living which gave a focus to the struggles of disabled people to organise themselves'.[37] The concept 'insists that biology is not destiny. Impairment does not necessarily create dependence and a poor quality of life, rather it is lack of control over the physical help needed which takes away people's independence'.[38]

The movements explicitly and determinedly connect the personal and the political. They highlight both agency and structure; the psychological and the social. Thus while the disabled people's move-ment has emphasised the structural relations of disability, there is an increasing concern, particularly among disabled women, not to lose sight of personal impairment and the feelings, emotions and percep-tions associated with it.[39] This concern is embodied in the centrality of the idea of empowerment in the movements and its definition to encompass the positive redistribution of both personal and political power.

Recently there has been some interest, as part of broader political realignments, in connecting politics and psychoanalysis. This is seen as offering a new route to understanding and reforming the interplay between personal and political forces.[40] Many survivors, however, have serious reservations about the so-called talking treatments, identifying their history of abuse, exclusion and Eurocentrism.[41] Their movement, however, offers an alternative route to reuniting the personal and political. As Peter Campbell says:

> For many of us, a central feature of our lives has been the way ... our perceptions, thoughts, ideas and feelings have been taken from us and possessed, processed, interpreted and described by others who have limited sympathy with who we are or who we might become ... The standard response to our distress sets us up beyond society and sets us at odds within ourselves. The challenge we face is to repossess our experience and to reclaim our dignity and value as citizens ... But we need not deny our distress to achieve acceptance. The boundaries of approved experience are narrow enough already. Through poetry and music, visual arts, writing and action we must fight for a broader understanding, a re-evaluation of individual experience.[42]

Survivors have particular reasons to connect the personal and the political. Their experience is of psychiatry and broader social structures which devalue, reject and control their experience, emotions, perceptions and interior world. The medicalisation of their madness and distress, and the chemical and mechanical 'treatments' they receive, are frequently both physically and psychically destructive and sometimes lead to death. Distress is increasingly presented in – often racialised – images of dangerous, threatening people, when the reality is a psychiatric system through which vulnerable people are particularly likely to pass, and where their rights are not just ignored, but routinely restricted, without adequate safeguards or accountability.

The disabled people's and survivors' movements are helping their members to redefine and reclaim their experience. The disabled people's movement has redefined disability[43] and enabled disabled people to rethink themselves,[44] 'transforming the individual and collective consciousness' of the disabled.[45] Survivors are increasingly challenging the medicalisation of their distress and perceptions and rejecting psychiatry's preoccupation with causation and its denial of their feelings and legitimacy. They are beginning to rethink madness and distress. For example hearing voices, which has long been treated as a defining sign and symptom of madness and mental illness, is now being reconceived in non-medical terms. Survivors and their allies are listening to, trying to make sense of, and accepting, voices.[46]

The survivors movement is not only concerned with the particular situation of mental health service users, but also with the broader impact of state, society and psychiatry on people's mental, emotional and spiritual well-being. It does not see madness and distress as confined to a deviant group, distinct from the 'rest of us', but as an inherent part of the human condition. Similarly, 'the politics of disablement is about far more than disabled people'.[47] Both movements are concerned with changing more than the position of a particular group in society. They challenge all forms of social oppression and the attacks which state and society make on our bodies and our selves.

REVOLUTIONARY AND REFORMIST

Both movements incorporate reformist as well as revolutionary politics. They are involved 'in the formal political system ... and the promotion of other kinds of political activity'. The disabled people's movement particularly has achieved some significant successes, in reactionary times, resulting in major legislative changes. Their campaign for civil rights legislation 'has succeeded in converting all the political parties and the vast majority of voluntary organisations to the idea of legislation to outlaw discrimination'.[48] It has also led to the conversion of some traditional disability organisations into democratic ones. The disabled people's movement, with the involvement of the survivors' movement, has produced new legislation enabling some disabled people and survivors to live independently by making it legal to pay them to run their own personal assistance schemes. The survivors movement has invested considerable effort in trying to reform the mental health system, responding to consumerist initiatives for user involvement. There is however a growing sense of disillusion with this route. One survivor has written:

> Reformism ... is still failing the user movement. Political parties do not see us as an important issue. If it is impossible to change or reform the system, then there is only one practical answer and that is to come out of the system all together.[49]

The politics of both movements is potentially revolutionary. The social model of disability focuses on 'what is wrong with the way society is organised'.[50] Its premise is that society must be changed for disability to end. The disabled people's movement has begun to change the social relations of disabled and non-disabled people; disabled people and society. Members of the survivors movement challenge the 'maddening' effects of society. Both movements are transformative in their implications. The analyses they have developed and the solutions they advance are groundbreaking and innovative.

Survivors are exploring various alternatives with increasing enthusiasm and determination. These include ideas, theories, research, structures, therapies, knowledge, nutrition and media.[51] Against the odds of inadequate funding and support, they are beginning to develop alternatives to existing services, from asylums and sanctuaries, advice and counselling services and personal assistance schemes, to training courses and complementary therapies,[52] as well as offering their own visions of the kind of support they want.[53]

Both movements are also based on a different economics in which all can contribute their labour if they wish to and are not, as now, frequently excluded. Disabled people, people with learning difficulties and survivors are groups with some of the highest levels of unemployment, as well as being restricted to employment with the lowest pay and poorest conditions.

The movements have made massive progress, but they still face a series of crucial tensions. These include tensions between whether to pursue participatory or representative democracy; between individual and collective rights; between parliamentary and extra-parliamentary activity; between reform and revolution; between supporting individuals caught up in the welfare and psychiatric systems or helping them to develop their own alternatives; between co-operation with and incorporation by government, and making change and ensuring equal involvement. Similar tensions exist for all new social movements and new politics. What is significant about the disabled people's and survivors' movements – and indeed what is extraordinary, given how recently they have developed and how extreme, stigmatic and punitive has been the exclusion of their members – is the way they have themselves identified, acknowledged and begun to work through these tensions.

Colin Barnes has described the disabled people's movement as 'one of the most potentially potent political forces in contemporary British society'.[54] Old and new politics still have to wake up to this. It's not just that there's a new force to be reckoned with. Even more important perhaps, there are a whole set of new principles and practices to be understood and learned from. The emphasis of the survivors' and disabled people's movements on participation, inclusion, autonomy and self-help, in practice and theory, is groundbreaking. It is a model with wider relevance. It offers much broader hope and promise for politics for the future.

NOTES

1. Frank Bangay, Jo Bidder and Hilary Porter (eds), *Survivors' Poetry: From Dark to Light*, Survivors' Press, London 1992.
2. Julie McNamara, 'Out Of Order: Madness is a feminist and a disability issue', in Jenny Morris, (ed), *Encounters With Strangers: Feminism and Disability*, The Women's Press, London 1996, pp194-205; Anne Plumb, *Distress Or Disability?: A discussion document*, Greater Manchester Coalition of Disabled People, Manchester 1994.
3. Mike Oliver, *Understanding Disability: From theory to practice*, Macmillan, Basingstoke 1996, p33.
4. Robin Means and Randal Smith, (eds), *Community Care: Policy and practice*, Macmillan, Basingstoke 1994.
5. Jane Campbell and Mike Oliver, *Disability Politics: Understanding our past, changing our future*, Routledge, London 1996.
6. P. Beresford and J. Campbell, 'Disabled People, Service Users, User Involvement and Representation', *Disability and Society*, V9. No3. 1994, p321.
7. Judi Chamberlin, *On Our Own: User controlled alternatives to the mental health system*, MIND, London 1988.
8. Cited in Suzy Croft and Peter Beresford, 'User Views', *Changes: An International Journal of Psychology and Psychotherapy*, March, Vol 9 No 1, 1991, p72.
9. Anne Plumb, 'The Challenge Of Self-Advocacy', *Feminism And Psychology*, 3(2), 1993, pp169-187.
10. Campbell, foreword to Bangay, Bidder and Porter, *op. cit.*, p6.
11. Jane Campbell and Mike Oliver, *op. cit.*, pp176-8.
12. Colin Barnes, *Disabled People In Britain And Discrimination*, Hurst and Company, London 1991.
13. E. Fry, *Disabled People and the 1987 General Election*, The Spastics Society (now known as Scope), London 1987.

14. B. Shepperdson and A. Fletcher, 'Invisible Voters', *New Statesman and Society*, 1992.
15. L. Ward, 'The Right to Vote', *Values into Action*, London 1987.
16. Campbell and Oliver, *op.cit.*, p177.
17. *Ibid.*, pp176-7.
18. Quoted in *ibid.*, p118.
19. Harrison, personal communication, 1996.
20. Campbell and Oliver, *op. cit.*, p22.
21. George McKay, *Senseless Acts Of Beauty: Cultures of resistance since the sixties*, Verso, London 1996.
22. Michael Jacobs, *The Politics Of The Real World: Meeting the new century*, written and edited for the Real World Coalition, Earthscan, London 1996.
23. The Land Is Ours, *We've Occupied The Derelict Land On York Road*, campaign leaflet, The Land Is Ours, East Oxford Community Centre, Oxford 1996.
24. John Vidal, 'The Seeds On Stony Ground', Second Front, The *Guardian*, 16 October 1996.
25. George Monbiot, 'Common Cause And Effect', Second Front, The *Guardian*, 16 October 1996, pp2-3.
    Monbiot later apologised for dismissing the occupation as a failure, saying that: 'It had to cope ... also with Wandsworth Council's closure of almost every other facility that might have been able to help the drunk, the drugged and the deranged. This was the only community able to care' (George Monbiot, 'Genius Will Out: On a dream that refuses to die', Society, The *Guardian*, 4 December 1996). Thus instead of recognising survivors as partners or pioneers in alternative politics, he perpetuated their traditional passive, welfare role.
26. Colin Barnes, *op.cit.*; Jim Read and Sue Baker, *Not Just Sticks And Stones*, MIND, London 1996.
27. Tom Shakespeare, 'Disabled People's Self-Organisation: A new social movement?' *Disability, Handicap & Society*, 8, 1993, p254.
28. Mike Oliver, *The Politics Of Disablement*, Macmillan, Basingstoke 1990, p13.
29. Ian Budge, *The New Challenge Of Direct Democracy*, Polity Press, Cambridge 1996.
30. Stephen Goodman, 'City Corporations Challenged By People Power As East Enders Seek A Share In Their Future', *Independent*, 18 November 1996.
31. Jenny Morris (ed), *Encounters With Strangers: Feminism and disability*, The Women's Press, London 1996, pp194-205; Campbell and Oliver, *op. cit.*

p132-8; Peter Campbell, 'The History Of The User Movement In The United Kingdom', in T. Heller, J. Reynolds, R. Gomm, R. Muston and S. Pattison (eds), *Mental Health Matters,* Macmillan, Basingstoke 1996.

32. Campbell and Oliver, *op. cit.,* pp152-6.

33. Oliver, *op. cit.,* pp147-9.

34. Terry Simpson, 'Beyond Rage', in Jim Read and Jill Reynolds (eds), *Speaking Our Minds: An anthology of personal experiences of mental distress and its consequences,* Macmillan, Basingstoke 1996, pp233-4.

35. Peter Campbell, 'What We Want From Crisis Services', in Read and Reynolds, *op.cit.,* p220-1.

36. Campbell and Oliver. *op.cit.,* p22.

37. Oliver, *op.cit.,* p155.

38. Morris, *op.cit.,* p10,

39. Morris, *op.cit.,* pp13-14; Liz Crow, 'Including All Our Lives: Renewing the social model of disability', in Morris, *op.cit.*

40. Andrew Samuels, *The Political Psyche,* Routledge, London 1993.

41. Suzy Croft and Peter Beresford, 'User Views', *Changes: An International Journal of Psychology and Psychotherapy,* Vol 12, No 3, September 1994, pp229-30.

42. Campbell, foreword to Bangay, Bidder and Porter, *op. cit.,* p6.

43. Frances Hasler, 'Developments In The Disabled People's Movement', in Jon Swain, Vic Finkelstein, Sally French and Mike Oliver, *Disabling Barriers – Enabling Environments,* Sage, London 1993, p284.

44. Sally French (ed), *On Equal Terms: Working with disabled people,* Butterworth-Heinemann, Oxford 1994, p80.

45. Campbell and Oliver, *op.cit.,* p123.

46. Marius Romme and Sandra Escher (eds), *Accepting Voices,* MIND, London 1993.

47. Barnes, foreword to Campbell and Oliver, *op.cit.,* pxii.

48. Campbell and Oliver, *op.cit.,* pp179, 170.

49. Pete Seeger, 'A Concise Political History Of The User Movement', *Asylum: A magazine for democratic psychiatry,* Vol 9, No 4, 1996, p13.

50. Morris, *op.cit.,* p11.

51. Survivors Speak Out, *Alternatives: Developing our own philosophy and responses,* workshop discussion, Annual General Meeting, 9 November, London 1996.

52. Vivien Lindow, *Self-Help Alternatives To Mental Health Services,* MIND, London 1994.

53. Campbell, *The History of the User Movement in the UK, op.cit.*; Jim Read, 'What We Want From Mental Health Services', in, Jim Read and Jill Reynolds

(eds), *Speaking Our Minds: An anthology of personal experiences of mental distress and its consequences*, Macmillan, Basingstoke1996.
54. Foreword to Campbell and Oliver, *op.cit.* p ix.

'NEW SEXUAL MINORITIES', OPPRESSION AND POWER: BISEXUAL POLITICS IN THE UK

Merl Storr

INTRODUCTION

There is nothing 'new' about sexual minority politics. Campaigns for sexual minority rights – or, more specifically, homosexual rights – have been active in 'the West' since at least the 1860s.[1] What *has* been hailed as 'new' in sexual politics in the 1990s is 'queer', a sexual and political style emerging from AIDS activism, which has angrily rejected what it sees as the assimilationism of earlier movements. 'Queers' have asserted a confrontational, transgressive, 'in your face' attitude, demanding not just legal and political rights but something like a permanent sexual revolution.[2]

Actually, one might question how 'new' queer really is and to what extent it is 'a new generation of gay and lesbian activists ... resurrecting old debates in new contexts and formulating new debates in old contexts they believe to be new'.[3] For example, a re-reading of Jeffrey Weeks' account of the Gay Liberation Front (GLF), active in the UK between 1970 and 1972, suggests many political and tactical similarities with queer, including a strong self-perception as radical and anti-assimilationist, and the assertion of an uncompromising political stance.[4] Moreover, even after the demise of the GLF, a number of lesbians and gay men were positioning themselves as 'outlaws' or 'transgressors' in relation to more mainstream lesbian and gay politics well before the emergence of queer. The most famous example is probably SM practitioners, whose exclusion from the London Lesbian and Gay Centre (LLGC) in the mid-1980s both arose from and fuelled lasting controversy.[5] Nevertheless, it would be incorrect to suggest that queer is simply 'the same as' any or all of its predecessors – queer clearly operates in political and material contexts, and with distinctive political features, quite different from those of the 1970s and 1980s, particularly in relation to AIDS. While the novelty of queer remains controversial, it continues to have a major impact on 1990s sexual politics.

A NEW POLITICS OF DIFFERENCE

One of these distinctive features of queer is its rejection of unitary and exclusive categories of 'lesbian' or 'gay' identity. In aspiration, if not always in practice,[6] queer politics is self-consciously inclusive: its participants can be queer *and* ... and that 'and' need not be 'lesbian' or 'gay'. As a much-quoted London queer leaflet of 1991 claims, 'There are straight queers, bi-queers, tranny queers, lez queers, fag queers, SM queers, fisting queers in every single street in this apathetic country of ours.'[7] In a paradoxical turn, queer political gestures, not just towards inclusiveness but perhaps even to *universalising* queerness as sexual transgression (igniting its potential in 'every single street') have led to an increase in visibility for *discrete* (and sometimes, though not necessarily always, smaller) sexual minorities alongside lesbians and gay men, including transgendered people, sadomasochists, fetishists and bisexuals.

Of course, just as the 'newness' of queer is ambivalent, so too is that of these 'new' sexual minorities. Strictly speaking, it is not the groups themselves which are new, but rather their (relatively) high profile within sexual minority politics. Nevertheless that high profile – the acknowledgement (albeit contested) of their presence – is in itself an important political turn in the history of sexual minority politics.

One of the most significant implications of this political turn is that it entails a serious re-thinking of notions of power and oppression. 'Power' and 'oppression' have been key terms for political movements of all kinds, both practically and theoretically. Indeed, certain theoretical approaches to what sociologists have called 'new social movements' tend to suggest that 'oppression' in particular is indispensable to the existence of those movements as such. Tim Jordan, for example, claims that the very thing that brings together any movement for political change is '*by definition* ... its project of emancipation and/or its experience of oppression.'[8] Jordan's definition of the latter is that 'oppression exists when one collective benefits because another collective is simultaneously deprived.'[9] But, as I shall argue, this notion of 'oppression' as a mechanism *by* a particular collective *against* another particular collective is not necessarily – and certainly not unproblematically – a notion being employed by activists in the sexual politics of the 1990s.

Oppression has been a key subject of debate in sexual minority movements since the rise of feminist and gay rights movements in the 1960s. From GLF struggles against sexism and heterosexism, to lesbian separatism and distinctive forms of lesbian, feminist and lesbian-feminist politics, sexual minority movements of the 1970s and 1980s articulated a sense of their own oppression. They also struggled (not always successfully) with oppressions of sexism, racism, ableism, ageism and class privilege within their own ranks.[10] While lesbian and gay politics couldn't agree who the oppressors were and how they were to be tackled, the general tendency, consistent with Jordan's formulation, was towards a view that certain groups in society were oppressed by certain other groups and that lesbians and gay men collectively formed an oppressed group. Political debate on the subject of oppression tended to revolve around the following: on the one hand, what were the main oppressions and who were the main beneficiaries of those oppressions; and on the other, whether and how particular lesbians and gay men (as white, middle-class, young and so on) may also be oppressors in some contexts.

In the queer 1990s, however, sexual minority politics has become an acknowledged arena not just for sexual minorities other than lesbians and gay men (including some heterosexual sexual minorities such as some sadomasochists and transgendered people), but also for same-sex lovers who supplement or simply reject lesbian or gay identitification by claiming alternative sexual identities (butch, lesbian boy, leather queen, daddy, bottom, femme, switch ...). It is therefore increasingly difficult to retain notions of oppression as a stable and definable structure, or of oppressors as a discrete social group who benefit in discernable ways from oppression. It is no longer simply a matter of dealing with multiple axes of oppression or with the complexities of being simultaneously oppressed along one axis (black, disabled), and being an oppressor along another (man, middle-class) – although that has already been difficult enough for many. The 1990s has seen the exacerbation, and in many cases arguably the creation, of politically significant sexual differences. Some of these differences are not just between, but actually *within*, sexual minorities, where each newly-emerging splinter identity paradoxically both refuses earlier lesbian and gay political claims to coherent, unified sexual and political identity, and at the same time insists on its own uniqueness, including its uniquely disadvantaged position in the internal hierarchies of lesbian and gay communities. In this scenario minority groups are accused of oppressing each other not on non-sexual grounds such as 'race' or class but, precisely, for their different sexualities. Notions of power and oppression are consequently in a state of flux and crisis.

Hence in what follows I shall chart a shift in sexual political thinking from the mid-1980s to the mid-1990s, away from notions of 'oppression' and 'oppressors' towards an understanding of power as more diffuse and pervasive than the concept of 'oppression' can encompass. Although I shall point out some of the specific reasons for this shift along the way, it must also be located more broadly in changes in the material organisation of power during and since the 1970s and 1980s. The successes of the New Right in industrialised nations, epitomised in the Anglo-American twin peaks of Thatcher and Reagan, presided over both free market capitalism in the economic and political mainstream and fragmentation and aporia among movements of social and political resistance. Such fragmentation and aporia, often dubbed 'postmodernism' by academic observers, can be seen as effects of, and forms of response to, the New Right and its legacy.

Some commentators have seen newly emerging emphases on 'difference' over 'unity' (particularly marked in feminist debates since the mid-1980s, but also present in other movements, including lesbian and gay politics which perhaps sees the apotheosis of 'difference' in queer) as the outcome of political pessimism, even defeatism, in the face of the New Right. Others, however, have more optimistically regarded them as realistic approaches to a changing political landscape.[11] These changes in emphasis have brought with them correlative changes in understandings of power, incorporating insights about 'difference' into notions of power as multiple and local rather than unified and global. While postmodernism by no means has a monopoly on such understandings of power – as I shall suggest below, recent discussions of power in such terms have also come from other countercultural political traditions – its continuing theoretical importance since the 1980s may be indicative of changing social and political conditions.

'New sexual minorities' are arguably key *loci* where these shifts in political thought can be seen emerging. In what follows I shall offer an analysis of one particular locus of this: the UK bisexual movement. Clearly, this is both local and specific: other sexual minority movements, and perhaps bisexual movements in regions other than the UK, will have different trajectories and offer different perspectives. Nevertheless I would argue that the emerging bisexual politics, and more specifically an emerging change in how the bisexual movement conceives of itself and its project in terms of power and oppression, are indicative of a new political direction. My discussion will give an account of this change, but in doing so I am not suggesting that the new conceptions are politically any 'better' (or 'worse') than previous conceptions, and am not intending to present a narrative of progress from outdated political positions to new, enlightened ones. Although I shall make some tentative final comments on current bisexual activism, evaluation of the political effectiveness of the turn to postmodernism and/or to 'difference' is too enormous a task to engage in here.[12] In any case, to speak of 'political effectiveness' in any obvious sense may be inappropriate in the context of sexual minority politics, as Jeffrey Weeks suggests:

> For the movements concerned with sexuality what matters more than a single set of goals or a defined programme is the symbolic focus of the activities of the movements themselves ... They cannot therefore be judged in terms of their political effectivity ... Their ultimate importance lies in their cultural, individual and informal impact on the lives of the individuals who align with them, and are addressed by them as active subjects.[13]

As my discussion below will make clear, this emphasis on the cultural, the individual and the informal as political arenas is strongly characteristic of current bisexual politics.

BISEXUAL POLITICAL DISCOURSES: THE 1980S AND 'OPPRESSION'
The history of bisexual movements in the UK been documented elsewhere, and I do not intend to repeat those details.[14] Briefly, the first bisexual organisation in the UK was the London Bisexual Group (LBG), formed in 1981 and still operating today; this was followed by the formation of a group in Edinburgh in 1984, and other groups in UK cities thereafter. At the time of writing (autumn 1996) there are over twenty such local groups currently active, alongside two telephone helplines, a sexual health project, special interest groups ranging from SM to penpal schemes, several internet discussion lists, and an annual national conference.[15] Some participants have expressed doubt over whether this still fairly disparate activity can be said to constitute a movement,[16] but within this disparate community there are individuals and groups who clearly see bisexuality as a political issue and who consider themselves to be either working towards, or already partici-

pating in, a bisexual political movement. Such views, and the debates sparked by them, are to be found in bisexual community newsletters, which offer a rich archive of bisexual thought and politics from 1984 to the present. Indeed, newsletters of 'new social movements' – characterised, like the UK bisexual movement, by informal networks between locally-based groups rather than by formal hierarchical organisation – function not just as movement archives but as significant factors in the movement in their own right, holding the network together.[17] Thus newsletters are not just records *of* the bisexual movement: they are, in an important sense, part of what *constitutes* the movement.

I intend, then, to proceed by an analysis of the UK's three national bisexual newletters: *Bi-Monthly*, *Bifrost* and *Bi Community News* (BCN). *Bi-Monthly*, issued by LBG, appeared (somewhat erratically) between January 1984 and March 1989; *Bifrost*, based first in Norwich and later in Edinburgh, appeared between summer 1991 and summer 1995; *BCN*, produced by a collective whose membership is dispersed around the UK, began publishing in September 1995 and continues to date. Each newsletter has its own very distinctive tone. *Bi-Monthly* is firmly located in the context of the 1980s, with a heavy emphasis on identity politics (a great deal of discussion revolves around whether bisexuals should identify politically as lesbian and gay), and opposition to Thatcher's radical Conservative government, including to the notorious Section 28 of the Local Government Act of 1988.[18] In tune with this political mood, *Bi-Monthly* is the only one of the three newsletters to include letters and articles by members of lesbian and gay organisations on a fairly regular basis (although both *Bifrost* and *BCN* include a few pieces from non-bisexual individuals, including heterosexuals). The move away from this trend in *Bi-Monthly*'s two successors might be read as an index of bisexual politics' increasing independence from lesbian and gay organisations. *Bifrost* is less seriously political in tone, with noticeably more fiction and light-hearted columns. Serious features are less concerned with lesbian or gay identification, more concerned with the establishment and viability of (relatively) autonomous bisexual organisations, and increasingly interested in queer politics as the 1990s progress. *BCN* is more political than *Bifrost*, and more self-confident about autonomous bisexual organising than *Bi-Monthly*: the emphasis is on reporting news about activist campaigns and debating current issues in bisexual politics, rather than on the agonising over definitions of bisexuality or the viability of bisexual identity that often characterised its predecessors. Doubtless these differences between the three newsletters arise from the different locations of their production, and the different individuals and groups contributing to them. As with all such movements, the numbers will-ing and able actively to contribute to such projects are always far smaller than the numbers who enjoy the results, and all three news-letters routinely appeal for readers' contributions to keep the publication running. Although this makes newsletters unrepresentative in one sense, on the other hand lack of copy does mean that all three publications appear to have published *all* readers' letters, and perhaps all readers' submissions.[19] In any case, lack of contributions can itself be significant, and readers' silence on particular issues itself a kind of contribution: as the editor of *Bifrost* points out, 'It is rare for people to write in when they are happy with what has already been said.'[20]

Despite their differences, the three newsletters share common themes: HIV/AIDS and safer sex; relations with lesbians' and gay men's organisations; connexions between bisexuality and feminism, particularly in terms of bisexual men's commitment to and relations with feminist concerns. The common theme that I wish to explore here, however, is the changing conception of power and oppression emerg-ing in the newsletters, and the particular tension in political thinking that appears in the 1990s.

Contributors to *Bi-Monthly* tend towards a fairly straightforward view of power as oppression. Although there is some disagreement over whether bisexuals (and others) are mainly oppressed by patri-archy, compulsory heterosexuality, the state or some combination of the three, the existence of oppressed groups and oppressor groups is simply assumed, as is the notion that different 'structures' or 'systems' of oppression are interconnected. It is standard for bisexual manifestos to include statements to the effect that 'our sexual liberation is an inte-gral part of the struggle against racism, sexism, heterosexism, homophobia and other forms of oppression'.[21] Moreover, although the question of whether to identify as lesbian and gay as well as (or even instead of) bisexual is a matter of some debate, it is a common view – at least in early issues – that 'it [is] important for bisexuals to be polit-ically active *within the lesbian and gay community* to work towards the reconstruction of sexuality without oppression.'[22]

In this respect bisexual politics as represented in *Bi-Monthly* is very much like both feminist politics and lesbian and gay politics of the time, which are similarly articulated around notions of oppression.

However, bisexual articulations of such notions are problematised by their relation to those very political movements. Firstly, bisexual politics has a peculiar relation to feminism because of its specific roots in *men's* politics: LBG grew out of an anti-sexist men's group,[23] and contributions to both *Bi-Monthly* and its successors indicate a continuing tension around the notion of 'men's oppression' and the need for autonomous women's (and men's) spaces. Female contributors to *Bi-Monthly* repeatedly complain of numerical and behavioural dominance of men over women at LBG, and male contributors express incomprehension of and even hostility towards women's demands for women-only spaces at bisexual events.

The idea that men are oppressed – not just by factors such as 'race' and class, but as men and by the same system(s) or force(s) that oppress women – is expressed on a number of occasions, particularly in *Bifrost*. One (male) contributor is especially clear about the implications of this for notions of oppression:

> The concept of oppression that most of the radical left has been using over the last few decades has in fact been a male defined concept of oppression: focused upon economics and visible power ... Under this concept many of the more subtle and personal means of oppression get ignored .... Men do well on external, visible forms of power (although only a small number really 'make it' in capitalist society), but are deprived relative to women in internal forms such as access to fulfilling relationships and self-awareness ... Whilst there is no doubt that women suffer greater limitations of their lives in general due to the patriarchy, this cannot be separated from men's oppression due to patriarchal norms, and these oppressions must be understood and fought together in a coherent way, rather than being simply blamed on the 'opposite' gender ... The bisexual movement has a key role in bringing together men and women who have a genuine interest in fighting the patriarchy.[24]

Men do not oppress women; rather, both men and women are oppressed by 'the patriarchy', which seems here to operate as a self-perpetuating structure with few clear beneficiaries. Although such views usually (but not always) provoke angry responses from women in subsequent newsletters, they recur often enough to constitute a significant feature of bisexual political thought, and are not confined to men only. This produces a construction of 'oppression without oppressors' which throws the whole notion of 'oppression' into crisis, and which might be seen as a stage in a transition away from the dominance of 'oppression' as previously understood in sexual political thought.

Secondly, bisexual politics has a peculiar relation to lesbian and gay politics in that bisexuals have been both attacked by and excluded from lesbian and gay organisations,[25] despite their pledges of allegiance to lesbian and gay politics in *Bi-Monthly*. Indeed *Bi-Monthly* is itself the arena for a particularly heated and long-running dispute with the Gay Youth Movement (later the Lesbian and Gay Youth Movement), which accuses bisexuals in general and LBG in particular of apolitical complacency. A series of events during the 1980s exacerbates this tension between bisexuals and lesbians and gay men: the exclusion of bisexuals from NALGAY, the National Association of Local Government Officers' lesbian and gay campaign, in 1984; the banning of bisexuals (as well as SM practitioners, as mentioned above) from the LLGC in 1985; the banning of bisexuals from the National Union of Students' (NUS) lesbian and gay campaign; the restriction of membership of the Organisation of Lesbian and Gay Action (OLGA) to lesbians and gay men, and OLGA's refusal to allow a 'specially oppressed group' caucus for bisexuals in 1988.

Indeed, perceptions of factionalism within organisations like OLGA contribute to a growing sense that bisexuals should organise separately from lesbians and gay men: 'We can learn a lot from the divisions in the lesbian and gay communities, the main thing is that we have to form a movement of our own!'[26] The particular question to emerge from all this controversy is whether lesbians and gay men *oppress* bisexuals. This is strongly denied by lesbians and gay men themselves. As one gay man writes:

> They [bisexuals at an NUS conference] somehow felt that the oppression from us was equal to, and in some cases worse than that dished out by the heterosexist anti-gay society we're all familiar with. I only wish that lesbian and gay propaganda was as abundant and universal as they make out ... I'm still trying to work out how me and [another gay man] alone managed to 'oppress' (their words, not mine) a room of 30 or so bisexuals.[27]

The view that bisexuals are 'oppressed' by lesbians and gay men continues to be common in *Bifrost*, with contributors writing of 'two sides to the oppression of bisexuals. One is from straight society, the other from the gay community.'[28] A handful of contributors continue to object to this view, but such objections are much rarer in *Bifrost* than in *Bi-Monthly* (not least because lesbians and gay men seem not to have contributed to the former), and the identification with lesbian and gay politics is much more ambivalent.

Clearly neither of these characteristics is unique to bisexual politics: it is not only bisexual men who claim to be oppressed by patriarchy and/or as men; it is not only bisexuals who have been attacked and excluded from lesbian and gay politics, particularly during the 1980s when the 'lesbian sex wars' were at their height.[29] But the convergence of these tensions around bisexual politics *has* been unique, producing on the one hand a notion of 'oppression without oppressors' and on the other a sense of being oppressed by groups who are themselves oppressed. These two apparently contradictory trains of thought in bisexual politics are relatively under-theorised to date, although attempts have been made to conceptualise the latter as 'biphobia' (oppression of or hostility to bisexuals) or 'monosexism' (belief that it is only possible to feel sexual attraction for one sex),[30] and indeed some bisexuals claim that biphobia oppresses everyone, thereby bringing the two trains of thought together into one grand political claim.[31] Under-theorisation notwithstanding, this tension is nevertheless producing a subtle but perceptible shift in understandings of power and oppression in bisexual politics. There is a growing tendency to abandon the notion of 'oppression' as such in favour of models of power which see social relations of domination and disadvantage in terms of complex and diffuse forces rather than fixed, stable systems or structures of oppression. This in turn is producing new forms of activism and new approaches to social change.

BISEXUAL POLITICAL DISCOURSES: THE 1990S AND 'VISIBILITY'
Bifrost sees a gradual convergence in the 1990s of three strands of bisexual thought on oppression as outlined above. Firstly, there is the notion of structures of oppression as interconnected; secondly, there is the notion that oppression is not – or at least not necessarily – perpetrated by discrete beneficiary or oppressor groups, as expressed in the view that men as well as women are 'oppressed' by patriarchy; thirdly, there is the related notion of bisexuals as 'oppressed' by other 'oppressed' groups, specifically lesbians and gay men. The convergence of these three produces a growing sense that there are few, if any, members of society who are not 'oppressed' in some sense by 'external' or 'internal' forms of power: in other words, power is everywhere and

traditional forms of protest are often inappropriate to the complexities of contemporary power relations.

This view is expressed both directly and indirectly in the pages of *Bifrost*. Direct expressions are a clear minority, although it is significant that none of them provokes adverse responses from readers. Such expressions come from quite different political perspectives. One, for example, takes up a recognisably postmodern stance:

> Yes, politics is about power, but only a tiny proportion of power is located in 'powerful' institutions. There is no Winter Palace of 'top-down' domination to storm ... It is mainly located in everyday understandings about what is 'common sense' and what is 'taken for granted' ... These shifting 'ways of understanding' are the articulation of mobile negotiations, alliances and affiliations between the representatives of different groups in society.[32]

Another gives a more anarchistic or countercultural perspective, arguing for 'creating an alternative culture and space apart from mainstream society ... [W]e are fighting a pervasive, psychological and conditioned oppression.'[33] Nevertheless, both perspectives agree that the way to deal with power is not by traditional forms of direct action. 'There are several models for the construction and growth of a radical movement: mass direct action; use of the electoral system ... and what could be termed "building a culture of resistance". The latter means creating an alternative culture and space apart from mainstream society ... [T]his continuous low-level process of resistance may be more appropriate than large scale direct action';[34] 'people can have power in interpreting their view of themselves and their society ... Unfortunately, this way of understanding "power" makes the traditional methods of protest (inherited from the nineteenth century) seem increasingly decrepit as we enter the fragmented, self-referential and resistance absorbing media world that is (or will be) the twenty-first century.'[35]

Indirect expressions of this view that power is 'pervasive', located in the 'psychological' and in 'everyday understandings', are far more common, and are indeed integral to the 1990s notion of bisexual politics as such. It would be quite wrong to suggest that bisexual politics is not interested in, or not directly active against, manifestations of 'top-down' power such as the outlawing of SM, the age of consent and other issues arising from the Criminal Justice Act of 1995, or civil rights for same-sex lovers. It is however very rare for bisexuals as such – rather than homosexuals – to be explicitly targetted by 'top-down' power such as that of the state (although there have been recent exceptions to this, to which I shall shortly return), and the most common political concern in *Bifrost* and *BCN* is with 'visibility' – the recognition of bisexuality and bisexuals as discrete entities. Almost every issue of *Bifrost* – particularly the earlier ones – carries at least one item about the inclusion (or, usually, exclusion) of bisexuals from particular organisations, or of the word 'bisexual' from the names of such organisations. One contributor sums up this concern:

> Much is made of bisexual 'invisibility'. At every bi conference and event it seems that I'm forever bumping into people muttering about the invisibility of our community. It's becoming clear that it's high time we did a little more to make our presence seen ... What's needed is a bit of visiBIlity'.[36]

The concern with visibility is carried over into regular media columns detailing coverage of bisexuality in both gay and straight media (a permanent feature of both *Bifrost* and *BCN*), and repeated protests at gay and straight refusal to recognise any orientation other than heterosexuality or homosexuality. Inclusion and acknowledgement of bisexuality, especially in lesbian and gay politics, is of course a key issue in *Bi-Monthly*, but the attention and relative importance given to visibility is much greater in its two successors: *BCN* gives 'be[ing] able to increase bisexual visibility' as one of its explicit aims.[37] This concern with the politics of visibility is, precisely, a concern with 'everyday understandings about what is "common sense" and what is "taken for granted" ... [T]he struggle to influence how we understand our lives and our society'[38] – that is, with power as 'pervasive' rather than 'top-down'. As another contributor puts it, 'The bisexual outlook ... [is] associate[d] with a blurring of boundaries, a rejection of traditional stereotypes and moral certainties, and the quest for freedom in the shape of alternative or queer forms of life'.[39]

Thus an increasing focus on 'visibility' and 'alternative forms of life' suggests the development of an implicit understanding of power as diffuse and ubiquitous, rather than more traditional notions of power as formal or hierarchical. While such an understanding clearly owes much both to the early feminist claim that 'the personal is political' and to the continuing legacy of 1980s identity politics, it operates in the

1990s with quite different approaches to power relations than that of 'oppression' which characterised bisexual politics in the 1980s. This shift in bisexual political thinking remains unformulated at a meta-discursive level, but is nevertheless a very real one. Whereas 'oppression' is an almost universal paradigm for understanding power in *Bi-Monthly*, the word itself barely appears in *BCN*, where contributors deal rather with 'visibility', 'stereotyping' and 'recognition'. The rise of a model of 'pervasive' power has in turn led to 'new self-criticism on the part of the bi community',[40] with examinations of power dynamics within bisexual organisations prompting debates over bisexuals' own exclusionary practices.

PROBLEMATICS

Despite these changes in political thinking, there are some manifestations of power with which bisexual politics consistently fails to grapple. Even when the 1980s politics of 'oppression' was at its height, racism in particular was rarely included in bisexual politics on anything other than a rhetorical level, and the new ways of thinking do not appear to have addressed it any better. As one black bisexual recently pointed out, 'The bi scene is not encouraging black bi involvement' even now.[41] Moreover, the effectiveness of bisexual politics as currently conducted can paradoxically mean an increase in precisely those forms of 'top-down' power which the new ways of thinking have decentered from political debate. Increased visibility of bisexuality – owing largely to the construction of bisexuals as 'conduits' of HIV infection from homosexuals to heterosexuals during the AIDS debates of the 1980s, but also to successful campaigns for bisexual inclusion and visibility in the broad arena of sexual politics – has resulted in the 1990s in the wholly unprecedented phenomenon of bisexuals being targeted *explicitly* as a discrete group by legislators and other authorities, even in cases where lesbians and gay men are not so targeted. Particularly notorious examples of this have been: the case of Labour MP and then shadow cabinet minister David Blunkett, who voted against an equal homosexual age of consent because he disapproved not of homosexuality, but of bisexuality;[42] cross-bench peer Lord Monson, who attempted to have bisexuals, and bisexuals only, removed from the Sexual Orientation (Discrimination) Bill of 1996;[43] and the Church of England, which in 1991 explicitly stated that bisexuality is always wrong.[44] Changing everyday understandings does not always have positive results.

Nevertheless, for better or worse, something is afoot in sexual politics in the UK, and the bisexual movement is, perhaps for the first time, very much a part of the new direction. According to some commentators, new ways of thinking about sexual politics in bisexual communities *have* produced more enabling modes of political activism. The *BCN* editorial collective suggests that there has been a shift away from large-scale, overarching struggles towards multiple small-scale and local campaigns, and that there appears to be less 'burn-out' among bisexual activists than previously as a result: rather than aiming for the overthrow of capitalism, patriarchy and the state, bisexual activists in the mid-1990s are more likely to concentrate their energies on maintaining a particular local group or service, or on achieving bisexual visibility in a particular media forum, or – one recent outstanding success – on gaining official inclusion in what at last became in 1996 the UK's Lesbian, Gay, Bisexual and Transgender Pride celebration. Indeed *BCN* sees its own role as pulling all these local campaigns together in its pages to produce a collage of bisexual politics, hoping that this will in turn contribute to yet more political change.[45] In this 'struggle to influence how we understand our lives and our society, a struggle to persuade rather than to force',[46] the bisexual movement may not quite be storming the millennium, but it plainly intends to see and be seen above the parapet.

Thanks to Paul Day, Jo Eadie, Clare Hemmings and Tim Jordan for their comments on earlier drafts of this article. Special thanks to the BCN *editorial collective for their assistance, and to Jo Eadie for kindly loaning me his collection of back issues of* Bifrost.

NOTES

1. See Lillian Faderman, *Odd Girls and Twilight Lovers: A History of Lesbian Life in Twentieth-Century America*, Penguin, London 1992; Jeffrey Weeks, *Coming Out: Homosexual Politics in Britain*, Quartet, London 1977.
2. See Cherry Smyth, *Lesbians Talk: Queer Notions*, Scarlet Press, London 1992; Simon Watney, 'Queer epistemology: activism, "outing", and the politics of sexual identities', *Critical Quarterly*, Vol.36, no.1, 1994, pp13-27.
3. Cherry Smyth, *op. cit.*, p28; c.f. Anna Marie Smith, 'Outlaws as legislators: feminist anti-censorship politics and queer activism', in Victoria Harwood, David Oswell, Kay Parkinson & Anna Ward (eds), *Pleasure Principles: Politics, Sexuality and Ethics*, Lawrence & Wishart, London 1993, pp20-40, esp. p24.
4. See Jeffrey Weeks, *op. cit.*, pp185-230.
5. For an account of struggles over SM and the LLGC controversy, see Susan

Ardill and Sue O'Sullivan, 'Upsetting the applecart: difference, desire and lesbian sadomasochism', *Feminist Review*, 23, 1986, pp31-57.

6. See e.g. Helen (charles), '"Queer nigger": theorising "white" activism', in Joseph Bristow & Angelia R. Wilson (eds), *Activating Theory*, Lawrence & Wishart, London 1993, pp97-106.

7. Cherry Smyth, *op. cit.*, p17.

8. Tim Jordan, *Reinventing Revolution: Value and Difference in New Social Movements and the Left*, Avebury Press, Aldershot 1994, p85; emphasis added. C.f. Jordan's contribution to this volume, chapter 9.

9. *Ibid.*, pp91-2.

10. See Caroline Ramazanoglu, *Feminism and the Contractions of Oppression*, Routledge, London and New York 1989.

11. See Anne McClintock, *Imperial Leather: Race, Gender and Sexuality in the Colonial Contest*, Routledge, New York and London 1995, pp391-396; Linda J. Nicholson (ed), *Feminism/Postmodernism*, Routledge, New York and London 1990; Anna Marie Smith, *New Right Discourse on Race and Sexuality: Britain 1968-1990*, Cambridge University Press, Cambridge 1994.

12. See Linda J. Nicholson, *op. cit.*; Caroline Ramazanoglu, *op. cit.*; Jeffrey Weeks, *Invented Moralities: Sexual Values in an Age of Uncertainty*, Polity, Cambridge 1995.

13. Jeffrey Weeks, *Invented Moralities*, p104.

14. Sue George, *Women and Bisexuality*, Scarlet Press, London 1993, especially pp184-99; Sharon Rose, Cris Stevens et al/Off Pink Collective (ed), *Bisexual Horizons: Politics, Histories, Lives*, Lawrence and Wishart, London 1996, pp215-88.

15. Up-to-date information on bisexual activism in the UK can be found in *Bi Community News* (hereafter *BCN*), available on subscription from BM Ribbit, London WC1N 3XX (homepage at http://www.bi.org/~bcn).

16. See Sharon Rose, Cris Stevens *et al.*, *op. cit.*, p216.

17. See Alan Scott, *Ideology and the New Social Movements*, Routledge, London and New York 1995, pp30-1.

18. See Madeleine Colvin, *Section 28: a Practical Guide to the Law and its Implications*, Liberty, London 1989.

19. *BCN*, certainly, has to date (September 1996) published all letters and submissions received, with some items edited for length only. Personal correspondence with *BCN* editorial collective, September 1996.

20. Editor's comments, 'Snail mail', *Bifrost* no.40, summer 1995, pp6-7, p7.

21. Manifesto of black bisexual caucus, *Bi-Monthly* no.21, February/March 1989, p7. (Some issues of Bi-Monthly are undated; in such cases estimated dates are given in square brackets.)

22. Anonymous report on 'Politics of Bisexuality' conference, *Bi-Monthly* no.7 [1985], pp2-3, p3, my emphasis.

23. See Sue George, *op.cit.*, p189.

24. Kevin Croydon, 'Conference feedback: bisexuality and anti-sexism', *Bifrost* no.17, November 1992, p11.

25. In fact bisexuals themselves arguably have considerable investment in the notion that they are 'excluded' from lesbian and gay political organising, in that exclusion acts as an alibi for the autonomy of bisexual identity as such: lesbians and gay men, in this context, act as the 'other' from which bisexuals are separate and distinct. Thanks to Clare Hemmings for this insight: c.f. Clare Hemmings, 'Locating bisexual identities: discourses of bisexuality and contemporary feminist theory', in David Bell & Gill Valentine (eds), *Mapping Desire: Geographies of Sexualities*, Routledge, London and New York 1995, pp41-55, esp. pp50-52.

26. Anonymous, 'An unbiased look at lesbian and gay politics', *Bi-Monthly* no.18 [1987/8], pp6-7, p7.

27. Anonymous article, *Bi-Monthly* no.7 [1985], p31.

28. Letter from Joy Hibbert, 'Letters', *Bifrost* no.21, March 1993, p2.

29. See Susan Ardill and Sue O'Sullivan, *op. cit.*; Emma Healey, *Lesbian Sex Wars*, Virago, London 1996.

30. C.f. Sue George, *op. cit.*, p187.

31. See Amanda Udis-Kessler, 'Bisexuality in an essentialist world: toward an understanding of biphobia', in Tom Geller (ed.), *Bisexuality: a Reader and Sourcebook*, Times Change Press, Ojai 1990, pp51-63. Thanks to Jo Eadie for this insight.

32. David: Birmingham, 'Power', *Bifrost* no.22, April 1993, p1.

33. Kevin Lano, 'Political bisexuality – a culture of resistance', *Bifrost* no.36, supplement 2, August 1994, p3.

34. *Ibid.*

35. David: Birmingham, *op. cit.*

36. Giles, 'VisiBIlity', *Bifrost* no.31, January 1994, p1.

37. Steve C., 'Bi Community News: what are we up to?', *BCN* no.5, March 1996, pp4-5, p4.

38. David: Birmingham, *op. cit.*

39. Tom Shakespeare, 'Last words', *Bifrost* no.38, winter 1994/5, p21. This article provoked a series of heated exchanges in the letters page – objections being to the author's views on monogamy, not to his characterisation of 'the bisexual outlook'.

40. Letter from Sue George, 'Letters', *BCN* no.5, March 1996, pp8-9, p8.

41. Jackie Hunt, 'Black, bisexual and where?', *BCN* no.7, May 1996, p3.

42. See Andrew Saxton, 'I made the right decision' (interview with David Blunkett), in *The Pink Paper*, 18 March 1994, p15.
43. See *BCN* no.6, April 1996, p1. The Bill sought to ban discrimination on the grounds of sexual orientiation, which is still legal in the UK. Monson's attempt failed, but the Bill itself was defeated later that year.
44. See Sue George, *Women and Bisexuality*, p12.
45. Personal correspondence with *BCN* editorial collective, September 1996.
46. David: Birmingham, *op. cit.*

THE ANTI-ROADS MOVEMENT: THE STRUGGLE OF MEMORY AGAINST FORGETTING

Patrick Field

INTRODUCTION

In his 1947 critique of the 'road safety' movement J.S. Dean described the motor-interests' 'dream-world' where ...

> ... nothing is to be seen except colossal roads, so long and wide that even the super-cars using them are scarcely visible and the minute pedestrians merely enter or emerge from subways, and then only in two's and three's or singly; in which, in fact nothing exists except "fast traffic" and the entire life of the community is held up to allow it to pass; but in which whatever else happens, everyone goes on buying more and more cars.[1]

By the 1960s people who could remember when the roads of Britain were free from the deadly hazard of motor-traffic were growing old and few and the fantasies of the motor-lobby had gained a powerful hegemony. In 1963 the report of the Buchanan Committee into the problem of urban motor-traffic congestion concluded that road 'improvements' could never accommodate unlimited motor-travel, that sooner or later restraint would be required. This was ignored whilst the report's other strand, that towns and cities should be remodelled to separate pedestrians from motor-traffic, received rapid concrete endorsement.[2]

In 1965 the newly formed Greater London Council initiated the 'Ringways' plan of motorway construction in London. It threatened 20,000 homes with destruction. The GLC expected 2500 objections to the Greater London Development Plan; it got 22,000.[3] The decisive political battle over these plans took place during the 1973 GLC elections when Labour fought and won on a 'homes not roads' ticket.

Wards straddling controversial sections of the proposed routes produced higher than average swings to Labour. From this period onwards new road proposals were revealed piecemeal as 'bypasses' and local 'improvements'. The era of self-confident grand design was over.

Two key events in the emergence of the more recent public consensus against unlimited motor-traffic and destructive road building were 'fares fair' and the opening of the M25. The former was a policy of cheap fares and better public transport implemented by Ken Livingstone's GLC which was successful and popular. Income from passengers went up, car crashes and traffic congestion went down. But before the 'fares fair' policy could be tested by the ballot box the GLC was abolished. In 1986 the M25 – an orbital motorway built outside the jurisdiction of the GLC – opened. Sections of it were immediately congested by flows of motor traffic far higher than its designed capacity.

In November 1984, having promised to abolish the GLC in their manifesto for the 1983 General Election, the Conservative Government announced the London Assessment Studies, widely interpreted as preparation for the construction of new roads. The response to these studies showed that public opinion was moving from a 'not in my backyard' attitude to a general distrust of car-based solutions to transport and land-use problems.

Within Inner London the unanimity was remarkable. Young, old, rich, poor, black, white: almost without exception the public were opposed to new highway construction and wanted more money invested in public transport.

The draft road plans published before the collapse of the London Assessment Studies were accompanied by assurances that any schemes chosen to progress further would be subject to public inquiry. Little comfort was taken from these words. By this time the public inquiry system – as applied to road construction – was widely discredited. As George Stern the celebrated campaigner against the widening of the A1 in North London put it, 'The record says that motorway inquiries result in a motorway in 99 per cent of cases. That sounds like Soviet democracy, Brezhnev-style, to me'.[4]

However, this opinion against road-building was confined to Inner London where it is impossible to escape the harmful effects of motor traffic. In the suburbs, where motor-dependence seems both less destructive and more necessary, the dream that increasing road capacity could reduce congestion retained currency.

THE GREAT NORTH ROAD

The first major showdown between campaigners and the Government came in 1973 when the Department of Transport tried, in a series of six public inquiries, to win consent to widen the A1 along Archway Road and Falloden Way. A vigorous campaign declared its opposition to the plans. The Archway Road campaigners developed tactics which combined posing difficult questions to the authorities with uncompromising ridicule. This approach drew on the experience of the Chiswick Motorway Liaison Committee which had, unsuccessfully, resisted the extension of the M4 through West London, and was aided by John Tyme, an environmental lecturer from Sheffield Polytechnic who terrorised the Department of Transport throughout the 1970s by helping similar campaigns all over the country. As this epic struggle unfolded the campaigners recognised that to be drawn into a polite debate was to take the road-lobby and the Department of Transport more seriously than they deserved. The projects of the motorisers, as J.S. Dean observed years before, have no more logic and reason than an opium-smoker's dream.

George Stern's influential samizdat paper, *How Not To Lose Motorway Inquiries* explains the theory of opposing an all-powerful foe with cunning, frivolity and implacable disrespect:

> Remember: they've come to destroy your home, your district, to make where you live into a slum beside a motorway. 'They' are the Ministry officials, the inspector and his side-kicks, the inquiry organisers, quite likely your MPs and your council. People understand this, but when they meet officials are fooled by superficial politeness. Well, Himmler was a polite little man too. You may, at times, be polite back. But never forget: this man wants to destroy everything you have. And he wants to do it not because he'll be shot if he doesn't. Not because his pay will go down. But because he's a nasty little toady who will condemn thousands to misery for life just to make his boss smile at him.

Stern's advice is don't waste energy making the case against the project. If the forces of 'progress' were susceptible to reasoning they wouldn't be trying to build it in the first place. More devious resistance is demanded:

> Little old ladies weeping in distress – he (the presiding inspector) loves it. He listens politely and then signs away their home. Your line is that

you can't put your important case until other things are right. The tactic has to be, we believe: make the enquiry as uncomfortable as possible for the inspector so that he wants to leave it, but give him a technical excuse. He won't just stop the inquiry (nothing wrong in asking for it though). But he may stop the inquiry for a few months – which may be forever – to get some more information, to ask for a reworking of wrong figures. So you need the pomposity puncturing but you do need a good argument about new data etc. as well.

The campaigners saw that the only way of redressing the awesome imbalance of power between the two sides is to keep the bureaucrats guessing as to what will come next, a detailed question to which they must provide a plausible answer or a piece of calculated lunacy:

Take things with you into the inquiry – you feel terribly alone and are terribly easily hypnotised into inaction. Looking at officials/inspectors through binoculars is good. Bird-call whistles, laughing cushions from joke shops – great.

The tactics were mad but the trees and houses that line the Archway Road are still standing. Archway was the motor-lobby's Stalingrad.

A BRIDGE TOO FAR

The East London River Crossing (ELRiC) was a plan to replace the Woolwich Ferry with a new bridge linking the North and South Circular Roads. This creeping ringway is well advanced in North London but hardly present in the South. The bridge's approach road was planned to cut through Oxleas Wood, the last patch of ancient woodland within Greater London. The plan was considered at a series of public inquiries, including Britain's longest ever hearing into a road scheme which ran from September 1985 to December 1986. But in August 1993, with tree-felling expected to follow the leaf-fall, ELRiC was summarily abandoned.

This raises the question: if public inquiries are so proper, how come the Department of Transport drew back – at the fifty-ninth minute of the twenty-third hour – from building the East London River Crossing which had been exhaustively examined by that system? If ELRiC was *'unacceptable on environmental grounds'* – as the Department claimed when it dropped the scheme – how did it get through so many public inquiries?

The public inquiry system asks what kind of road shall we build? It cannot question the assumptions underlying road-building itself, and which maintain the demand for road-capacity. Contempt for the public inquiry system – even amongst volunteers who dedicated years of their lives to fighting within it – allows activists to consider a whole spectrum of tactics: lobbying politicians, public agitation, bureaucratic opposition in the law courts, symbolic stunts, disobedient mass-action and clandestine sabotage. These may be conducted by different groups – albeit with considerable interchange of personnel – but with an understanding that many different forms of resistance are appropriate for different situations. They are all valid and complementary.

'UNLIKELY ALLIES'

'I'M NOT an anarchist, I'm a Conservative voter the elderly man said'. The quotation begins a story, headed *'Unlikely allies confront bulldozers as motorway crosses the water meadows'*, which was run in the *Independent* on Wednesday 18 March 1992. The 'unlikely allies' slant has since become a cliché in news reports of actions against road construction. It has also generated acres of feature material often accompanied by photographs of wild-haired young outlaws (nose-rings preferred) chatting sweetly or linking arms with patrician types in tweed. The young are supposed to disrespect their elders while the old are supposed to respect the law.

That some of England's conservatives chose to support those willing to step outside the due process of law to fight for their country should not surprise anyone who has read Larkin, Betjeman or especially Kipling. The mystical significance ascribed to the landscape of England in *Puck of Pook's Hill* is not so far from contemporary neo-paganism.

In addition, the denial of natural justice implicit in the public inquiry system, where the Executive conducts inquiries into its own proposals and is also the body making the final decision, is liable to provoke previously respectful citizens to the point where direct action can be supported or even engaged in.

Once destroyed, landscapes, communities, trees and houses cannot be remade. The struggle to defend something that cannot be replaced demands more desperate measures than the fight against less concrete policy; hence the Earth First! slogan. 'If not you who? If not now when?' To young people, who have no memory of the world without the ecological imperative, the fury with which their elders may fight to defend their localities and homes is easily transferred to the whole globe. 'Not in my backyard' becomes 'not in my biosphere'.

Young people taking an anti-authoritarian posture for the thrill of youthful rebellion find being supported (with soup, old clothes etc.) or even joined in action by mature companions confirms that they are not just being naughty for the sake of it. Likewise older people, inhibited from direct action by years of unquestioned obedience, can be inspired by youth's reckless example.

The state has proven strategies for dealing with bourgeois campaigners: engage and exhaust them with inquiries, commissions and committees, then apply the steam-roller. Those who choose physical resistance are likely to be crushed with overwhelming force and the threat or use of violence and prison. However, when respectability and rebellion are combined the campaign can prove more troublesome. Following eighteen months of outrage over the Winchester bypass the prospect of Oxleas Wood filled with tree-houses each staffed with two determined outlaws nursing secret dreams of martyrdom and one 'excuse-me-do-you-know-who-I-am' professional person, equipped with a mobile phone whose memory contains the numbers of several national newspapers and a lawyer, was just too daunting. The East London River Crossing was abandoned and the direct action movement had its first uncontested victory.

Rebellious youth has often presented a public order problem. In the twentieth century accelerating change justified generational conflict. Only the young, lacking a sentimental attachment to the past, could fully understand, appreciate and benefit from the opportunities offered by the unprecedented present. Twenty-something Phil Mcliesh explains why he is against the proposed M11 Link Road even though it would, supposedly, take six minutes off a motorist's journey into Central London:

> It is the logic of growth, change and movement for its own sake, that is being called into question. Six minutes or sixty, it makes no difference how fast you go if you're not going anywhere. In the rejection of mobility for its own sake there is implied a rejection of the whole restlessness of modernity.[5]

The busy world of the 1990s is managed by people who came of age as the first teenagers in the 1950s or in the white heat of the technological revolution of the 1960s. Commentators surprised by the multi-generational appeal of campaigns against road 'improvements', against change for the sake of change, miss the delightful paradox that today's rebel generation can reject the values of their parents by respecting the wisdom of their elders. When Neil Goodwin edited 100 hours of interviews and actuality to tell the No M11 Story on video tape he put a quote from Milan Kundera on the front *'The struggle of people against power is the struggle of memory against forgetting'.*[6] The inclusive nature of anti-road campaigning reflects a desire to value wisdom and the recognition that many kinds of opposition are valid.

PRINCIPLES AND TACTICS

Non-violence as principle and tactic allows the maximum number of people to participate. It maintains public support. It keeps the focus on the issues of transport policy, land use planning, public health, the right to protest. The road builders would certainly prefer violent resistance which would give the conflict a public order slant. Allegations of violent conduct by private security guards working for contractors have generally been more convincing than any slurs against activists.

Non-violence is self-preservation, cameras aren't always present, and there are proven examples (such as the fire-bombing of a bender at Wanstead in 1993) of potentially lethal force being used against campaigners. Rumours persist of anonymous paramilitary eviction squads operating at Newbury. In general non-violence does not have to be enforced since it is implicit in much of campaign methodology. Work site invasions are carnivals with drums, whistles and fancy dress. Fortified camps are adventure playgrounds with tree houses and aerial walkways. Evictions are house parties, street festivals, performance.

THE SINGLE ISSUE

The *Independent*'s 18 March 1992 *'unlikely allies'* story suggested the action on the water meadows 'may prove to have been the last stand against the M3 extension'. In fact, actions continued for another sixteen months. 'Last stands' and 'last ditches' have proved to be another repetitious theme in coverage of direct action against road construction.

Resistance to road building is not just about stopping a particular project. Every delay, every disruption, every extra one thousand pounds spent on police or security is a victory: money that is not available to be spent elsewhere. *'Double the cost of one road and you have prevented another being built'* is an opinion often expressed by activists. In such an unequal struggle, to resist is to win. Resisting draws attention to destruction that would otherwise go unnoticed. It draws attention to the lack of arguments in favour of building the road. It was worthwhile, at Claremont Road on the line of the proposed M11 Link Road, to spend months fortifying and defending houses so neglected that, even if the road had been scrapped before the eviction, they would have been demolished anyway.

This is the difference between demonstration and protest. (The *Independent*'s 18 March 1992 story called the action on the water meadows a 'demonstration' even though it halted the bulldozers). 'Actions' may involve a symbolic element. They may, like the occupation of the roof of the Secretary of State for Transport's house on 26 April 1994, be designed to generate images that reveal the issues involved. But they also always aim to disrupt. Protest and demonstration are only symbolic, action never is.

The 'last stand' angle may be employed to add drama but it also tends to marginalise the action. The commentators from the busy world like dynamic stories. They love sieges in trees or houses especially if they involve photogenic danger. They are not so good at putting the action in an ideological context. Resisting the construction of a new road is often described as a 'single issue campaign'. It is. The single issue is the future of human life on earth.

In June 1994, at the height of the worst asthma epidemic ever recorded, a team of scruffy liberty-takers from Claremont Road climbed the scaffolding around the Department of Transport's Westminster tower block, let off a clutch of smoke bombs and flew a giant banner reading – 'Build an M11 Link? You must be choking'. Parliament was sitting, which made the demonstration illegal. The action was carried out with good humour, but letting off big fireworks in Victoria can only be called provocative. The police were all smiles and seemed under no pressure to take the matter further.

No matter how big a splash an event on the M11 Link road made there was a conspicuous absence of national politicians popping up to defend the value of a new expressway to bring motor traffic into London. A few days after the pyrotechnic stunt the minister for roads and traffic was sacked in a reshuffle.

THE END OF THE ARGUMENT

In October 1994 the report of the Royal Commission on Environmental Pollution (chaired by Paul Channon a former Conservative Secretary of State for Transport) called for an end to new road construction. Just before Christmas of the same year an even more conclusive government report came from the Standing Committee on Trunk Road Assessment. This finally admitted that new or wider roads make new and bigger traffic jams. Only shock-jocks and motoring correspondents still resist the idea that motor-dependence must be limited but the Government restricts itself to futile appeals: 'Please leave your car at home today the air is bad', or talks of measures to be applied 'in the long-term'.

Viewing a retreat from motor dependence as a chance to increase health, happiness and conviviality is very much a dissident position even though a critique of motor culture offers answers to many problems: marine pollution from grounded oil tankers, brutal oppression in the Niger Delta, road rage. Even the live export of food animals can be analysed as an issue of unnecessary road freight.

The Australian urbanist David Engwicht uses graphs to explain why motor-dependence destroys communities and social harmony: even highway engineers can understand his argument. His study of the relationship between movement and exchange explains how greater use of private vehicles sets up a series of downward spirals that ultimately increase the length and frequency of journeys without any resulting increase in exchange. Finally more and more time is spent travelling with less and less benefit.[7]

A third of British ten-year-olds do not even walk for ten minutes a week. Many are taken to school by car and avoid sports, preferring to watch TV and play computer games. Dr Ian Baird of the British Heart Foundation says, 'There is overwhelming evidence that children who do not exercise are at greater risk of developing heart disease. The trend towards a sedentary life-style among school children is potentially disastrous'. This public health issue is also a land-use issue, a traffic issue and an issue of motor dependence.

In the autumn of 1996 a furore gripped British media and politicians concerning contemporary society's inability to socialise certain of its male children. No one suggested that loss of autonomy and social interaction precipitated by motor dependence may be a contributory factor, even though the startling decline of children's independent mobility in the last twenty years is a matter of record.[8]

Those whose lives have been made harder by motor traffic – children, women, the elderly and the poor – the people who previously used streets for more convivial purposes than the movement and storage of motor vehicles, who used the local facilities that motorisation has reduced or removed, who don't have access to private motor vehicles – have always been in the majority. This majority has lately been reinforced by many of the traditional beneficiaries of motorisation. Whatever your political persuasion, disposable income or preferred mode of travel, an atmosphere that is not toxic to oxygen-breathing organisms should rate high on your list of requirements for prosperity and satisfaction. The social-justice and public-health consequences of unrestrained use of the motor car cannot forever be excluded from the arena of political debate.

NEW OFFENCES
The end of road construction will not curtail direct action against motor traffic. On 13 July 1996, the short stretch of road known as the M41 was captured for a party by 'Reclaim the Streets', a disorganisation many of whose personnel have experience of resisting road-construction. 7000 people danced and socialised on the roadway. Under the skirts of a giant carnival puppet the tarmac was dug up and trees were planted.

Critical Mass is a global phenomenon which began in San Francisco. Critical Mass is a very big sociable bike ride, with minimal pre-planning. All that is fixed is a regular date and time. The only certain element is the unpredictable. In London, on the last Friday of each month, several hundred riders are always expected. Mainstream media and the police commonly tag it as 'protest' or 'demonstration' whereas the atmosphere is more carnival or party. How does a leisurely Friday night bike ride come to be interpreted as contentious? Is there a clue in the politicisation of other no-brain-no-headache pursuits? In the summer of 1996 'Surfers Against Sewage' was claiming a UK membership of 23,000. The idea that going out for a bike ride with your mates to celebrate the start of the weekend can be an act of political resistance ties in nicely with the phenomenon of the politically-conscious surfer.

Well within living memory the opinion that 'the best things in life are free' was commonly expressed. This is no longer the case. The rapacity of the busy world threatens to devour fresh air, clean water, silence, darkness and contentment. The urge to treasure what was once free and is now priceless is most easily recognised and expressed by people distanced from the levers of economic and political power, semi-detached from the short-termism of the busy world.

The desire to protect 'the best things in life' is not however confined to outsiders. When Cecil Parkinson, then Secretary of State for Transport, gave consent for the construction of the Winchester Bypass, a *Times* editorial stated: 'Twyford Down has a value too and that also belongs on the balance sheet.'[9] The vogue for nostalgia amongst politicians – 'back to basics', 'family values' – can be analysed as symptoms of this desire.

In the busy world earning and spending are the paramount forms of human activity, and 'work' (which in this context means 'paid employment') has an almost sacramental status. Work, 'efficiency' and increasing consumption are the targets of left, right and centre. 'Standard of living', 'gross national product' – presume to measure our fulfilment by how much we can waste. Health and harmony do not appear in the balance sheet. Economic growth is the automatic key to increasing human happiness.

Only armaments, drugs of addiction and motor vehicles are wasteful enough to sustain this growth. Increasing the world-wide consumption of the first two has obvious problems. Thus the motor-car occupies a central position in the mythology of satisfaction through consumption. Abandoning the road programme means much more than taking business away from some heavy contributors to Conservative Party funds. Humans in motor-vehicles, polluting town and country with noise, danger and poison gas – frustrated, angry and alienated – are victims of a crisis in human organisation. This crisis concerns our philosophical relationship to the earth, nature or God. The theory of 'work hard and consume more' may have served humanity tolerably well for 7000 years but now we know that continued, unplanned growth is not a target but suicide. The argument is no longer about how we divide the cake but over the origin and content of the cake itself.

Climatic change – the scariest component of the ecological imperative – has an old testament ring. Counter-measures demand a millennial, 'first-shall-be-last-and-the-last-shall-be-first' shift of priorities. The whole project of social progress through increased consumption is a steam-roller running down hill without a driver. Our nominal rulers have no programme except crisis management. They are hobbled by short-term agendas. Waiting for them to take action is waiting for an apocalypse.

In a sustainable future the mainstream's hero, the amoral workaholic, is a liability. People content with a simpler life that allows more time for reflection (poverty and idleness in the busy world) are better role models. Taking action against the busy world is a no-lose option. Win and sustain the future or everything goes down into chaos which would have happened anyway. As the contradictions of the busy world become more obvious (who would have dared predict the scale of the mad-cow crisis of 1996) as it disappears up its own exhaust pipe, resistance becomes easier – climbing a tree, surfing, going for a ride on your bike, having a street party. *'The desire to live is a political decision.'*[10]

A MONUMENT

On Sunday 4 July 1993 a mass trespass broke into the new cutting through Twyford Down. It was a cloudless day and the cliffs of clean chalk reflected heat and light. In the previous six months sediments deposited over millions of years had been removed, transforming the soft green downland into a harsh white desert. Hundreds of people cavorting through the unfurnished canyon served only to emphasise its scale: a mile long, 400 feet wide and 100 feet deep, a triumph of humanity's power and ingenuity. Emptiness is fitting monument to the people who understand the 'how' of working such miracles but daily grow less certain of the 'why'.

NOTES

1. J.S. Dean, *Murder Most Foul ... a study of the road deaths problem*, George Allen & Unwin Ltd., London 1947.
2. Buchanan et al., *Traffic in Towns: A study of the long-term problems of traffic in urban areas*, HMSO 1963.
3. Mick Hamer, *Wheels Within Wheels – A Study of the Road Lobby*, Routledge Kegan Paul, London 1987.
4. George Stern, *Archway*, unpublished, 1990.
5. *A BE SEA magazine*, Claremont Road Celebration issue, Sebastien Boyle, London 1995.
6. *Life in the Fast Lane*, for details send an SAE to: PO box 10834, 44 Tottenham Lane, London N8 0AW.
7. David Engwicht, *Reclaiming our Cities and Towns*, Jon Carpenter Publishing, PO Box 129, Oxford OX1 4PH.
8. M. Hillman et al., *One False Move*, Policy Studies Institute, London 1991.
9. *The Times*, 28.2.1990.
10. Graffiti from the wall of the No M11 Office, Claremont Road, 1994.

New Space, New Politics: The Electronic Frontier Foundation and the Definition of Cyberpolitics

Tim Jordan

Hopes and fears in cyberspace and on the Internet

Cyberspace's nature is most simply captured by John Perry Barlow's saying that 'cyberspace is where you are when you are on the telephone'. It is the place we enter when we communicate with each other but are physically separated. Under this definition cyberspace has existed for a long time. However, with the marriage in the last thirty years of computer and communications technology, whole communities have erupted there. This shift should not be underestimated, as it is the point at which cyberspace stops being subordinate to 'offline space' and becomes its own sphere with particular rules of society, time and space. The size of this global community is difficult to measure, but in 1997 it was at least 19.5 million and at most 100 million.[1]

The material basis of this community is the ability of people to communicate with each other using computers, the Internet being the main means for this. Computer-mediated communication allows the creation of virtual communities that have several characteristics which are different to non-virtual communities: global many-to-many communication, anti-hierarchical communication, identity fluidity and the importance of information.[2] From online fantasy worlds to corporate electronic mail: people have married in cyberspace, had sex there, argued and, in Timothy Leary's case, (almost) died there, and through all this activity have built a new social space.

When the results of computer-mediated communication are understood as a space, the question 'what is the politics of this place?'

becomes appropriate. Rather than simply the reflection of a politics that already exists, which might be the case, cyberspace is sufficiently its own place to warrant the question, 'is there a specific form of cyber-politics?'[3] This chapter will offer the beginnings of an answer to this question by examining an activist group that was born in and concerns itself with cyberspace. There are a number of organisations that campaign on behalf of cyberspace users, Centre for Democracy and Technology (CDT), Computer Communicators' Association, Voters Telecommunications Watch and others, but the longest lived and best known activist group is the Electronic Frontier Foundation (EFF). A case study of EFF forms the central part of this chapter.[4]

To explore the cyberpolitics of EFF, a brief history will be offered, followed by a statistical assessment of EFF's politics as they have appeared in its newsletter *EFFector*. Then an overall characterisation of EFF's politics will be given. All analysis will be supplemented by interviews with some of the leading actors in EFF and CDT (see appendix) and any unreferenced quotes are from these interviews. In conclusion, the extent to which the politics of EFF relate to cyberpolitics in general, and the questions posed for a new politics, will be raised.

EFF: HISTORY, NEWSLETTER AND POLITICS

History
The following history provides an introduction to EFF and the major political changes it has undergone. Changes can be correlated with EFF's four locations: Cambridge, Massachusetts; Cambridge and Washington DC; Washington DC; and San Francisco, each of which will be dealt with in turn.

> Each of the moves reflects major changes in where EFF was going, what it was going to focus on, the issues that came from the Board and so on. Those moves were reflected by changes in how we did things, things we said, what kind of stances we took, what kind of funding and audience market we went for. There are very big differences between the EFF of Cambridge and Washington DC or of DC and San Francisco. (Stanton McCandlish, online activist, EFF)

Cambridge: December 1990 to January 1992. In late 1989 and early 1990, the US secret service and various State and Federal police bodies conducted a crackdown against computer hackers, known as

Operation Sun Devil, and explored a number of other computer crimes, such as the theft and anonymous mailing of some of Apple's proprietary software. The ignorance of many of the police pursuing computer crime and the draconian methods employed alarmed a number of cyberspace users. For example, there is the legendary policeman who was asked to copy a floppy disk and promptly put it in the photocopier, thereby getting a copy of the disk's label and scrambling all the data. Not only is ignorance evident here but also destruction, as that disk's data would not be recovered.[5] John Perry Barlow, then a cattle rancher in Pinedale Wyoming, one-time chair of his state Republican committee, lyricist for the Grateful Dead and an inhabitant of cyberspace, wrote an account of a baffling visit he received from his local policeman who was pursuing computer crime. As a result, he was contacted by the co-founder of the Lotus corporation, Mitchell Kapor, who had also been interviewed by the police. They decided to found a civil liberties organisation for cyberspace called the Electronic Frontier Foundation. After posting this intention on the net, Steve Wozniak (co-founder of Apple) and John Gilmore (early employee of Sun Microsystems[6]) added their financial and intellectual weight and the organisation was founded in 1990 in Cambridge, Massachusetts USA.

> We had this notion of ourselves as Butch Cassidy and the Sundance Kid. It was just going to be Mitch and John alone against the governments of the free world! But we felt so electronically amplified we felt we could probably do just as well that way as any way.
>
> (John Perry Barlow, co-founder, board member, EFF)

During the period in Cambridge, naturally enough, EFF picked up the fall-out from Operation Sun Devil. First, EFF constituted itself as an organisation with some members of staff (the first being staff counsel Mike Godwin) and a Board.[7] Early activities consisted of a number of high profile court cases to establish the rights of hackers and others affected by law enforcement operations. EFF also attempted to educate law enforcement and the media about online life and those online about their rights. An online newsletter called *EFFector*, several online discussions and a site on the Internet to provide documents and information all began. EFF began to lobby the US government and bureaucracy, which resulted in a second office in Washington. Barlow recalled this change as being largely a response to cable and telephone companies having the objective of:

> turning cyberspace into a one-way environment. It would be a place, but it would be a place where there would be a speaker on every light-pole and it would all be coming downstream. We thought that was a pretty loathsome prospect and we thought the best way to stop or mitigate it was going to be Washington. We'd already met Jerry Berman and he was all over it, with a lot of old connections in telecommunications' lobbying. We thought, 'well, you know, let's set up another office with Jerry in Washington'. So we did.
>
> (John Perry Barlow[8])

Cambridge and Washington: January 1992 to June 1993. This period is marked by the emergence of a central concern with the developing nature of the net and with a widening gulf within the organisation between the policy/lobbying office in Washington and the education/community office in Cambridge. EFF worked on policy in two directions. First, it tried to ensure cheap and widely available ISDN (Integrated Services Digital Nerwork) to ensure people could have powerful and economical access to the Internet. Second, it developed the Open Platform policy, which eventually appeared in the Clinton/Gore administration's National Information Infrastructure proposal (the famed and failed Information Superhighway). The Open Platform policy aimed at opening access to online life and at ensuring that, as networks developed, they would communicate with each other. Community or educative work proceeded much as it had in the period prior to establishing the Washington office, but tension between the two approaches became exacerbated by personal differences such that it became impossible for the two offices to work together. EFF's Board made the decision to focus on policy and lobbying and closed its Cambridge office, sacking a number of staff.

> It was really untenable, the culture division was so great. I remember at one point we went to a retreat, the whole staff and Board at Lake Tahoe. I could sense from my contacts on the net that people were ready to form chapters, to grow the organisation ... And there was a general consensus to go ahead. Jerry Berman was very upset about this because his experience at ACLU (American Civil Liberties Union) was that the problem was you were always getting pressure from below or above and you were always getting your hands tied and second-guessed by other

people who didn't know what you knew about how to operate. He wanted to have an organisation with some clout where he had a very small constituency that he was responsible to; that was what EFF became.

(Mike Godwin, staff counsel, first employee, EFF)

Only Washington: July 1993 to July 1995. As would be expected, this period was marked by a deeper focus on lobbying and policy. Issues already taken up continued. In addition, a number of Clinton/Gore administration initiatives began to focus attention on privacy. Most importantly, the various incarnations of the Digital Telephony Bill and the Clipper chip emerged, all of which would attempt to mandate automated wiretapping into the USA's communications infrastructure. At the same time, the controversy over pornography on the Internet was taken up and resulted in a series of battles that would culminate in the Communications Decency Act. As a result of these battles, EFF became heavily enmeshed in the particular politics required to influence government legislation and bureaucracies.

The end of this period can be related to the Digital Telephony Bill that EFF was thought by many to have supported, causing outrage among many on the net and some civil libertarians. In fact, EFF supported certain provisions of the Bill and opposed others, but it also opposed the Bill as a whole unless the provisions it rejected were removed. This amounted to opposition to the Bill but was a complex position that was widely misinterpreted.[9] The difficulty created by the decision to support part of the legislation and the reaction to that decision, led to a review of the shift into legislative politics.

> The Washington office had gotten incredibly good at bringing in lots of money from our erstwhile enemies, like AT&T, and we'd been suckered into the belief that this was what we needed to be effective. Now that the scales have fallen from my eyes I just feel 'Doh'[slaps forehead], but at the time I was going for it.
>
> (John Perry Barlow)

During the process of staff and Board members reviewing what EFF had become, a decision was taken to shift direction back to grassroots and legal work, away from policy work. The initial decision was for Jerry Berman, then Executive Director, to move with the policy staff into a new EFF project concerned only with policy. In the interim

Berman would become Policy Director and Drew Taubman was hired as Executive Director. However, friction between Berman and Taubman led to the shelving of this plan. Berman then left EFF with EFF's policy and lobbying staff to found the Centre for Democracy and Technology. As Godwin noted: 'Suddenly EFF was no longer a policy organisation.' While there were undoubtedly personal battles that contributed to the split between EFF and CDT, different political beliefs constituted the key components.[10]

> What happened was a difference in vision ... at the bottom line it was a question of strategy differences and political differences; a question of how does one effect change inside Washington? And that's why we are here and they are in San Francisco.
>
> (Jonah Seiger, online activist, CDT)

The difference was, in some ways, the re-emergence of the community-based vision of politics that had been sidelined with the move to Washington. Two of the founders described their experiences in Washington and what they felt had been lost there, in these ways:

> I saw that the only thing we could do in Washington was to prevent bad things, we couldn't actually catalyse good things to happen. And it became very disheartening because we would work and work and work and stave off a bunch of bad things and still some of them would happen, and nothing good would happen.
>
> (John Gilmore, co-founder, Board member, EFF)

> Then there we were in DC and we found ourselves dealing more and more with the art of the deal in ways that made people feel increasingly uncomfortable. Finally we felt we just had to leave to save our mortal souls. We also had to get back to where we had been since, personally ... I felt there was no way to play the game in Washington and not get too much dirt on you; that merely accepting their terms for the game was enough to let them win it. We were better off going off at a distance and creating our own terms.
>
> (John Perry Barlow)

San Francisco: Beyond 1995.[11] The shift to San Francisco can be seen both as a return to previously sidelined community politics and as a move to a new definition of EFF's politics. Stanton McCandlish, who joined the staff in Washington, sees it as an accumulation. He argues that in its first phase EFF focused on individuals, in its second it added government and in its third it added the industry that creates and sustains Internet technology, and by moving to San Francisco all three levels could co-exist. However, it is also largely true that the policy record of EFF was created by staff who left to form CDT. Somewhat ironically, EFF's work in San Francisco was initially chiefly dominated by a legal and judicial matter being passed in Washington: the Communications Decency Act. However, even with this necessary focus on a piece of legislation, EFF worked on generating grassroots and corporate criticisms of the act and policy work largely passed to CDT and other organisations. EFF has also managed to generate a new programme in e-TRUST, which attempts to build trust in online privacy and attempts to pre-empt legislative or state involvement in such change (see section three below).

A brief history of EFF drawn from available documents and interviews suggests two sides to EFF's politics. First, there is a split between a broader focus on cyberspace though educative and community building work and a narrower focus on the state and legislature. Second, a number of issues that characterise online politics emerge; access, privacy, censorship and individual rights (that is, having the same rights online as offline). It is the first side of cyberpolitics that dominates the organisation's history: its move into the power politics of government (in the process losing a community-based role), and then the attempt to move away from Washington style politics to recover its own agenda. To explore this further we can turn to an analysis of EFF's online newsletter, *EFFector*.

Analysis of *Effector*

EFFector is received by over 7000 people in the form of email and is read by countless more as it is posted widely online. *EFFector* can be treated as a record of EFF's activism as it is one of the key places where EFF educates and organises its community. A content analysis of *EFFector* should, then, provide a measure of EFF's politics generated from publications produced at the time various issues emerged. It will provide a check on the politics outlined by activists in interview.[12] The analysis' methodology is outlined in an attached appendix and it explores two types of politics. First, a comparison of typical online and offline issues. Second, a comparison of policy versus community building politics. All editions of *EFFector* up to edition number 9.08, 12 June 1996, are included, 107 editions in all.

Nine types of politics have been constructed to compare online with offline and to explore EFF's politics. To this end five types of online politics have been created from analysis of the nature of cyberspace, from analysis of EFF and CDT's documents and from discussion with interviewees. The five types are as follows: access TO cyberspace which covers issues of who gains access (and how) to cyberspace; access IN cyberspace, which covers issues related to which information sources are available (and to whom) online (for example, lobbying for government documents to be placed online); privacy, which covers issues of who can read messages sent online, and includes encryption debates; censorship, which covers attempts to control content that is provided online; and finally, hacking, which covers issues of the rights of those involved in unauthorised computer intrusion. The four categories of offline politics are: gender, race, class and ecology. These have been chosen because they represent four undeniably central issues in modern Western societies. This does not mean other issues could not have been chosen, only that these four should provide a measure of whether offline politics is evident in online politics. The first graph shows the overall numbers of these nine types of politics found in *EFFector*.

Chart 1: EFFector: all politics by total instances

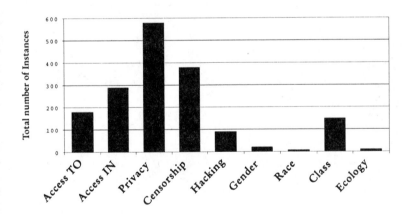

The first conclusion is that EFFector clearly reflects a cyberpolitics. The categories of gender, race and ecology show up in such insignificant numbers as to be irrelevant. Class politics appears in significant quantities, but further analysis indicates that it follows very closely the cyberpolitics of access TO, particularly around the Open Platform proposal. This is simply because EFF's articulation of access TO issues integrated a free market approach to the developing economic basis of cyberspace. Class should accordingly be taken as a subsidiary of access and so, as with race, gender and ecology, will be omitted in further analysis of EFFector.

Chart 2: EFFector: politics by location per edition

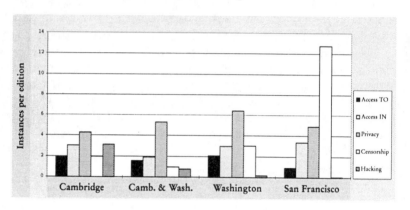

The second chart uses instances of politics per edition grouped by location to track whether a distinctive type of politics can be found for each location of EFF. The changes clearly show the diminution of hacking as an issue;[13] the rise and fall of access TO cyberspace (which correlates with the rise and fall of the National Information Infrastructure), the fall and rise of access IN cyberspace, the constancy of privacy and a surprisingly low level of activity around censorship until the emergence of the Communications Decency Act. The relationship between initiatives from outside EFF (principally Operation Sun Devil for hacking, the National Information Infrastructure for access TO and the Communications Decency Act for censorship), and the constancy of privacy, suggests that rather than EFF's locations having particular political identities, *EFFector* has often reacted to initiatives. The possibility that *EFFector* shows EFF to be a reactive organisation was vigorously denied by the Board and staff of EFF. This denial seems correct, because a reaction to initiatives from elsewhere is inevitable for any political organisation; it is the manner of reaction that is important. Godwin commented:

> Organisations of this sort are prone to being reactive, that's necessarily correct ... I knew that as a person without many resources it was always going to be the case that we were going to be reactive. The question was how to turn that into something useful. What we did was in every case, every case, I'd explain it as a free speech case if at all possible ... I would talk again and again. I took my job as being primarily to shape the First Amendment understanding of this media.
>
> (Mike Godwin)

Chart 3: EFFector: community/policy politics by location

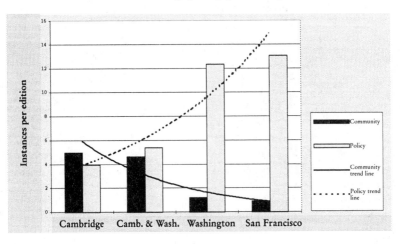

The third chart tracks the second axis of cyberpolitics, policy/community, and here the importance of EFF's locations seems clear, with a massive increase in policy activity between Cambridge and Washington. In addition, there is a rise in community activity between Cambridge and the establishment of dual offices, and the collapse of such activity with the closure of the Cambridge office. It is difficult to tell if the gradual bottoming out of community activity will be followed by an upturn, partly because of the short amount of time analysed in San Francisco and partly because this time has been dominated by a piece of legislation, the Communications Decency Act.

There are two conclusions from this analysis of *EFFector*. First, *EFFector* shows a particular form of online politics, one in which the usual axes of offline politics seem to be largely absent. Instead a range of issues emerge that are known in the non-electronic world but are not constitutive of offline social divisions. Online social divisions are constituted around specifically virtual issues.

> it's not 'haves and have-nots' from a monetary perspective, it's 'haves and have-nots' from an understanding perspective. I think we need an Educational Party, rather than a Green Party or Perot's Party. We need a Party that just focuses on making sure that everybody has knowledge.
>
> (Lori Fena, Chair of Board, EFF)

The second conclusion is that EFF's cyberpolitics do not escape some of the well-known dilemmas of offline activism. This can be seen in EFF's shift towards the power politics of government and then away from this potentially narrow definition of politics. Neither is this a rejection of policy work but an attempt on EFF's part to strike a balance. Here the formation of the Centre for Democracy and Technology is a key moment in understanding EFF's shifts. The formation of CDT, in a sense, allowed EFF to move away from the legislative process because it could be assured that work around policy will go on. Both Stanton McCandlish and Jonah Seiger stressed a co-operative and coalition building approach to cyberpolitics that allowed each organisation to focus on its strengths. However, these two conclusions still leave open the question, why has EFF's politics in *EFFector* not involved categories like race, gender or ecology?

> I was surprised when I saw the axes of traditional European political discourse in your analysis of EFFector. I thought, 'there isn't going to be any of that in here'. I was actually surprised to the degree that class showed up in relation to access. My initial reaction was that this stuff just doesn't fracture along those lines. The rest of it was pretty familiar. I hadn't tried to look at it that way, but if I had I would have expected what you showed us.
>
> (John Gilmore)

The explanation for a lack of concern with race, gender or ecology is, then, that there is a particular cyberpolitics that EFF addresses and this is constituted by issues such as privacy, censorship, access and intellectual property. Cyberspace is simply a different space to meta-space and we should not be surprised if the familiar categories of offline politics are not present.

EFF's political framework

The outline of EFF's history combined with the analysis of *EFFector* produces a picture of EFF's cyberpolitics in terms of issues and organisation. The question remains whether cyberpolitics is anything more than these two sets of issues. Is there a general cyberpolitics that frames cyber-political issues? Outlining such a framework involves a shift to a higher level of abstraction, since it provides a backdrop to particular issues. Such a framework was articulated by interviewees as two-sided, with anar-chist, libertarian and free market beliefs on the one hand and concern for the nature of technology that constructs cyberspace on the other.[14]

John Perry Barlow's articulation of cyberpolitics demonstrates this general model in four principles. First, cyberpolitics for Barlow is 'small "l" libertarian'. He argues that people experience a 'genuinely functional, large-scale anarchy' online and this convinces many that government could be smaller or need not exist at all. Second, Barlow argues that 'awareness that there is some relationship between the free market and free speech and belief in the ultimate fairness of free markets' is another key part of cyberpolitics. He notes that this has two sides, in relation to the free markets both of goods and ideas. Third, online life is charac-terised by a high degree of tolerance for others' views. He says, 'There's one thing about not having the means to shut anybody up that makes it easier for you to listen to what they have to say.' Finally, Barlow quotes Mitch Kapor's slogan that 'architecture is politics', meaning that 'rights bearing technology' is a greater guarantor of rights than 'rights bearing legislation'. If we note that libertarianism and the free market are closely connected, as are tolerance and technology (because technology deprives discussants of the ability to shut each other up), then we have a two-sided model of cyberpolitics. On one side is a concern for co-operative self-government, and on the other consideration for the social nature and social results of technology.

Libertarianism and the free market form one side of cyberpolitics, with the underlying social nature of the net being seen as self-govern-ing, even ungovernable.[15] McCandlish defined this as an axis of politics stretching from authoritarianism to libertarianism and noted that this axis does not map onto that other common axis of politics, left versus right. Part of this view is that online life has attained a near-perfect market that allows self-governability online.

> People who say things that further investigation shows are bogus, just don't get listened to. People who say things that are true can build followings. People who do things that don't tend to work, don't get adopted on the net and there are very low barriers to adoption ... There's just been a very positive trend on things that bear truth in reality, things that turn out over a period of time or through a lot of discussion to be true. And I think that the politics of people on the net has tended to follow that rule.
>
> (John Gilmore)

Gilmore here explains cyberpolitics as having been influenced by the existence online of a properly functioning free market. In addition, the online market must be understood in relation to, at least, two related markets. The first is the market of ideas. Given wide and virtually universal exchange of ideas, the online community simply takes up those that work without any need for some intervening bureaucracy or government. The second market is the market of goods. Exchanging software is an economic activity whether this is realised, for example as it is in Cygnus Support (that Gilmore co-founded), by giving away software but asking for payment to support it or, like the famed game Doom, by giving away a limited version of a programme to entice people to buy the full version or even, as in much shareware, by giving away a full version of the programme but asking for payment if it is used. Placing a software package online seems equivalent to owning a factory and distribution system, because once online that package can be copied again and again. For both goods and ideas, themselves nearly indistinguishable in a product such as software, the net provides open competition, because barriers to entry are very low, and it therefore provides near-perfect information for consumers, because products can be freely tested (what better information is there about a product than using it?). Also results of these tests can be widely disseminated. Unlike many markets, the net fulfils some of the essential criteria of a self-regulating, productive free market. Though distinguishable, the two markets of goods and ideas are not entirely distinct. As Barlow says, 'Class struggle is really an industrial manifestation. You've got capital and you've got labour, well in this instance the labour is the capital. It changes the whole equation.' The labour to produce ideas and embody them either in software packages or in web-sites and documents that appear online automatically produces the capital investment of products that can be tested in the anarchy of the net.

The other side of cyberpolitics begins with the connection between the particular technology of the Internet and the nature of online society. The simplest example is the way discussions conducted through text avoid many of the personal signs – age, sex, race – that are used to judge people. John Gilmore notes, of the absence of race and gender in the analysis of *EFFector*; 'I was actually pretty happy to see that ... On the Internet nobody knows you at all, on the Internet nobody knows what your race is or your sex. That whole colour and sex-blindness is a positive force for a lot of people, they feel welcome.' Cyberactivists do not, however, adopt a technological determinist position, rather they are concerned to monitor the nature of technology and its effects. When Jonah Seiger discussed creating an active rather than reactive politics as part of CDT, he picked up a software package that allows parents to screen out certain Internet sites. Seiger was pointing to a means of dealing with parental concerns over the availability of things like pornography on the Internet – user-control – that is premised on the creation of certain pieces of technology, like the packages Surfwatch or Cyberpatrol, and is consonant with the already existing technology of the net. One of EFF's explicit aims in relocating to San Francisco was to re-connect with the industry that produces much of the technology that underlies the net. Lori Fena notes that one of EFF's intentions is 'to work with industry before they release products, to ask them these questions: how does this affect the individual? how does this affect society?' Here the aim is to affect the technology as it is being produced. The politics of architecture is a major part of cyberpolitics.[16]

Generated from an analysis of EFF is a general model of cyberpolitics that is two-sided; libertarian and anti-technological determinist. The hinge between the two is the recognition of the collapse of some offline distinctions, particularly in the collapse of a clear distinction between the generation, production and marketing of, first, goods and, second, ideas. It is this framework that operates in the background of cyberpolitical issues like privacy and censorship. For example, the fear of a Balkanised net was, at least in part, a fear of losing the functioning free market because information would no longer travel to all. The preference for user-control in relation to censorship rather than government regulation can be understood as a defence of free flows of information, because it offers people ways of controlling the content they or their children access on the net while simultaneously allowing all content to be available on the net. The defence of free speech on the net, often too easily interpreted as a particularly American politics related to the USA constitution, appears within this framework as an essential element of a free and open net. Cyberpolitics, as practised by EFF, consists of a number of issues – privacy, censorship, access, online rights – that spread across the two axes of a libertarian free market of goods and ideas and the social nature of cyberspace's technology.

Cyberpolitics: liberation and the new elite

A libertarian or anarchist belief in small government and the ability of people, working with rights-bearing technology within a free market of ideas and goods, to create their own communities underlies EFF's issue-based politics. To further explore this cyberpolitics a critical analysis can now be outlined. For example, for those of a nervous political disposition the mention of a positive attitude towards free markets will have marked EFF as a right-wing organisation, whereas McCandlish argues EFF is centrist on a right-left axis but libertarian on an authoritarian-civil libertarian axis. To make an appraisal, a return to the notion of cyberspace as a place will be useful because it suggests two obvious questions. First, who can get access to cyberspace? Second, what goes on in cyberspace?

The answer to the first question has been fairly consistent across a range of measurements, with users being overwhelmingly white, wealthy, highly educated and, until recently, male. However, a change to this picture is that the gender gap seems to be closing quickly, with surveys in 1996 pointing to a ratio of over 1:3 of users being women, compared to 1:10 in 1995 or earlier.[17] EFF's politics of access in response to this particular profile are interesting. Initial evidence can be found in a comparison of the categories of access TO cyberspace with access IN cyberspace.

The chart shows a concern for access TO and access IN moving in different directions during EFF's history. The reasons for this can be explored by analysing EFF's main campaign on access, which was ongoing during the period 1992-94 when, as already mentioned, two related issues emerged: fear of a Balkanised net and the National Information Infrastructure (NII). To affect both of these they worked on the Open Platform policy which specifically warned against the possible emergence of a society of information 'haves' and 'have-

Chart 4: EFFector: access by location per edition

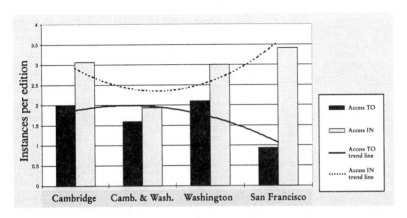

nots'. While such a goal might be read simply as endorsing universal access (that is everyone who wants to will have access), it has been interpreted by EFF as universal service (that is a service providing reasonable access should be available in all areas of the USA). The difference here is between the right to have access and the opportunity to have access. Policy differences that result from this distinction are, for example, that universal access would be served by ensuring freely available terminals connected to the net in public libraries, whereas universal service would be supported by the existence of Internet Service Providers offering good and economic access in all parts of the country, even if some cross-subsidy were needed from metropolitan centres to ensure a service in distant or rural areas. This is a clear, if fine, distinction that sometimes causes confusion. For example, the EFF press release announcing this policy refers to universal service but the policy document that is being announced refers to universal access.[18] Mitch Kapor's testimony, when chairman of EFF's Board, to the USA's Senate Subcommittee on Communications in 1993 offers a flavour of this conversion of the need for all to have access to cyberspace into the provision of a service that would allow access:

> The universal service guaranty in the Communications Act of 1934 has, until now, been interpreted to mean access to 'plain old telephone service' (POTS). In the Information Age, we must extend this guaranty to include 'plain old digital service.' Extending this guaranty means ensuring that new basic digital services are affordable and ubiquitously

available. Equity and the democratic imperative also demand that these services meet the needs of people with disabilities, the elderly, and other groups with special needs. Failure to do so is sure to create a society of 'information haves and have nots.' In a competitive telecommunications environment, regulatory paradigms must be industry neutral and treat all similarly situated providers equally. [This legislation] sets out just this kind of framework by defining interconnection and universal service fund obligations for all entities that provide telecommunications service, regardless of which traditional industry category they are associated with.[19]

The concern for a society of information 'haves and have-nots' creates a policy of ensuring that service is universally available and then, with some safeguards, leaves the market to provide access. Kapor's statement moves immediately from concern for 'have-nots' to the regulation of the telecommunications industry. Many in EFF now argue that the market has solved problems of access by driving down the price of equipment and connection. The need for activism on access to cyberspace is therefore minimal.

> The evolution of the computer communications industry has been driven by a fundamental technology of chip application that reduces costs at a tremendous rate, an exponential rate. This is a phenomenon that most people have a hard time trying to understand because they don't tend to see exponential forces happening elsewhere ... We used to hear these things about access, you know 'we have to put terminals in libraries so that the underprivileged can get at them'. These days for $5 and $10 a month you can get all the Internet access you want and it doesn't matter whether you're rich or poor you can still find $10.

> (John Gilmore)

However, access is not simply a matter of cost. Godwin draws an analogy to public libraries which, he notes, have open, free access but are mainly used by wealthier people. He argues: 'The lesson for cyberspace is that there are some cultural barriers that are vastly more important than economic barriers in terms of getting access to the tools and information necessary to fully empower yourself ... I think that the access issue springs from that and not dollars.' EFF's work around cultural issues of access TO was also concentrated in its work on Open Platform when it called for easier interfaces between users and the net, in order to overcome some of the cultural problems in using Internet technology. But such issues did not receive much attention after it became clear that the net was not going to be Balkanised and the NII failed to pass USA legislatures. Given these two shifts, EFF felt forced to remove attention which had been given to access, in order to accommodate issues around online authority. Access issues principally shifted to those of public access to government information and to further issues of access IN cyberspace. When assessing these shifts, it must always be borne in mind that EFF's resources were limited and not all possible issues could be taken up. However, even given the certainty that EFF would not be able to deal with all issues that can be defined in the abstract, the allegiance to an essentially free market implemented universal service to solve problems of access to cyberspace raises questions about the nature of EFF's politics.[20]

For example, some of the USA's ethnic communities are among the most notable absentees from cyberspace. It might be hypothesised that if EFF were centrally concerned with access to cyberspace and the effect on cyberspace of the absence of such communities, then it would have to take account of the fact that one in four Native American and Inuit households do not have a phone-line.[21] The lack of a phone at home does not mean Internet access is impossible but it undermines the idea that everyone can simply purchase this access. Further, though this failure of universal service in relation to telephones might be interpreted as evidence for a more market-led understanding of universal service, this failure also raises questions over whether or not universal access should be set aside entirely in favour of universal service. The different communities that might be better (or less well) served by universal service or access are little analysed by EFF. The point is not that EFF should be taking-up the all too obvious struggles of offline life, but that its conception of cyberpolitics perhaps leads its attention away from the effect on cyberspace of differential access to cyberspace.

Further evidence is available from a number of statements by EFF of its mission, though such statements need to be treated with caution because, as in many institutions, they may function less as a statement of what an institution is actually doing and more as what it would like to do or feels it is expected to do. EFF's mission announced at its founding included four goals, of which the last was fostering 'the development of new tools which will endow non-technical users with full and easy access to computer-based telecommunications',[22] raising issues of cultural barriers to non-technical users. In addition, one of the three sections outlining key issues was about information 'haves and have-nots'. Yet when announcing the move to San Francisco, EFF affirmed its mission in the following way:

> EFF's overall mission has not changed. We are dedicated to promoting civil rights *and* responsibilities in cyberspace. Especially now that governments have discovered the net and are trying to figure out how to regulate it, it is important to establish a clearer understanding both in the public mind and within governments worldwide. Cyberspace should not be a lawless arena, but its diverse communities should be self-governing as much as possible. Specifically, we are dedicated to free speech, freedom of association, diversity in cyberspace, protection of privacy, the right to anonymity, and *proper* accountability (including immunity from liability for sysops not directly involved in illegal acts).[23]

Issues of access to cyberspace are absent by the time of the shift from Washington. A further mission statement in August 1996 when EFF had been established in San Francisco did not mention access.[24]

The point is not that EFF is somehow covertly racist or plotting to keep cyberspace for an élite. The point is that 'access TO' is the key point at which online life meets offline and EFF does not seem to question whether the free market seen in cyberspace is the same as the free market of offline life. The free market of online life supports open and largely self-governing communities that they believe have certain in-built barriers to discrimination. The market of offline life produces undoubted inequities that, in turn, relate to the differential access individuals have to cyberspace. The point about the typical net user being white, wealthy, educated and male is that this mirrors the profile of the most powerful sections of USA society in offline life. The growing access of women to cyberspace supports this as it coincides with growing female access to higher education and professional jobs. Given that the growing number of women entering cyberspace has yet to affect the racial, economic and educational profile of net users, it can be hypothesised that it is a particular, privileged group of women who are gaining access to cyberspace.[25] Once again, the importance of this relation between offline and online is not that EFF should drop focus on cyberspace in favour of a campaign to eliminate offline inequities, but that EFF does not seem to take into account the effect on cyberspace of its privileged, in offline terms, community. Cyberspace and cyber-politics have so far been constructed around a privileged community.

NEW SPACE, NEW POLITICS

In this respect, EFF seems like an organisation that is part of the new power bloc dominating USA politics which Manuel Castells argues replaced the New Deal or liberal power bloc during the time of Reagan's presidency. This bloc consisted of 'the alliance of multi-national business and the technical-managerial middle class' and in particular the beneficiaries of the information technology revolution.[26] Far from being an organisation working within a liberating social movement, EFF can here be interpreted as part of a new offline élite, who happen to be the norm online. If EFF's nature as an organisation born on and concerned with cyberspace is recalled then this is perhaps unsurprising, yet it alerts us to the fact that cyberpolitics as EFF practices it may well be blind to cultural and economic issues of concern to those who are not the norm in cyberspace.[27]

If we turn to the second question to be asked of EFF's cyberpolitics: what goes on in this place?, then the Open Platform is again relevant. Barlow has already been quoted as saying that a key reason for EFF moving to Washington was that a number of large corporations were attempting to transform cyberspace into something like television, a 'one-way environment'. Much of EFF's work around the Open Platform and NII tried to ensure that cyberspace remained an open, interactive environment. Here the work of EFF looks far more like an activist organisation fighting to ensure the rights of users against any corporate or bureaucratic desire for an authoritarian medium. Similarly, the e-TRUST initiative demonstrates a concern to build an open cyberspace.

> Most people ... don't know that when you cruise to a web-site all kinds of web-tracking,[28] that is now embedded in just about every browser, is available to pull down information ... Most people worry about electronic commerce working, but not just because they don't have strong security (which is one issue) but also over who has information taken from web-sites and what are they doing with it?
>
> (Lori Fena)

Personal information can automatically be harvested from cyberspace users and many web-sites ask for personal information as the price of access. One use of this information is for sites to sell themselves to advertisers and so keep the site free to users. But there has been no means of knowing what will be done with information taken knowingly or unknowingly. EFF has helped set up a system of logos that can be attached to web-sites; these logos are monitored and offer the first real guarantee of the use of personal information. This is not, of course, an earth-shattering development but it is one element in the construction of online society.

> Governance is a lot less obvious than government. Essentially, governance is what really keeps you from running over people on the street; it's not the government that tells you it's against the law, it's your culture that tells you it's wrong. I think governance is the dominant ordering principle in cyberspace and it's working pretty well, but it doesn't have flags and it doesn't have divisions and it doesn't have gold braid.
>
> (John Perry Barlow)

From this perspective the anti-government, libertarian philosophy that underpins EFF's work appears as a serious attempt to ensure that the net will survive the attention of large corporations and government, that it will be a medium that can reverse many of the power relations of offline life.

If the answers to the two questions raised in this section are drawn together, EFF can be interpreted as being both an expression of that part of the US elite that has developed closely with information technology, and a grass-roots liberating organisation. EFF seems most clearly an elite in relation to access to cyberspace and most clearly liberating in their pursuit of the key issues of cyberpolitics. EFF cannot be dismissed, as Castells might lead us to believe, as simply a representative of a new USA elite, playing in its high-tech sandbox. But neither can the absence within EFF of a concern for communities that are not moving into online life be ignored; a concern, that is, about the consequences both for cyberspace and for these communities. It is the combination of genuine grass-roots and elite that is characteristic of EFF and perhaps of cyberspace itself.

CYBERPOLITICS AND NEW POLITICS

Two questions remain to be briefly considered. First, is this analysis of EFF representative of cyberpolitics in general? Second, what significance does this analysis of EFF have for new politics?

The first question cannot be answered in the space available.[29] Instead, the simple point can be made that EFF is one of the creators of cyberpolitics. As Barlow says, 'We are literally the canary in the coal mine. Before us, nobody was starting to complain about the air. Nobody else recognised that there was air in there to complain about or that there was an in-there to complain about.' The politics of EFF have been a major formative influence on cyberpolitics. A related question is: to what extent does EFF represent a peculiarly USA version of cyberpolitics? Again this question is impossible to answer fully in the available space, only a quick indication can be given. Naturally enough, EFF as a USA-based organisation concerns itself with USA political processes and ideas. But EFF has also grown in intimate embrace with the global space of cyberspace and it would be astonishing if its politics did not generate some of the key elements of cyberpolitics. For example, anarchy and libertarianism are not as distinct from each other in online politics as might be thought, with both having a central component of anti-authoritarianism. If both were broadly understood in this way, anarchism could be substituted for libertarianism in the preceding analysis, which would make EFF appear to be part of one of the great traditions of European radicalism without changing the essence of EFF's politics or of cyberpolitics.

EFF is also part of new politics. This analysis of EFF could be related in several ways to theories of new politics or new social movements. There is, again, not the space to do this here but one particular conclusion emerges from this chapter although not from any of the preceding analyses of movements. How do we judge the effect of new social movements? What sort of radical social change do we want or expect from new politics? The example of EFF points to the need for critical work that explores the meaning of new political movements because EFF is not unambiguously a liberating movement. It seems probable that part of EFF's cyberpolitics is best understood as the politics of a new elite. It is all too easy to study grass-roots political movements that can be intuitively and emotively supported and in doing so assume an answer to the hardest question new politics poses: What is liberation? What is a radically better society? EFF pose this question because in some ways it has been saving cyberspace for a radical future (often for radicals who had no idea they would want cyberspace), but in other ways we cannot be certain of its effect. These are questions posed in the Introduction to this book and will be taken up in Part Two. EFF's importance to new politics and to cyberspace is its contradictory state of being both a grass-roots liberator and an element of a new elite.

NOTES

1. 19.5 million is the number of host computers in mid-1997 and 100 million an estimate of electronic mail users. See network wizards host count at

http://www.nw.com; J. Rickard, 'The Internet by the Numbers', *Boardwatch Magazine*, 9(12), 1995; J. Quarterman, 'The Global Matrix of Minds', in L. Harasim (ed), *Global Networks*, MIT, Cambridge, Massachusetts 1992, pp35-56. There is also some terminological difficulty in naming the two different spaces of cyberspace and 'meatspace'; for convenience I will mainly use the terms online and offline. Finally, thanks to Sally Wyatt, Alan White and Stanton McCandlish for comments.

2. For discussions of these see, among others, S. Jones (ed), *Cybersociety: computer-mediated communication and community*, Sage, London 1995; R. Shields (ed), *Cultures of Internet: virtual spaces, real histories, living bodies*, Sage, London 1996.

3. Most work that addresses cyberpolitics tries to read this politics from the particularities of its technology. One example of this is the way online life is sometimes held to be inherently free of racial and gender politics. Important and interesting work has been done this way but two problems emerge. First, technological determinism is always, at least, in the background. Second, it produces an abstract analysis with no necessary relevance to how politics on the net has actually developed.

4. Of course this does not mean that EFF's politics are being endorsed, nor does it mean that the study of other cyberpolitical organisations is irrelevant.

5. B. Sterling, *The Hacker Crackdown*, Viking, London 1992.

6. Gilmore explained how he became a founder in this way: 'Someone forwarded me an email that came off the WELL that said John Barlow and Mitch Kapor were starting some sort of electronic freedom foundation. Once I got some details about what was going on I thought "this is something I want to be involved in". So I sent them a message that said, "I'm not as rich as some of you guys but I can probably send some support"'. Quittner claims that 'support' was at least $100,000. J. Quittner, 'The Merry Pranksters go to Washington', *Wired US*, 2 June 1994.

7. EFF did not constitute itself as responsible to a membership: the board and staff set EFF's direction. EFF does allow membership, though it does not allow its membership a direct say in setting policy, and has flirted with setting up chapters, which led to a number of now independent organisations that use the EF name such as Electronic Frontiers Australia or Electronic Frontiers Austin.

8. Jerry Berman was Policy and then Executive Director of EFF and is now working with CDT, which he co-founded.

9. Some of the misunderstanding can be traced to an article in *Wired* that was largely inaccurate. R. Van Bakel, 'How Good People Helped Make Bad Law', *Wired UK*, 2 February 1996. Godwin noted that this article was *Wired* magazine's 'hit' piece about EFF to go with *Wired*'s 'puff' piece in J. Quittner,

NEW SPACE, NEW POLITICS

op.cit.. The Digital Telephony Act is a complicated episode. Godwin argues that the telephone companies were already implementing eavesdropping technology outside of any legal constraint at the informal request of law enforcement agencies and that it was necessary to legislate to bring these agencies back under control. It was these sorts of provisions that EFF supported, while also opposing the bill as a whole. As of March 1997 the constraints Godwin refers to have been in operation for several years but the funding to build the eavesdropping infrastructure has not yet been allocated. Effectively, this means that greater control was gained while the feared automated eavesdropping has yet to appear. However, such automated eavesdropping is now legally possible.

10. This move should not be read as a total rejection by EFF of policy work. The retention of a staff member, Shari Steele, in Washington most clearly indicates this.

11. A further change was the departure of Drew Taubman and his replacement in mid-1995 by Lori Fena as Executive Director.

12. This is not to say that the analysis can be taken as a complete or perfect record of EFF's activism. Rather, the combination of interviews and content analysis will provide a broad analysis of EFF's politics.

13. This result finally refutes, if it still needs to be done, the accusation that EFF is a 'hackers' defence fund'.

14. It must be stressed that the following analysis is not drawn solely from the analysis of *EFFector* but from an integrated analysis of documents, *EFFector* and interviews.

15. This does not mean that all online activists, especially those interviewed for this research, are fully committed libertarians. As Godwin commented, 'Welfare, my god! Of course you should have welfare, of course you should, how could you not?'. It is simply that they all see libertarianism as a key constituent of cyberpolitics. Further, the meaning of 'libertarian' varied between interviewees, the common denominator being an opposition between libertarian and authoritarian. That is, libertarian in this context can perhaps be interpreted as anti-authoritarian, though not all would agree.

16. A distinction needs to be drawn between what some activists say and how they treat technology. A 1996 mission statement of EFF begins with the following point: 'Technology is a neutral but unavoidable agent of change.' This was reiterated by Fena in interview. These claims do not change the fact that e-TRUST and much online activism involve attempts to influence the design of technology in order to affect social and political issues.

17. An NOP survey for the UK in 1995 confirms this: see http://www.nopres.co.uk; and the Seventh GVU World-Wide Web User

Survey confirms this for the USA and Europe in 1996. The GVU User Survey also confirms the shift in gender composition with less than 10 per cent of women users found in the Second User Survey in 1994, but 31 per cent found in the Seventh User Survey in 1996 (though there was little shift between the fifth survey in early 1996 and the seventh in early 1997). For GVU, see http://www.cc.gatech.edu/guv/. The O'Reilly and Associates 1996 survey, like NOP a random telephone survey rather than GUV's online form that produces a self-selecting population, also found 33 per cent of online users to be women.

18. EFF (1994) 'Open Platform Campaign: Public Policy For The Information Age; Open Platform Policy 2.1' and 'Open Platform Campaign Summary', are available at http://www.eff.org/archives.html.

19. Mitchell Kapor's testimony to the Subcommittee on Communications of the Senate Committee on Commerce, Science and Transportation regarding the Telecommunications Infrastructure Act of 1993 (s. 1086) on September 8, 1993, is available at http://www.eff.org/archives.html. Brackets added.

20. EFF's policy on universal service is not entirely free market, though there seems to have been an evolution in that direction over the course of the first articulation of these problems and their later judgement that access is a subsidiary issue to all the other issues they have to deal with, because technology and the market have driven down prices. EFF has been, for example, committed to some tariffs on companies providing access to densely populated regions in order to support those in thinly populated regions, and they have a deep concern that cyberspace be developed with open network standards that ensure the online free market is not dominated by any one operator.

21. W.Wresch, *Disconnected: haves and have-nots in the information age*, Rutgers University Press, New Brunswick 1996.

22. John Perry Barlow and Mitchell Kapor (1990), 'Across The Electronic Frontier', available at http://www.eff.org/archives.html.

23. Editors, *EFFector Online*, 8 (11), 6 July, 1995. 'Sysops' is short for systems operators: the operators of computer systems.

24. EFF (1996), 'EFF – The Big Picture', unpublished.

25. For example International Labour Organisation statistics show that women filled 51 per cent of professional jobs in the USA in 1992, representing a historic point at which women achieved equality in some of the best paid jobs that are available, but that only form 17 per cent of all jobs. I.L.O., *International Labour Office Year Book of Labour Statistics*, Geneva, International Labour Organisation, 1992.

26. M. Castells, *The Informational City*, Basil Blackwell, Oxford 1989, p304.

27. The germ of this interpretation can perhaps be seen in Sterling's interpretation of EFF's origins: 'It dawns on me that Mitch Kapor is not trying to make

the world safe for democracy. He certainly is not trying to make it safe for anarchists or utopians ... What he really hopes to do is make the world safe for future Mitch Kapors.' (Sterling, *op.cit.*, p301). The figure of Kapor is ambiguous. He is the multi-millionnaire software entrepreneur who could afford to begin and run EFF from his own funds, and also the grass-roots libertarian who rejected large scale corporate life to defend free speech and an open, interactive computer network.

28. 'Web-tracking' is the way sites that are visited on the web can take information from the visitor's software that identifies the visitor. Site visitors can in this way be tracked and personal profiles built up. Go to http://www.cdt.org for a privacy check that will tell you what information can be collected from you as you surf the Web.

29. An attempt is being made to characterise cyberpolitics in general and will appear in T. Jordan, *Cyberpower: the politics and culture of the Internet*, Routledge, London, forthcoming 1998; see also M. Godwin, *Cyber Rights*, Random House, New York 1998.

30. K. Krippendorf, *Content Analysis*, Sage, London, 1980; R.Weber, *Basic Content Analysis*, Sage, London 1985.

APPENDIX: METHODOLOGY AND LIST OF INTERVIEWS

Interviews

All unreferenced quotes from the following people are from semi-structured interviews conducted in August/September 1996 in San Francisco, Washington DC and London.

John Perry Barlow	Co-founder and board member of EFF
Lori Fena	Then Executive Director, now Chair of Board, EFF
John Gilmore	Co-founder and board member of EFF
Mike Godwin	First employee and staff counsel, EFF
Stanton McCandlish	Online activist, EFF
Jonah Seiger	Online activist, CDT.

All interviews were conducted after the analysis of the eight categories of online and offline politics in *EFFector* was presented to the EFF's staff and board in August 1996. All interviewees except Jonah Seiger were present for this discussion. Subsequent discussion in interview and at the board meeting led to the generation of the categories of policy and community politics. Thanks in particular to Stanton McCandlish who stressed the need for such an analysis.

EFFector analysis
The analysis of *EFFector* was conducted according to the methodological principles of first stage of content analysis as developed by Krippendorf and Weber.[30] Each category of politics was defined by a number of keywords and the content of all EFFectors was searched for these words. Where a legitimate reference to the politics the keywords intended was found a 'hit' was recorded. This was done by generating a report which included two lines of text on either side of each key word hit and by reference to the relevant issue of *EFFector* if these five lines of text were unclear; the combination of these two sources allowed a clear judgement to be made for each hit. This ensured that the mention of someone like Judge Green did not result in a hit being recorded for ecological politics. Hits were counted and analysed. Keywords used could be part-words (i.e. educat rather than all the variants of educate). The only variation to this technique was with the categories of Access To and Access In. Criticism of the keywords used for the initial definition of Access and the emerging importance of access to in the analysis of EFF led to a re-analysis of Access. This was achieved by generating a far larger number of keywords, a search that focused on whole words or phrases rather than partial ones and caused the generation of the two categories from the one list. The difference between Access IN and Access TO is such that it would make no sense to generate different lists with different keywords (which category would use the word 'access'?) but it lent itself to a combined generation, but separate recording, of instances according to the meaning of each hit.

EFFector by location:
Cambridge: sixteen editions 15 per cent of total (1.00-1.12, 2.01-2.03); 387 days (10 December 1990 to 7 January 1992)

Cambridge and Washington: thirty-three editions, 31 per cent of total (2.04-2.09, 3.00-3.09, 4.00-4.05, 5.01-5.11); 517 days, (18 January 1992 to 25 June 1993)

Washington: forty-two editions, 39 per cent of total (5.12-5.15, 6.01-6.08, 7.01-7.15, 8.01-8.14); 737 days, (9 July 1993 to 26 July 1995)

San Francisco: sixteen editions, 15 per cent of total (8.15-8.22, 9.01-9.08); 273 days and counting, (9 September 1995 to 12 June 1996)

Political categories and their keywords:

Access TO and Access IN: access, statistic, statistics, demographic, demographics, demograph, gatekeeper, FOIA, freedom of information, open, public, monopoly, centralisation, balkan, balkanise, balkanisation. (See note under methodology.)

Privacy: privacy, crypto, cryptography, pgp, private, personal, clipper.

Censorship: porn, CDA, decency, Rimm, pornography, freedom, speech.

Hacking: hack, hacker, crime, phreak, hackers, cracker, crackers.

Gender: sexism, sexist, misogyny, feminism, feminist, gender, violence, women, woman.

Race: race, racism, ethnic, ethnicity, bigot, bigotry, afro, African, Asian.

Class: economic, ruling, trade, union, business, financial, commercial, fiscal.

Ecology: green, ecology, ecological, environment, environmental, sustainability.

Lobbying/policy: legislat, lobby, congress, senate, senator, administration, policy

Community/educative: educat, community, communal, social, society, BBS, Fidonet.

'TOO BLACK TOO STRONG'?: ANTI-RACISM AND THE MAKING OF SOUTH ASIAN POLITICAL IDENTITIES IN BRITAIN

Shirin Housee and Sanjay Sharma

The question of Black, in Britain ... has its silences. It had a certain way of silencing the very specific experiences of Asian people. Because though Asian people could identify, politically, in the struggle against racism, when they came to using their own culture as the resources of resistance, when they wanted to write out of their own experience and reflect on their own position, when they wanted to create, they naturally created within the histories of the languages, the cultural tradition, the positions of people who came from a variety of different historical backgrounds. And just as Black was at the cutting edge of a politics *vis-a-vis* one kind of enemy, it could also ... provide a kind of silencing in relation to another. These are the costs, as well as the strengths, of trying to think of the notion of Black as an essentialism.[1]

There was a Black community in the 1960s and 1970s in the political sense – the sense of an anti-racist bloc. But in the last two decades, multi-culturalism and subsequently ethnicism have fragmented Black politics, have negated Black political culture. And what you have today is cultural politics, ethnic politics, identity politics.[2]

The hegemony of the anti-racist signifier 'Black' is over. The promise of 'Black' as a political identity symbolically uniting diverse social group-ings experiencing racism in Britain is no longer apposite, according to many cultural commentators and theorists. Stuart Hall has made a timely recognition of the limits of Black – as an essentialism, and in response to the assertion of an emerging Asian political cultural expression in Britain.

Somewhat in contrast, Ambalavaner Sivanandan more emphatically mourns the end of Black politics and remonstrates with its displacement by myopic and reactionary forms of identity politics. The longing for a unified anti-racist struggle now appears only as a utopian moment in the days when politics was made out to be a simple matter of mobilising already constituted identities for radical social transformation. Not only has a coherent national or European anti-racist movement failed to materialise over the last decade, while racial terror and violence reach unprecedented levels, but the primary agent – the Black subject – has been problematised, deconstructed, de-essentialised and rendered obsolete in the face of contemporary discursive conditions of identity production and more complex modalities of (racial) oppression.

In this chapter we do not wish to romanticise the signifier 'Black' or present a revisionist account, although we argue for a more nuanced and contextual understanding in relation to anti-racist struggles. A premature dismissal, and the move to theoretically dissolve this category, belies the valency of how Black was actively *produced* in and through struggles against racism. We recognise that the promise of a unified anti-racist movement has passed, and (re)evaluate the status of the political utility of Black in mobilising or exhaustively describing contemporary expressions of anti-racist political identities. Most significantly, the deconstruction of Black and critiques of anti-racism and identity formation have opened up alternative political spaces, and legitimised the emergence of more culturally specific and even essentialising identities.

We do not believe it coincidental that, concurrently, there has been the emergence of an Asian identity discourse.[3] The problem is that while the identity category 'Asian' has gained a visibility and ascendancy in political and popular discourses, little attention has been paid to exploring incisively its recent historical emergence as a site of cultural identification that does not exclude or proscribe other political positionalities. Placed within a discussion of (post-)Black identifications and anti-racist politics, in this chapter we interrogate the status of the signifiers 'Black' and 'Asian' by raising relevant questions about political struggle and organisation. One of our contentions is that in both common sense popular and academic discourses, the sutured category of 'Asian' operates reductively as an ethno-cultural identity. But through a critical engagement with the idea of cultural hybridity, we aim to de-centre normative and culturalist notions of 'Asian-ness'. By locating our critique within some recent political events and organisational strategies, we tentatively suggest an alternative way of imagining the signifiers 'Asian' and 'Black' as contestable and unfinished sites of political identification.

BLACK IS ...

The politically charged discourses governing Blackness are far too complex to unravel in this short chapter. One of the problems of entering into this debate is delineating the specificity of the operation of Black as a signifier in the discursive field. Much of the discourse of Black fails to locate what particular social configuration and context the signifier operates in. Often, Black as a set of political, cultural and aesthetic representational practices is conflated, and framed, as lying outside of history and social processes.[4] Nevertheless, as a point of departure, Hall's seminal critique of the 'end of the innocent notion of the essential black subject' marks out a territory for us to imagine and rethink new modes and practices of anti-racist struggle.[5] It forces us to recognise, as Hall suggests, that Black is composed of a 'diversity of subject positions, social experiences and cultural identities ...', and is 'a politically and culturally constructed category'.[6] The difficulty for Hall is when Black became an essentialism, when it silenced or excluded other cultural identities, and failed to recognise how Black subjects were also being positioned by patriarchy, capital and other cultural differences. It follows that 'there is no guarantee, in reaching for an essentialised racial identity of which we think we can be certain, that it will always turn out to be mutually liberating and progressive on all the other dimensions'.[7] Hall's critique makes it clear that just being Black does not command a predetermined emancipatory political location, and nor is it possible to determine in advance that the identity of a group will necessarily be articulated to a specific liberatory type of politics. For example, the increasing calls for separate Muslim state education by certain educational groups and critics from a 'pro-Islamic' position[8] – whilst legitimately based on grounds of racial and religious discrimination in current state schools – has nevertheless been supported by sections of a neo-racist New Right.[9] This latter group's project is one of cultural separatism for the preservation of an untainted white British national identity. The emergence of this kind of perverse 'alliance' illustrates that a subaltern identity politics does not automatically secure a progressive political position on other fronts, and that it can be re-articulated to other more conservative positions.

Ali Rattansi, in a critical exploration of anti-racist orthodoxy, has added to an anti-essentialist critique of Black by arguing that the notion of 'the community' has been reified in the construction of a unitary conception of 'the black struggle', in which a cultural essentialism has operated at the core of the category Black. He has further stated that, '"Black" ... denotes not simply an often successful political alliance against racism. It operates as a profoundly cultural category, an attempted representation of particular experiences and particular construction of unity around those experiences.'[10] However, the questions we wish to pose are: 'was Black ever that innocent or essential in anti-racist struggles?';[11] and what kind of anti-racist practices and formations are actually being described or alluded to in the anti-essentialist critiques against a closed Black identity? Here, alongside Hall and Rattansi, we share the post-structuralist desire to deconstruct identity, as this move is crucial in imagining new forms of politics that live in and through difference. But there is a danger that in the legitimate and important *theoretical* move[12] to de-essentialise Black, it is not only *re*constructed as the cardinal anti-racist signifier, but has become an overdetermined site – overburdened as a vehicle for racial emancipation on all fronts. What we are claiming is that there has been a tendency to fail to specify and adequately locate the operation of the signifier Black in particular sets of discourses, and this has led to an overly generalised critique. Similarly, we take issue with the assumption that the political identity of Black was simply 'innocent' or 'essential', as there is a failure to acknowledge sufficiently its multi-accentuality in locating the signifier in particular sets of social struggles. As an organising strategy against specific forms of racism, the signifier Black (and Asian) has held many common-sense meanings dependent on the political effects desired for in the act of self-naming. There never has been a universally agreed acceptance of any one version of the category 'Black', but only particular (strategic) claims made by specific groups or institutions. This has been the case even from the very moment 'black' was reclaimed in North America by the Black Power movement, against its pejorative and racialised usage. Kobena Mercer has written, 'What made 'Black Power' such a volatile metaphor was its political indeterminacy: it meant different things to different people in different discourses. It appeared in the discourse of the right ... as much as in the discourses of the Left or the liberal centre'.[13]

In the British context, the redefinition of 'black' from a racial to a political category ('Black') has occurred in a variety of situations, and various typologies of 'Black' and attempts to periodise it have been forwarded recently.[14] However, Tariq Modood's criticism of what he terms 'political blackness', as being hegemonic and suppressing an Asian subjectivity, fails to make, for example, an adequate political distinction between the operation of Black in local grassroots anti-racist struggles, and the appropriation of the term in the palliative anti-racist language of local authorities. Alistar Bonnett and Kabir Shukra are more discerning, and their delineation of 'Black' attempts to locate how this signifier emerged and functioned in a number of different discourses. Nevertheless, their accounts, alongside Modood, fail to acknowledge sufficiently the implication that an anti-racist Black identity did not pre-exist or belong to a particular group, but rather has been *produced* 'through political antagonism and cultural struggle'.[15] We have learned from Foucault that not only are discourses conflictual, embodying particular interests, and delimiting what can(not) be said, but also that they are permeated by power and institutionalised as practices.[16] The meaning and deployment of Black can only make sense within the particular discourses it has operated in, and at particular moments. Avtar Brah has made the important point that 'the usage of "black" ... or "Asian" is determined not so much by the nature of its referent as by its semiotic function within the different discourses'.[17] We would want to emphasise, contra Modood, that in grass roots anti-racist activism and self-defence campaigns, 'Black' was never simply imposed onto 'Asian' groupings.[18] Now this is not to privilege local grass roots organisations in order to claim the production of an authentic anti-racist Black subject (or to suggest that activism is the only mode of doing 'real' politics). Rather, it highlights that in certain kinds of spaces, in particular anti-racist practices, Black has been constantly struggled over, and produced in contestation.[19]

By way of a more explicit example, we can turn to a contemporary formation – the Black People's Alliance (BPA) in Manchester. BPA came into being as a response to the brutal racist murders of Siddak Dada and Mohammed Sarwar in Manchester in 1992. This organisation provided a forum where Black (mostly Asians, Caribbeans and Africans) came together to organise anti-racist activities and to work towards the court hearing awaiting those apprehended. Alongside the BPA, there also existed a Memorial Committee in support of the families of the two who were murdered. This Committee was based on the principle of a broad alliance, which included anti-racist sympathisers from different organisations and groups. Most importantly, it nurtured close links with family members of the victims and negotiated the Campaign's activities. The role of the Committee was very specific in providing support for the family and organising the funeral procession, as well as organising demonstrations outside the courts. The rationale behind the existence of the Memorial Committee was that, once its demands were met and the accused were brought to justice, the Committee would have served its purpose and could fold. In contrast, the BPA held longer-term political strategies and goals. It came together in response to the murders, but its existence was not limited to this specific event. It had been about organising and politicising the various communities of Manchester who continue to face racial terror and attacks. In the words of one member of the BPA:

> As the news of the racist murders spread, different sections of our 'communities' – Muslims, Sikhs, Hindus, and Caribbeans – were emotionally moved and outraged. This was reflected in the spontaneous, massive turnout at the funeral procession – the biggest ever in Manchester. BPA was formed recognising that whilst there were anti-racist organisations such as ARA [Anti-Racist Alliance] and ANL [Anti-Nazi League] and other anti-racist groups operating locally and nationally, we needed a political organisation in our area which challenged internal divisions, and called for unity which built alliances amongst Asians and Afro-Caribbeans.

Those male and female members involved in the Memorial Committee and the BPA did not encounter these organisations as confining members' political outlooks or silencing their specific 'differences' and experiences based on class or gender. Through constant discussion and active negotiation – sometimes involving conflict and dissension – those participating became aware of the role of these organisations and the respective strengths and limitations that these modes of organising engendered. Additionally, members of these groups did not limit their political existence within one organisation, but were simultaneously involved in other groups, some of which were specific to their cultural and national differences (and not necessarily of the traditional left).

The BPA was founded on political actions based on sharing common experiences which are structured, but not exclusively *determined*, by white racism. This mode of organising is hardly a sedate process, and is not based simply on a 'shared socio-economic position or colonial history', as James Donald and Ali Rattansi have contended in what still remains an authoritative critique of anti-racism.[20] Discordance and difference have been as much a part of creating the conditions for a strategic 'unity' in the BPA as have sameness and consonance. In this respect, the organising principle under 'Black' has never intended to 'silence' other cultural differences. As Brah maintains:

> Its specific meaning in post-war Britain cannot be taken to have denied cultural difference between African, Caribbean and South Asian people when cultural difference was not the organising principle within this discourse or political practice. The concrete political struggles in which the new meaning was grounded acknowledged cultural differences but sought to accomplish political unity against racism.[21]

It has also been highlighted by a number of commentators that the project of Black anti-racism has been underwritten by a masculine politics and has silenced feminist stances, as well as feminist cultural differences.[22] However, feminist organisations such as Southall Black Sisters and Birmingham Black Sisters specifically enabled Asian women to find a voice on anti-racist platforms, and to raise and connect 'race' and gender issues both inside and outside of their communities. Similarly, in the BPA, linkages have constantly been sought in relation to gender and other types of oppression and social exclusion, and a priority has been to work with those sections of the 'community' traditionally excluded or marginalised.[23] Moreover, it is important to recognise that issues of 'Blackness' and 'Asian-ness' in relation to gender and womanhood have been much debated within the Black feminist literature. As espoused by hooks, Brah and Parmar, for example,[24] the reality of the multiplicity of identity positions for Black women has always been present – identities which cut across class and gender as well as 'race' and ethnicity. These different points of identification have informed and structured the modes of political organisation and types of solidarity. A member of Birmingham Black Sisters echoes this position in recalling the political and social solidarity 'Black' engendered: '... I remember how our differences were always still articulated under the one banner of "Black". Our political aspirations and desires cut across our social interests and activities. Our Caribbean sisters would come along to our Bhangra events, whilst we went to their Blues'.

The line of argument we are forwarding does not wish naïvely to deny that the signifier Black has in the past operated as an essentialism, and silenced other subjectivities and experiences. We acknowledge that this signifier has always been 'split' along the lines of the political and the cultural and it is common to find the culturalist terms 'black and asian' being deployed – denoting a shift more towards ethnic particularisms.[25] Neither are we trading on isolated empirical examples to defend the continuing (though now more limited) success of anti-racist organisational strategies against the tide of opinion dismissing the viability of political Blackness in the 1990s. Our citing of counter-examples is more indicative: that the discourses governing an anti-racist Blackness and politics of change is, and always has been, a site of struggle in Britain. To valorise the 'Black struggle' and universalise its modes of political practices constructs a hegemonic essential notion of 'Black' that suppresses other narratives, of a more contingent practice of anti-racist Blackness, from emerging and claiming a legitimacy. Moreover, our contention is that in particular kinds of struggles a non-essentialising and more self-reflexive category of 'Black' has been invoked, and that it has the potential to be articulated alongside other emerging political positionalities such as 'Asian' or 'Muslim'.

ASIAN AIN'T ...

Having argued for a more open-ended notion of Blackness in relation to anti-racist politics, we now want to go on to explore the category of 'Asian' which has increasingly become a popular umbrella term for the more specific identifications predicated on overlapping national, regional, or religious identities of the South Asian diaspora in Britain. An account of the genealogy of the term 'Asian' remains to be written, but it is notable that in comparison to 'Black', it shares a different historical emergence.[26] Most significantly, it has not undergone a transformatory political redefinition as did 'Black' during the 1970s and early 1980s. According to Harry Goulbourne,[27] 'Asian' has principally been an imperial/colonial construction originally used to describe certain groups from the Indian subcontinent, which sought to distinguish between 'Europeans' and 'Africans' in a tripartite racial categorisation. (Although it is arguable that the discourse of Orientalism may include 'Arab' and 'Chinese' groupings within a definition of 'Asian', making the division of humanity more complex and shifting than it appears in Goulbourne's account). Nevertheless, whilst its earlier usage appears to be founded on a racial/geographic characterisation in colonial discourse, it is notable that 'race' has always been articulated and imbricated with 'culture'.[28]

In post-war Britain the historically specific nature of racial classification continued to operate within a Manichean binary logic that included all those deemed to be 'non-white' under the racist categorisation of 'black' (as inferior, sub-human etc.). However, the category 'Asian' has also represented a certain 'excess', more specifically signifying an Orientalist cultural particularity of Otherness. It is not then surprising that the dominant sociological writings of the 1970s about 'Asian-ness' emphasised specific cultural aspects of these identities.[29] The multifarious regional, linguistic, religious, class and gender differences were homogenised and/or essentialised, leading to culturalist and caricatured descriptions of South Asians in Britain. This work tended to concentrate on Asian patriarchy, cultural conflict and identity crises within the pathology of the Asian family. Asian identity was constructed either lying outside, or in opposition to, 'British culture', exemplified by the popular thesis of 'caught between two cultures'.[30] However, more recently a greater attention and positivity has been attached to the signifier 'Asian' (or its particular ethnicities). This has been promoted through official discourses as found in ethnic monitoring categories, the media, and in academic writings.[31] Nevertheless, it is still evident that the term 'Asian' in contemporary politico-academic discourse operates only as a narrow ethno-cultural identity category. At the heart of this discourse is a reductive notion of culture (or more specifically cultural difference), that attempts exhaustively to describe and delimit the cultural specifities of a discursively produced Asian identity.

Modood's misplaced critique against 'political blackness' has compelled him to assert the utility of the identity category 'Asian' as more accurate in describing peoples of the South Asian diaspora in Britain. He has argued that we ought to begin from the way an ethnic group *experiences* its oppression and mode of being, and not be made to fight in the name of a spurious (Black) identity imposed upon them.[32] Modood attempts to construct a form of identity politics based on 'ethnic self-definition' and 'ethnic pride', in which 'Asian-ness' is wholly determinate of an individual's cultural and political outlook. The problem with this account is that there is an essential relation assumed between culture and identity. It offers an almost primordial notion of ethnicity, one that is shared by the ideology of a liberal state multiculturalism in its search for a cultural authenticity in determining political representation and being. We would not deny that the signifier 'Asian' has a greater popular appeal and potential to mobilise, in some contexts, than has 'Black' in 1990s Britain. But any suggestion that the signifier 'Asian' is already given, or can claim, a privileged experiential cultural authenticity outside of political processes or history, needs to be challenged.

The sutured category of 'Asian' can only be understood in relation to the political and hegemonic operations involved in the construction and maintenance of a cultural identity, and in the policing of community boundaries in the interplay of both multicultural state processes and self-group definition. Cultural identity and the boundary-making processes of community formation are produced by competing modes of cultural authority, and struggled over in particular cultural and political configurations. There is no doubt that the signifier 'Asian' offers places for us to speak from, but there is a need to reclaim this signifier against its culturalist moorings.[33] Modood's tract closes down the political opportunities over this struggle and articulates dynamic modes of diasporic Asian cultural specifities to an essentialist standpoint. For example, Modood has highlighted the failure of much leftist anti-racism over the 'Rushdie Affair', exemplified by their simplistic slogan, 'fight racism, not Rushdie'.[34] However, the Rushdie Affair engendered a multiplicity of political responses in Britain amongst racialised 'minority' groups, and demonstrated how the act of political organisation is complex and riven with antagonisms. Many different groups found that their allegiances cut across religious, national, class and gendered interests. During the Rushdie Affair, some groups organising themselves as Muslims came together to raise their voices against religious and racial discrimination. Under different circumstances these same groups might, during cultural and national events, locate themselves as, say, Kashmiris, Pakistanis, Africans, (British) South Asians or Black. A sense of difference, structured by particular struggles, can under some circumstances lead to separate and incommensurable or even hostile interests; while in other situations difference can be used as a source to strengthen solidarity for marginalised groups. A pro-Islamic anti-Rushdie position could not readily express an equivalence to leftist anti-racism. Black feminist groups such as Southall Black Sisters and the group Women Against Fundamentalism found their anti-religious fundamentalism stance was articulated – though on different grounds – in the same way as the neo-racist anti-Muslim position of some liberal commentators and fascist groups.[35] However, alongside the anti-racists he accuses, Modood offers only an equally reductive response to the Rushdie Affair. He argues for an ethnically sensitive anti-racism predicated on a closed and finalist Asian/Muslim identity.[36] In doing so, there is a failure to explore the hegemonic operations that maintain a bounded notion of an authentic Muslim community, and which silence or marginalise alternative political positionalities.[37]

CULTURAL SPECIFICITY/POLITICAL SOLIDARITY

Solidarity implies readiness to fight and joining the battle for the sake of the other's difference not one's own.[38]

... Seeking simply to appropriate the experience of 'Otherness' should not separate the 'politics of difference' from the politics of racism.[39]

In an attempt to problematise the issue of essentialism in relation to questions of difference and Black anti-racist and feminist politics, Brah has asked: 'At what point, and in what ways ... does the *specificity* of a particular social experience become an expression of an essentialism?'[40] In responding to the practices of Black or Asian/Muslim identity politics and anti-racist strategies for political solidarity, it has been tempting to adopt a fashionable anti-essentialist postmodern perspective over the discursive conditions of identity formation. A certain nihilistic logic of anti-essentialism, however, suffers from a tendency to erase all forms of cultural specificity and political agency in the quest for a contingent and de-centred subject. But as hooks further points out: 'Should we not be suspicious of postmodern critiques of the "subject" when they themselves surface at a historical moment when many subjugated people feel themselves coming to voice for the first time'.[41] To navigate between the excesses and politically suspect position of extreme anti-essentialism, and its antithesis – the problems of an essentialist standpoint – at least two alternatives may be identified.

First, there is the idea of 'strategic essentialism', especially put forward by Gayatri Chakravorty Spivak and Hall.[42] This would, for instance, in principle support the practice of a Black or Asian identity politics as far as they are apposite for political organisation and action in response to particular conditions of racial oppression – although Hall has, on reflection, also commented on the potential weakness of the 'essentialising moment', saying that it functions with a binary logic of opposition against other political positionalities and is always in danger of naturalising what are historically produced identity categories.[43] While recognising the limits of strategic essentialism, from an alternative account our contention has been that the signifier Black in certain anti-racist practices has been an open-ended and unfinished mode of identification and has not necessarily collapsed into an essentialism, excluding or silencing other political positionalities. The question of a strategic or otherwise Asian (or Muslim) identity politics is rather more problematic. As we have pointed out, Asian (or its particular 'ethnicities') has been articulated productively alongside Black in anti-racist struggles, such as found in the BPA or in Southall/Birmingham Black Sisters. However, as advocated by Modood, its current dominant invocation and manifestation operates increasingly within a culturalist discourse. Attempts to organise around this signifier are liable to lead to an essentialising identity politics of ethnicity unless, as we argue, it is actively *re-articulated* in relation to the formation of other political alliances and solidarities.

The second alternative to emerge against the political limits of an essentialist standpoint, without erasing the subject altogether, employs notions of (cultural) syncretism as a form of hybridity in the formation of identities in contemporary multicultural spaces – especially in relation to describing the transformations of British national culture.[44] The powerful arguments made about the emergence of syncretic identities have been useful in disrupting exclusionary (white) notions of Britishness which rest on a new cultural racism.[45] However, the condition of syncretism cannot be marked as being inherently radical, and nor is it guaranteed to challenge forms of racial oppression. We would want to stress that the multiracial areas, which have been celebrated for their syncretic youth cultures and identities,[46] have been concurrently the very centres which continue to produce the most virulent forms of anti-Black (and especially anti-Asian) racism.[47] Moreover, there is a danger that the aggrandisement of an anti-essentialist syncretic hybridity results in the disavowal of cultural specificity – although, concomitantly, the condition of hybridity is often constructed as particular only to marginalised, ethnically marked groups. This practice can sublate the hybrid, by first claiming and then rejecting a supposed anterior cultural purity for those identities marked as non-syncretic.[48] Its logic can produce readings of an 'Asian' identity and an affiliated range of cultural practices as being 'traditional', 'pre-modern' or 'backward'. For example, identifying oneself as Islamic could easily be equated with being 'fundamentalist' – as occurred during the Rushdie Affair.

In an attempt to rethink cultural identity and specificity outside of the terms of essentialism and ethnic absolutes, we can briefly turn to a reading of Homi Bhabha's elaboration of the 'third space' of cultural hybridity and identification.[49] Bhabha contends that the problems of cultures emerge most intensely at their boundaries, at points of social conflicts and crisis. But the articulation of cultures is possible because they are a 'signifying or symbol forming activity', lived out through forms of representation which can never be complete in themselves. He understands cultural difference as a 'process of translations' which implies that it '... can never be said to have a totalised prior moment of being or meaning – an essence'.[50] Bhabha points to the inherent process of the hybridity of culture, which is not dependent on an accumulative process of synthesis and accretion of difference.[51] Neither is it predicated on cultural interaction of unmediated exchange, but more on the grating against each other of different (sometimes incommensurable) knowledge systems and cultural practices – the things that don't quite fit together. It is at the boundaries where these already de-centred cultural practices are contested that cultural hybridity as a form of cultural difference 'gives rise to something different ... a new area of negotiation of meaning and representation'.[52] Bhabha labels this as a nascent 'third space'. It opens up possibilities for new structures of counter-authority and novel political initiatives that may not fit into our conventional frames of reference or rules of interpretation. What is important in Bhabha's account is that it does not jettison cultural specificity for difference in order to fulfil an anti-essentialist move. The third space imagines the construction of forms of solidarity or alliances which conceive 'political subjectivity as a multi-dimensional, conflictual form of identification'.[53] This understanding of cultural hybridity does not first essentialise and then disavow or erase cultural specificity in order to propose a more politically radical syncretic or fusional notion of hybridity. It points to the contested and ambivalent nature of cultural specificity as difference in the making of political identities. The third space is not necessarily replete with ambiguity and voluntaristic identification, because, as Peter McLaren has emphasised, 'differences are produced according to the ideological production and reception of cultural signs'.[54] He argues that we need to understand cultural specificity as differences in terms of a politics of signification, in order for

120

different cultural identities both within and across different social groupings to be understood and located in political terms.

This reading of the third space as a site of 'becoming' enables us to recognise the cultural liminality of an 'Asian identity' and to see that the politics of the signifier 'Asian' is expressed by incommensurable interests, antagonisms and discursive and ideological contestation over its meaning. As we have argued, the Rushdie Affair expressed a multiplicity of competing and contradictory political positions and could not be contained by a conventional left anti-racist politics. The making of political identities and solidarities for future anti-racist strategies cannot be based on some finalist Asian (or Black) identity and agency or pre-determined political location. The formation of the BPA and its political projects has been founded on the political processes of 'becoming' in cultural spaces that have attempted to promote solidarities and alliances amongst Asians, African-Caribbeans and other groups subjected to popular and state racisms. Although these sites have not been without their antagonisms and antinomies, we believe that the projects of anti-racism are still important spaces in which new identities can be produced *and* made contestable. The act of reclaiming the category 'Asian' against an ethnic essentialism is one forged in political struggle and re-articulation. Similarly, the unique moment of 'Black' in the making of anti-racist political identities in Britain should not be so readily erased from memory in a rush to embrace and celebrate more contemporaneous and heterogeneous formations of identity. During a time of escalating racial terror and violence, the urgent task remains: how are we to think through and build *new* forms of anti-racist political alliances and solidarities?

We write this chapter in the spirit of keeping open a dialogue for re-imagining better Black political futures. Many thanks to the following folks: Mukhtar Dar, Ashwani Sharma, Barnor Hesse, Raminder Kaur and Virinder Kalra.

NOTES

1. Stuart Hall, 'Old and New Identities, Old and New Ethnicities' in Anthony D King (ed), *Culture, Globalization and the World System*, Macmillan, London 1991, p56.
2. Ambalavaner Sivanandan, interviewed in *Campaign Against Racism and Fascism (CARF)*, No 24, 1995, p3.

3. See Sandip Hazeersingh, 'Racism and Cultural Identity: An Indian Perspective', in *Dragons Teeth*, No 24, 1986; Tariq Modood, ' "Black", Racial Equality and Asian Identity' in *New Community*, Vol 14.3, 1988; 'Muslims, Race and Equality in Britain: Some Post-Rushdie Reflections' in *Third Text*, No 11, 1990; and 'Political Blackness and British Asians', *Sociology*, Vol 28.4, 1994; Paviter Sanghera, 'Identity Politics and Young "Asian" People' in *Youth and Policy – Journal of Critical Analysis*, No 45, 1994; and Kalbir Shukra, 'The Changing Context of Race in Britain: A Symposium. A Scramble for the British Pie' in *Patterns of Prejudice*, Vol 30.1, 1996.

4. See especially writers such as Hazareesingh, *op.cit.*, and the articles by Modood, *op.cit.*, for positing an ahistorical account of Black identity formation in Britain. The signifier 'black' has a long and complex history. Its historical antecedents from W. E. B. Du Bois and the Black Power movement in the USA suggest that it was organised primarily (though not exclusively) as a 'cultural' identity category via the African diaspora. However, the manifestations of 'black' in the Caribbean, India (in the Dalit movement) and in Britain also suggest that it has operated as a 'political' identity category and has been reworked in different national contexts. (We would like to thank Barnor Hesse for bringing this to our attention.)

5. Stuart Hall, 'New Ethnicities', 1988, in James Donald and Ali Rattansi (eds). *'Race', Culture and Difference*, Open University & Sage, Milton Keynes 1992, p254.

6. *Ibid*.

7. Stuart Hall, 'What is this "Black" in Black Popular Culture?' in Gina Dent (ed), *Black Popular Culture*, Dia Centre for the Arts, Bay Press, Seattle 1992, pp31-32.

8. For example, see S.A. Ashraf and S.S. Hussain, *Crisis in Muslim Education*, Hodder and Stoughton, Sevenoaks, 1988; and John M Halstead, *The Case for Muslim Voluntary-Aided Schools: some philosophical reflections*, The Islamic Academy, Cambridge 1986.

9. See M Hiskett, *Schooling for British Muslims: Integrated, Opted-out or Denominational*, Social Affairs Unit, Research Report Number 12 London, 1988. For an analysis of the New Right, see Paul Gordon and Francesca Klug, *New Right New Racism*, Searchlight Publications, London 1986.

10. Ali Rattansi, 'Changing the subject? Racism, Culture and Education' in James Donald and Ali Rattansi, *op.cit.*, p40.

11. Also see John Hutnyk, 'Adorno at Womad: South Asian Crossovers and the Limits of Hybridity-talk' in Pnina Werbner and Tariq Modood (eds), *Debating Cultural Hybridity: Multi-Cultural Identities and the Politics of Anti-Racism*, Zed books, London 1996.

12. We are not making a crude distinction between 'doing theory' and practice (such as political activism). We see theory as much a form of practice as is the messy business of attempting to organise politically 'on the ground' for social change. In relation to the discourse surrounding 'Black' these two modes have been bifurcated and reified, often leading to over-valorised accounts of both Black identity formation and anti-racist political action respectively.

13. Kobena Mercer, *Welcome to the Jungle*, Routledge, London 1994, p302.

14. See Alistar Bonnet, *Radicalism, Anti-Racism and Representation*, Routledge, London 1993; Tariq Modood, *op.cit.*, 1990, 1994; and, Kalbir Shukra, *op.cit.*

15. Kobena Mercer, *op.cit.*, p292.

16. Michel Foucault, 'Truth and Power' in Colin Gordon (ed), *Power/Knowledge: Selected Interviews and Other Writings 1972-1977*, New York, Pantheon Books, 1980.

17. Avtar Brah, 'Difference, diversity and differentiation' in James Donald and Ali Rattansi, *op.cit.*, p130-131.

18. Tariq Modood has also argued that 'Black' has been a too 'politicised identity' imposed on Asians, and that an Asian or Muslim identity is based on a more subjective act of ethnic self-definition. One may question Modood's notion of the 'political' and his voluntaristic account of identity formation. Moreover it could be argued that Asian/Muslim identifications have been produced out of specific discourses of 'race', gender, class and the condition of post-coloniality, both in and outside of Britain, *op.cit.*

19. It is important to stress that we do not wish to privilege 'activism' over other modes and sites of political struggle. For example, see Sanjay Sharma, John Hutnyk and Ashwani Sharma (eds), *Dis-Orienting Rhythms: the Politics of the New Asian Dance Music*, Zed Books, London 1996, for an exploration of how emergent identities and anti-racist alliances are being articulated through new forms of Asian musical expressive culture.

20. James Donald and Ali Rattansi, 'Introduction' in James Donald and Ali Rattansi, *op.cit.*, p4.

21. Avtar Brah, *op.cit.*, p128.

22. For example, see Floya Anthias and Nira Yuval-Davis, *Racialized Boundaries*, Routledge, London 1992; Stuart Hall, *op.cit.* 1992; bell hooks, *Yearning: race, gender and cultural politics*, Turnaround, London 1991; and Kobena Mercer, *op.cit.*

23. For a more general account of these issues see Shirin Housee, 'Contemporary theories of Inequality – identity, subjectivity and difference', in Andy Cooper, Paul Grant and Barbara Gwinette (eds), *The Sociology of Inequality*, MacMillan Press, Basingstoke, forthcoming.

24. hooks, *op.cit.*; Pratibha Parmar, 'Gender, Race and Class: Asian Women and Resistance', CCCS, *op.cit.*, and 'Young Asian Women: A Critique of the Pathological Approach' in *Multi-Racial Education*, Vol 9.3, 1981; Brah, *op.cit.*
25. Even with all the (somewhat dubious) talk of hybridity and new ethnicities, the continuing presence of 'old' ethnicities and singular identity politics are very apparent. For example, Stuart Hall, 'Black Bodies', *New Times*, 1 February 1997 confidently asserts the emergence of a 'new ethnicity, a new black [Afro-Caribbean] British identity' that is 'autonomous' and 'distinctive'. Hall's account of black identity formation is unrelated to other minority political positionalities. Moreover, he ostensibly slides towards a culturalist version of a new black ethnicity which may close off the possibility of rethinking a contemporary urban anti-racist cultural politics. For an engagement with Hall's contentions, see Ashwani Sharma, 'Afterwards', *new formations*, forthcoming.
26. The label 'Asian' is a diasporic identity category existing outside of South Asia. For one account of how this identity has emerged through migration processes in Britain, see Shirin Housee, 'The journey that travels a complex route', in Raminder Kaur and John Hutnyk (eds), *Travel Worlds: journey into contemporary cultural politics*, Zed Books, London, forthcoming.
27. Harry Goulbourne, 'Aspects of Nationalism and Black Identities in Post-Imperial Britain' in Malcolm Cross and Michael Keith (eds), *Racism, the City and the State*, Routledge, London 1993.
28. Robert Young, 'Colonial Desire: Hybridity' in *Theory, Culture and Race*, Routledge, London 1995.
29. For example, see especially the collection Verity S Khan (ed), *Minority Families in Britain: Support and Stress*, Macmillan, London 1979.
30. *Ibid.* For a seminal critique of this 'ethnicity school' position, see Errol Lawrence, 'In the abundance of water the fool is thirsty: Sociology and black "pathology" in CCCS, *The Empire Strikes Back*, Hutchinson, London 1982. Also see articles by Pratibha Parmar, *op.cit.*
31. Marie Gillespie, *Television, Ethnicity and Cultural Change*, Routledge, London 1995; Tariq Modood, *The Guardian*, 17 June 1995; Pnina Werbner, *The Migration Process: Capital, Gifts and Offerings among British Pakistanis*, Berg, Oxford 1990.
In sharp contrast to a more autonomous practice, a 'decentred' notion of Asianness is also being articulated in Asian dance music culture in Britain – see Sanjay Sharma, 'Noisy Asians or Asian Noise' in Sanjay Sharma, John Hutnyk and Ashwani Sharma *op.cit.* For a critique of Gillespie's work, see John Hutnyk, 'Media, Research, Politics, Culture. Review Article', in *Critique of Cultural Anthropology*, Vol 14.4, 1996; and, for a critique of Werbner's position

see, Simeran Man Singh Gell, 'The Gatekeepers of Multiculturalism', in *Critique of Cultural Anthropology*, Vol 14.3, 1996.

32. Tariq Modood, *op.cit.*, 1990.

33. See Sanjay Sharma, *op.cit.*; Raminder Kaur and Virinder S Kalra, 'New Paths for South Asian Identity and Musical Creativity', in Sanjay Sharma, John Hutnyk and Ashwani Sharma, *op.cit.*

34. Tariq Modood, *op.cit.*, 1990.

35. Southhall Black Sisters, *Against the Grain*, SBS, London 1990.

36. Tariq Modood, *op.cit.*, 1990.

37. See Gita Saghal and Nira Yuval-Davis, 'Refusing Holy Orders' in *Marxism Today*, March 1990; and, Nira Yuval-Davis, 'Fundamentalism, multiculturalism and women in Britain' in James Donald and Ali Rattansi, *op.cit.*

38. Madan Sarup, *Identity, Culture and the Post-Modern World*, Edinburgh University Press, Harvester Wheatsheaf 1996, p62.

39. hooks, *op.cit.*, p26.

40. Avtar Brah, *op.cit.*, p126, original emphasis.

41. bell hooks, *op.cit.*, p28.

42. Stuart Hall 1988, *op.cit*; Gayatri Chakravorty Spivak, *In Other Worlds – Essays in Cultural Politics*, Methuen, New York 1988, and, *Outside in the Teaching Machine*, Routledge, London 1993.

43. Stuart Hall, *op.cit.*, 1992.

44. See for example, Paul Gilroy *op.cit.*, Hall *op.cit.* 1991, Kobena Mercer, *op.cit.*, and Ali Rattansi, *op.cit.* See Robert Young, *op.cit.*, for a useful distinction between hybridity as 'syncretism' or 'fusion', and hybridity as 'translational'. (Although Young's conclusion about the dangers of hybridity as inherently racialised for use in contemporary theory misses the point about how terms may be reappropriated for political struggle).

45. Martin Barker, *The New Racism*, Junction Books, London 1982; CCCS, *op.cit.*; and, Paul Gilroy, *op.cit.*

46. For example see Les Back, 'Coughing Up Fire: Soundsystems in South-East London' in *new formations*, No 5, 1988; Paul Gilroy, *op.cit.*; and, Simon Jones, *Black Culture, White Youth*, Macmillan, London 1988.

47. See Koushik Banerjea and Jatinder Barn, 'Versioning Terror: Jallianwala Bagh and the Jungle', in Sanjay Sharma, John Hutnyk and Ashwani Sharma, *op.cit.*

48. For other critiques of hybridity, see Manthia Diawara, 'The Nature of Mother Dreaming' in *Third Text*, No 13, 1991; John Hutnyk, *op.cit.*; Ashwani Sharma, 'The (Im)possibility of theorising Asian Musical Cultures' in Sanjay Sharma, John Hutnyk and Ashwani Sharma, *op.cit.*

49. Homi Bhabha 'The Third Space' in Jonathan Rutherford (ed), *Identity*,

Lawrence & Wishart, London 1990; *The Location of Culture*, Routledge, London 1994.

50. Homi Bhabha, 1990, *op.cit.*, p210.

51. For a more detailed account of Bhabha's notion of hybridity, see Nikos Papastergiadis, 'Restless Hybrids' in *Third Text*, No 32, 1995.

52. Homi Bhabha, *op.cit.*, p211.

53. *Ibid*, p221.

54. Peter McLaren, *Critical Pedagogy and Predatory Culture*, Routledge, London 1995, p214.

NOT MAKING A VIRTUE OF A NECESSITY: NANCY FRASER ON POSTSOCIALIST POLITICS

Pam Alldred*

INTRODUCTION

Nancy Fraser is one of the most influential voices of contemporary Anglo-American feminist theory. Her work can be located within the encounters between socialism and postmodernism, and those of feminism with postmodernism. She insists on the necessity of developing feminist theoretical perspectives that are not immobilised by critiques of 'big sister' feminism or 'big brother' socialism and has articulated a position that remains productive for political critique, retains some kind of feminist or critical project and finds a way beyond the impasse. In her book, *Unruly Practices: Power, Discourse and Gender in Contemporary Social Theory*, Fraser described herself as a democratic socialist and feminist.[1] However she is highly critical of old-style socialist politics, especially for their lack of feminist and ecological analyses. Since this interview Fraser published her second book *Justice Interruptus: Critical Reflections on the 'Postsocialist' Condition*.[2]

Fraser works on theory for the sake of politics. She writes for an academic audience, addressing problems generated within political practice, particularly some of the personal and political dilemmas that emerge. She maintains a 'bifocal' approach to developments in theoretical work and to current political conditions. Fraser's academic background was in philosophy and she is currently Professor of Political Science at the New School for Social Research in New York City. In her work she reflects upon the tensions and contradictions of trying to do critique within the academy. Being a radical academic is not, she argues, a contradiction in terms.[3]

* Karen Triggs also participated in the conversation with Nancy Fraser.

STILL A SOCIALIST AFTER ALL THESE YEARS? DESCRIBING A CONTEMPORARY 'POSTSOCIALIST CONDITION'

Pam Alldred and Karen Triggs (PA/KT) In *Unruly Practices* you describe yourself as a socialist-feminist. Would you still use that term to describe yourself or, perhaps, in the late 1990s, would you want to qualify it in any way?

Nancy Fraser (NF) I would use it, but I would want to be extremely frank about the fact that I don't any longer know what I mean by socialism. Nor, I think, does anyone else. For me, the word is a marker for the need for some vision of an egalitarian and liberatory political economy, even when we don't know its precise content. I don't believe it's possible to have a liberatory cultural politics without a political-economic under-girding. Thus, I tend to think of the present moment as – with apologies to Jean-Francois Lyotard – a 'postsocialist' condition. By this I mean two things. On the one hand, there's a lot of ideological garbage about the triumph of neo-liberal capitalism and so on, which we must criticise and demystify. On the other hand, the collapse of communism in 1989 was not simply the delegitimation of the Soviet Union and formerly existing institutional socialism; rather, there's been a larger crisis of confidence and crisis of vision on the left. I am willing to claim the term socialism, if I can qualify it. For me, the word must be dissociated from any pretence of certainty and nostalgia. It can only be the sign of something that has yet to be invented.

PA/KT Even if we don't want to lose the critiques provided by socialism, are there some positive aspects within the loss of vision that you mention?

NF It's good to lose a vision that was flawed and I think that the major understandings of socialism were quite flawed on many levels; they were androcentric, de facto based on masculinist and majority nationality-based cultural assumptions. In so far as traditional models presumed the notion of a command economy or the nationalisation of large-scale industry, they are increasingly out of touch with the political economy of post-fordism, which is highly flexible, differentiated and transnational. In addition, the traditional socialist vision was production-centred and largely blind to ecological considerations. Thus, the loss of that vision opens the way for better alternatives.

PA/KT Your essays in *Unruly Practices* are interventions within feminist and political debates of the late 1980s. What do you think are the most important challenges for feminists in the late 1990s?

NF A major challenge has to do with the emergence of a very strong anti-feminist backlash. Even as many important feminist ideas have been widely disseminated and absorbed into the culture, there is a very articulate, mobilised backlash. At the same time, the movement has become differentiated and specialised. Academic feminists, for example, are increasingly engaged in very sophisticated debates amongst themselves that are sometimes out of touch with the larger changes in the Zeitgeist. We sometimes talk as if we need only bring our thoughts and our demands to 'the great unwashed masses', whereas in fact there is an enormous right-wing anti-feminist mobilisation which we haven't yet figured out how to address. Today there's more of a problem in terms of how academic USA feminism relates to currents outside of the academy than there was when I was writing *Unruly Practices*. Increasingly so, because although the book was published in 1989, many of the essays were written much earlier. At that time I didn't have such a strong sense of disconnection between academic feminism, and feminism and anti-feminism outside the academy.

This separation has to do with the more general challenge posed by the larger shift in the political winds- which I called our 'post-socialist' condition. I put that term 'postsocialism' in quotes in order to signal the need to interrogate it and maintain a critical relation to it. What I mean by it is that the horizon in which we're all operating is one in which we no longer have any credible vision of an alternative to the present order, which socialism provided, for better or worse, for a hundred and fifty years. In the USA we've got a very strong, resurgent free market neoliberalism, as well as a very strong cultural authoritarianism. To the degree that feminism of the second wave grew out of the movements in the 1960s, this was a time of ascendant radicalism and progressive emancipatory movements. For me, and many people of my generation, which is the 1968 generation, it went without saying that one could go forwards in a kind of ascending line and whatever gains one had one could build upon. What we're now confronting, and it's a terrible traumatic existential shock, is the idea that you can actually regress, lose things that you thought you'd won. Maybe only a very naïve American optimism prevented us from realising that before! But my generation of feminists assumed relative economic prosperity. We also assumed that the civil rights and legal gains we won one day could not be lost on the next. Today, therefore, we feel that the rug is being pulled out from underneath us.

THE POLITICS OF REDISTRIBUTION AND THE POLITICS OF RECOGNITION

PA/KT Your recent work articulates a conceptual division between two political forms or strategies: a politics of redistribution, and a politics of recognition. A paradigmatic example of the former would be socialism because it addresses the economic exploitation of workers, and a paradigmatic case of recognition politics would be lesbian and gay struggles or multiculturalism. You go on to describe how a redistributive approach is likely to reduce the distinctiveness of dominant and subordinate groups vis-à-vis each other, whereas recognition politics may be about increasing the recognition of specificity and hence emphasising differences between groups. Gender struggles, however, traverse both forms of politics. Gender inequalities require both a politics of redistribution, to remedy women's economic subordination, and a politics of recognition, to challenge cultural devaluation. You refuse a socialist position that subsumes cultural subordination within economic subordination, but insist on retaining a materialist analysis. You reject the idea that one can assume that justice of either type will necessarily follow on from the other: both types of struggle are necessary and neither is sufficient.

NF You have given a very accurate picture of the main lines of argument in my recent book *Justice Interruptus*.[4] Since it was published I've done more work on this project and it's developing in a slightly different way from the original formulation, which I was not entirely satisfied with. Nevertheless, the impetus for this project remains relevant. It was conceived as an intervention in contemporary new social movement politics in the USA, although I think the idea probably applies elsewhere as well. What concerns me is the relative eclipse within these social movements of social politics, especially egalitarian redistributive politics, and the relative ascendancy of cultural politics, especially identity politics and the politics of difference. I worry that we're losing the balance here and that, frankly, it fits much too conveniently with the 'postsocialist' condition. How convenient for the right if we fail to insist on material equality just at the moment when neo-liberalism is ascendant! My intervention is aimed, therefore, at advancing the slogan: *no recognition without redistribution*. At an earlier moment of Marxist hegemony on the left I may have said the opposite: *no redistribution without recognition*, but now I think the slogan that's needed is no recognition without redistribution.

However, I'm now trying to get away from what I feel was the overly additive character of my original formulation of these ideas. In the book I have said that we should be for socialism in the economy and deconstruction in the culture, as if these were two spheres or levels of society. The real point should be to think integratively about the relation between cultural struggles and social and economic struggles. The example I give, and it's one that I've been working on for many years, is welfare. At one level, everyone understands that rethinking the welfare state is a redistributive project, but what is less clear is that it also requires reinterpreting the dominant norms and cultural meanings of gender, sexuality, what counts as work, what counts as a contribution to society, what is the basis for entitlement. These cultural norms and social meanings are so completely interfused with distributive questions that we can't really separate them. As a result, struggles to transform the welfare state for the sake of egalitarian redistribution cannot succeed unless they are joined with struggles of cultural change. And vice-versa. Thus, welfare can be seen as an example of how the cultural and the social interpenetrate one another.

PA/KT A particular example for the UK would be that, until recently, if you were a woman who was receiving unemployment benefit and were in a partnership and cohabiting with a man, your unemployment cheque would be addressed to him. The welfare state was here constructing the meanings of gender and of heterosexual relationships. Is that what you're describing?

NF Absolutely. In the USA, it's constructing being a single mother, especially a poor single mother, as sexually deviant, irresponsible, being a 'scrounger', having babies to avoid employment. As if raising children were not work and a contribution! Meanings and norms permeate all the institutions of society, be it the welfare system, the legal system or whatever. So when it comes to evaluating proposed institutional reforms, we must take two different standpoints: the standpoint of recognition and the standpoint of distribution. From the standpoint of redistribution, we must ask: who benefits and who loses materially?

From the standpoint of recognition, in contrast, we must ask: how does this policy construct different subject positions? What status differentials or hierarchies does it constitute? Who is constructed as normative and worthy of respect and who is stigmatised as undeserving? In other words, we should consider how policies affect the relations of recognition as well as the distribution of resources. Policies that are economically redistributive can have the unintended effect of harming people's status. When properly analysed, many issues have these two dimensions, which I insist are irreducible to one another. Redistribution and recognition are equally primary and yet completely imbricated with one another. They cannot be addressed separately.

PA/KT Do you feel a post-structuralist approach to discourse would stop you from disentangling these issues, that is, disentangling meanings from the material?

NF Not at all. Some post-structuralist approaches to discourse provide very useful tools for analysing the relations of recognition. The mistake is in thinking that this is a substitute for analysing the relations of distribution. In contrast to those who treat post-structuralism as a total *Weltanschauung*, I defend what I call a 'perspectival dualism'. That means I insist on the need for two different standpoints of critique. One is the standpoint of cultural analysis, which concerns the status order and the construction of subject positions, including whether some people are relegated to second class citizenship in society. Here is an area where all the sophisticated new developments in cultural studies, including post-structuralism, can be extremely useful in unpacking how status differentials and hierarchies of value are established and played out in social institutions. You don't have to confine that sort of analysis to things that we think of as paradigmatically cultural; as I just indicated, the welfare system is just as cultural as a movie is. But there's also a second, absolutely crucial, standpoint of evaluation and critique that one has to adopt as well, namely, the standpoint of distribution, which concerns material resources. The cultural dimension and the distributive dimension are fused together and yet they don't map one on one. You can't assume that once you've got the cultural analysis you can read off the economic or vice versa. There's a certain autonomy even as they're interfused. That's my current view on these things.

THE USES OF FEMINIST THEORY, OR, DO WE MIND THE GAP
BETWEEN THEORY AND PRACTICE?

PA/KT The social protest movements of the 1960s and 1970s inspired
and propelled theoretical analysis of various kinds whereas, as you've
noted, a gap seems to have grown between social movements and critical theory in the following decades. Feminist activists have been
suspicious of feminism's 'turn to theory'. While women are active in a
range of new political movements, and are visible as organisers as well
as activists, specific campaigns addressing the inequalities that still exist
for women do not seem apparent. What light can feminist theory shed
on this? Does the recognition that there is not a simple unity among
women rightly complicate campaigns about women's issues or undermine them? Does this relate to the fact that young women in Britain
tend not to identify as feminist, even though their expectations can, in
many respects, be seen as feminist?[5]

NF With respect to the 'turn to theory', I would want to distinguish
between different currents. Feminist theory has made possible an enormous array of techniques for cultural criticism. I think we really need
to analyse film, video, advertising and so on. Approaches have become
very sophisticated and this is extremely useful, assuming it can be
rendered accessible, which I think it can. What I worry about is that
this has taken over as almost the only game. I see much less that's
creative and sophisticated in social and economic theory and in political theory, in the more traditional sense. Thus there is a disconnection
between feminist cultural theory, which is very rich and ascendant, and
social/economic policy analysis, which doesn't seem to be very lively
at this point.

At another level, the culturalist ascendancy is manifest in a theoretical impasse. We are spinning our wheels over identity politics. There's
a constant to-ing and fro-ing between essentialism, anti-essentialism
and strategic essentialism, without ever getting to anything else. Many
feminist theorists want to get out of the terrain of identity politics. But
they don't succeed. They just go back and forth between essentialism
and anti-essentialism.

Put another way, the time is past when feminism, or any movement, can focus on elaborating a specific identity in isolation from
other movements and currents. Feminists have undergone a healthy
self-criticism about that. Yet the way the self-criticism is being
formulated is not actually getting us to anything else. One tendency

133

is just to complicate identities by looking not only at gender but at other strands of the construction of identity, including 'race', class, sexuality and so on. Taken in one direction, this leads to ever smaller and more specific identities, whereas my sense of what we really need is to get beyond this identity terrain altogether. My suggestion for how to do that is to reconnect our current preoccupation with 'the politics of recognition' to a renewed focus on 'the politics of redistribution'.

PA/KT What kinds of politics of recognition do you support then?

NF 'The politics of recognition' covers a range of possible approaches to group identity. If the aim is to redress status harms and value hierarchies one could assume a deconstructive approach aimed at destabilising current identity categories. But there are also other ways of transforming the status order, including the kind of liberal universalism which tries to affirm universal humanity, and the kinds of politics of difference which try to revalue the undervalued identity. These represent three different politics of recognition, and although I'm very partial to deconstructive strategies, it's probably more useful to think about them not as simple alternatives to each other, although they are in tension with one another, but rather as levels. What one wants is recognition of universal humanity at one level and then recognition of difference at another level and then deconstruction at another. So somehow we must combine all three: with one another and with redistribution!

PA/KT Are you disappointed that specific local struggles don't have a vision, and appear to have abandoned larger stories?

NF I wouldn't use the term 'disappointed'. But I do feel strongly that it's important not to make a virtue of a necessity. This is a feature of the time we live in, that none of us can simply will ourselves out of. Part of what I mean by the 'postsocialist condition' is precisely the lack at present of a comprehensive vision of an alternative to the present order. Thus in one sense we don't have any choice but to do specific campaigns, even though we don't really know how they might connect to one another and to a broader project of social transformation. But what I find really pernicious are theories that attempt to say that any attempt to envision a broader picture is Stalinist, totalitarianism and so on: fill in your own term of abuse. The absence of a broader vision is not a permanent condition. Francis Fukuyama is wrong.[6] This is not the end of history. Alternatives to the present order will emerge at some point in the future.

PA/KT Is there an element of historical determinism there? That 'this is the time when this is happening and that there will be a time when it isn't so'?

NF There's no determinism in reflecting on the horizon in which we are operating, which is, of course, an historical horizon. The motive for doing so is, as I suggested earlier, the sense of having the rug pulled from under you. It's a very different moment from the one that gave birth to feminism twenty years ago, and I feel the need to step back and think about it. I use the word 'horizon' in a sense that does not involve determinism. What I called the 'postsocialist condition' is the horizon in which we are, for the time being, necessarily operating, but I believe that it's possible both to be within this horizon and to interrogate its limits critically from inside.

From this perspective, it's worth thinking about how the word 'coalition' is functioning now in USA discourse about new social movements. It works as the sign of an aspiration to connect various local initiatives and struggles to one another. The term 'articulation' in Mouffe and Laclau is another marker of this desire.[7] This is a completely proper, appropriate aspiration because we all know that significant change does require massive co-ordination. The problem is that these words 'coalition' and 'articulation' will remain empty unless we begin to talk about what the basis for a coalition might be. That is, unless we begin to think programmatically. In the USA, for example, we must try to develop a non-zero-sum way of thinking about affirmative action.

PA/KT We've rejected the unitary subject of feminism and this leads to not presuming commonality, but merely acting with certain women on certain issues. What's exciting about coalitions is precisely the fact that there isn't a pre-given basis. What you just referred to as the emptiness of coalitions is what seems to allow novel alliances to be made.

NF It depends on what one means by a pre-given basis. To begin to try to articulate the basis for coalition is not, in my view, to constrain activity and political processes. Political processes are highly evolving, contingent and not really constrainable. But all the more reason, therefore, to be pushing oneself at every point to articulate what it is one's trying to do and where it is one's trying to go.

My instinct is to try to think big. I would say that one always does implicitly have some bigger picture in mind. It's just that, usually, it's the status quo. People take for granted the existing background institutions. For instance it's usually assumed that there have to be jobs, and that jobs are how people get their income. Thus it's not that there's no big picture, it's just that the picture in place has the status of common sense. It's critically useful, in contrast, to try to imagine how local struggles might look different, might take a different form, if we re-imagined the implicit picture. That's what I mean about a non-zero-sum game. It's the case now that in current taken-for-granted, large-scale, institutional arrangements, people who we think all have just claims and who we think should all be on the same side, have interests which are constructed as opposing one another. Thus the gains of some seem to come at the expense of others. What one has to do, if one is serious about coalition, is to imagine different sets of background conditions and background institutions in relation to which people might begin to reinterpret their interests, so that they no longer appear to be opposed to the interest of their potential allies. This is difficult but I think it's what Trotskyists used to mean when they spoke of transitional socialist programmes. I am trying to conceive local struggles in ways that are transitional and lead to something else, rather than being, ostensibly, only local struggles.

Contemporary USA/UK feminisms and their institutional contexts

PA/KT We began by talking about the USA feminist movement facing a backlash. Can we speak of USA feminism as a movement, as a single unified project?

NF Yes and No. It was easier to speak of a movement when feminism was a very visible, dramatic counter-cultural formation that could be found in the streets and that had certain unique social practices like consciousness raising. What we have now is quite different. Much of what began as counter-cultural has become institutionalised. I'm not sure exactly when one stops speaking of a movement and when one starts speaking of something else, but today we find feminist consciousness and initiatives in every social institution throughout the social order. There are, in addition, a small number of overarching *leitmotif* concerns, like abortion rights, where you can still put together a large demonstration. But maybe the term 'movement' is less appropriate now for this kind of political formation. Especially since, in the USA, political parties are not primarily ideological to the degree that they are in Europe, and feminist energies are dispersed. We don't see much of anything we could call a feminist agenda at the level of political parties.

PA/KT Do you think the existence of official initiatives dents the 'radicalness' of this thing that we're not going to refer to as a social movement?

NF It depends. There are cases where official state institutionalisation does not dent 'radicalness', as it is an expression of a successful conquering from the grass-roots. But there are also cases where institutionalisation involves co-option. Generally, institutionalisation is double-edged. The fact that right-wing politicians sometimes think they can get votes by drawing from a certain kind of feminist discourse shows something about the inroads that feminist ideas have made. Yet any time a movement's claims get valorised enough to become incorporated into the state apparatus, they necessarily get changed into something else. The incorporation of feminist claims into government social programmes definitely has an effect on the 'grammar' of those claims. The movement loses some control over its own project. A good example of this is legalisation. What it takes to translate a demand into a legal claim that can stand up in court can change your sense of what the injustice is and what the remedies are going to be. Yet it's undeniably a sign of progress that certain kinds of feminist demands do obtain legal status.

Feminism, in its counter-cultural and radical phase, was very much about self-transformation through consciousness raising and so on. Thus, it has been susceptible to various depoliticising currents, which are very strong in the USA with its cultural stress on voluntarism and individualism. We have the same problem in the Black movement. That movement is today in a terrible crisis, much worse than that of feminism. There is an understandable sense of giving up – on membership, integration and transformation of American society – which goes along with the emergence of voluntarist politics of self-help. Many Blacks feel they have to do everything on their own, they can't expect anything from the government, from whites and so on. And some conclude that 'we'll take care of our own lives', perhaps becoming Moslems, or by marching with a Million Men on Washington, saying 'we'll atone, we'll get ourselves spiritually in order', while not making any demands on the government. This is all very American.

PA/KT Does such individualism explain younger women's lack of interest in feminism?

NF I really don't know exactly how to account for this, except to mention again the success of the right, and the media also, in portraying feminism as something *passé*. Although this is very strong it's also complex, because the same young women who distance themselves from feminism and don't want to use that word about themselves clearly hold aspirations and expectations that I would say are feminist. They expect to combine career and family, for example. Incidentally, some polls have shown that Black women are considerably more likely to say they are feminists than white women in the USA. That's very interesting and requires reflection and explanation.

PA/KT If we can't speak of *a* movement any more, do we then talk of movements? Even then, are we simplifying to pre-given groups gathering around identities? For instance, the way gender and 'race' intersect is more complicated than simply to speak once again of a Black women's movement.

NF What is usually perceived as a gender issue, say in respect of reproduction, has racialising subtexts and the critical task is to explicate these, to think critically about them. Any issue is going to involve intersecting strands. Usually, understandably, one strand tends to be salient and central but that does not mean one can ignore the others.

PA/KT It's *movements* plural rather than, say, a movement which has fractured?

NF Not exactly. When one gets involved in a struggle, say around reproductive rights, it is usual that the actors engaged in such struggles position themselves as women and in that sense gender is initially the salient focus. But it very quickly becomes clear that there are dimensions which may be in the background but which are there and are important, that have to do with sexuality, 'race', or class, and so on. Feminists certainly have become sensitive to the inadequacy of focusing too single-mindedly on gender at the expense of other strands. Now you might say, well, how can one translate that multi-strand awareness into a set of demands, a form of campaign or a set of struggles? I think that this can and does go on. I don't think complications are a bar to activism. We don't have to simplify the heterogeneity in order to have a strong activist ability.

PA/KT Perhaps this is something of a caution to academic theorists, not to imagine we need to iron it all out in the academy before we can do anything at the weekend.

NF Yes, absolutely. I agree there!

NOTES
1. Nancy Fraser, *Unruly Practices: Power, Discourse and Gender in Contemporary Social Theory*, Polity, 1989.
2. Nancy Fraser, *Justice Interruptus: Critical reflections on the 'Postsocialist' condition*, Routledge, 1997.
3. The interview was conducted in London in June 1996 by Pam Alldred and Karen Triggs, who planned and conducted the interview jointly. Pam wishes to thank Tim Jordan for his extensive editorial help with the original edited transcript and Nancy Fraser (NF in the text) for her time and quick, detailed responses to drafts.
4. And an earlier piece: N. Fraser, 'From Redistribution to Recognition?: dilemmas of justice in a "Postsocialist Age"', *New Left Review*, 212, 1995, pp68-93.
5. See H. Wilkinson, *No Turning Back: generations and the genderquake*, DEMOS, London 1994.
6. F. Fukuyama, 'The End of History?' *The National Interest*, 1989, 3-18.
7. For example, E. Laclau and C. Mouffe, *Hegemony and Socialist Strategy: towards a radical democratic politic*, Verso, London 1985.

Too Many Universals: Beyond Traditional Definitions of Exploitation

Tim Jordan

If there is to be revolution, we would rather make it than suffer it.

Otto von Bismark 1866[1]

INTRODUCTION

The time when the left mourned itself has passed. The left has forgotten not only how to make revolutions but why radical change is needed. The left now only suffers under radical changes. It is time the left perceived that revolutions we should, and must, recognise as our own are being made again. Amid all the movements that are still struggling for radical change are some that ignore the left's paralysis – in fact often simply ignore the 'left' altogether – and yet are aiming for radical change the left could easily recognise as its own. It is time the left embraced the changes that again make revolution possible. The time for self-pity has passed.

We all breathe air, drink water and eat food. Threats to any of these, and there are many, threaten us all. We each have a gender: a maleness, a femaleness or a mixture of these two. The imbalances between them, and their failures, are imbalances and failures for us all. We each have a race: a blackness, a whiteness or a deeper feeling for these differences. The prejudices of races, and their tyrannies, offer inequalities and tyrannies for us all. And as the left has always known, we all have a class, a socio-economic definition: an upper, a middle, a working, an under or a complex combination of these distinctions. The exploitations of class and the subjugations of classes are exploitations and subjugations for us all. Ecology, gender, race and class are all universals and all are part of active, at times revolutionary, movements to change society. And there are more universals than these: sexuality, nationality, age, species and more. It is not that a universal is necessary to create a political movement, but many of the movements that have emerged since the 1960s can constitute a universal as one of their principles.

There is no longer one universal; there are now many universals. One way of defining the central problem of left or liberatory politics is the despairing cry, 'There are too many universals'. The present argument is that the despair in this cry reflects three linked points: the left has had a commitment, often unspoken, to one unifying framework for both liberatory theory and movements; this assumption of one liberatory universal has failed; and while this failure destroys the basis for much of what has been known as the left, it also creates new political possibilities that are being enacted even as the left comes to terms with its own crisis. The first part of this chapter will explore the universalism of the left and its failure, while the second and third parts will explore the new emancipatory frameworks that have emerged.

WE AIMED FOR THE ONE

It is of course true that the left has never agreed, never been united and never, ever, pursued the one end by the one means. However, the present argument is that the left, in nearly all of its elements, thought the transformation from a capitalist to a socialist society would come when the one end, of a working class revolution, violent or parliamentary, was achieved. Laclau and Mouffe noted the same point in 1985:

> What is now in crisis is a whole conception of socialism which rests upon the ontological centrality of the working-class, upon the role of Revolution, with a capital 'R', as the founding moment in the transition from one type of society to another, and upon the illusory prospect of a perfectly unitary and homogeneous collective will that will render pointless the moment of politics.[2]

The focus on class politics as the central politics of liberation and the failure of this politics, noted by Laclau and Mouffe, forms a central component of the crisis of the left and liberatory politics. This crisis and its roots in the inability of class to be the universal framework of emancipation can be seen in many places.

One example is from the parliamentary left in the rewording of the British Labour Party's Clause IV, which sets out the overall aims of the Labour Party. A comparison between the Clause IV that existed from 1918 with the one that replaced it in 1995 shows that, even for a party explicitly devoted to Labour politics, a change away from a purely production-centred approach has occurred. (See Appendix for wording of the two clauses.) The language of class, of 'workers by hand and brain', contained in the first Clause IV is stripped away in favour of a broad sense of community 'in which power, wealth and opportunity are in the hands of the many not the few'. Even further, the contradictions of class are consigned to the past through an explicit commitment to combining the 'rigour' of the market and competition to the 'forces' of partnership and co-operation. Justice, democracy and the environment then join the market as the four pillars of Labour's aims and values in 1995.

This change is remarkable when it is remembered that this is a political party born out of class contradictions and dedicated to the interests of the working class. The Labour Party reacted to a changing political climate by making itself other than 'labour'. In this it offers an example of the left rethinking its fundamental vision of politics. The new Clause IV seems to offer little that is substantial, preferring what appear to be empty abstractions, hiding behind the words 'market', 'justice', 'democracy' and 'environment' to the substance of nationalising the means of production. This also reflected not just the desperate desire of a parliamentary party to win an election, but also a more general left-wing failure to rethink a political vision following the collapse of solely class-based aims and values.

A second example can be found in the interview with the editors of the new journal *Soundings: a journal of politics and culture* in this book. In that interview Stuart Hall, Doreen Massey and Michael Rustin can be found making fine distinctions according to their ultimate allegiance or not to class as an overarching framework.[3] All three of the editors have clear allegiances to open and flexible forms of Marxism, particularly influenced by Gramsci, and to the New Left. And, just as with the Labour Party, the strains in maintaining a Marxist or even class based framework are clear. The distinctions they draw are clearly delicate ones, and their point that the substantive distinction between the positions of Hall and Rustin are quite small is important, but it is also clear that the belief that the capital/labour distinction forms the overriding framework for understanding the left's project is under question.

> I would say that nothing about feminist politics could be understood without understanding their articulation to questions of economic capital, but certainly the economy and capital do not constitute the

problem of feminism ... Capitalism may shape it very urgently and maybe you can't disentangle the two, but you are nevertheless talking about an articulation between two formations or two antagonists or two contradictions, not the same contradiction with two manifestations. I think that is the deeper and more difficult distinction and I suppose I am more committedly on the second of these two.

Stuart Hall

I think that the nature of our antagonist has changed rather less than the nature of the resources of agency, culture, and programme we might be able to mobilise against it. What I mean by our antagonist comes back to the nature of capital, and property- capitalism itself.

Michael Rustin

I think I also no longer suspend judgement. I do not think capitalism (or the economy) is 'determining in the last instance'.

Doreen Massey

Further examples of this tension or change can be found but there is no need to extend the point.[4] It is enough to reinforce my present claim with the following summary, by Jan Pakulski, of the class interpretation of social movements:

Since the 1970s, the class interpretation has been in steady decline. Studies of the American civil rights movements, West European ecological and anti-nuclear (eco-pax and green) mobilisations, fundamentalist movements in Iran and the Middle East, and the more recent wave of anti-partocractic movements in Eastern Europe, have prompted further critical revisions of the class interpretation. Neither the social composition and identities of actors nor their key concerns could adequately be accounted for in class terms. The shortcomings of the class accounts became particularly apparent to students of 'new social movements', especially the Green and the feminist movements.[5]

It seems clear that the left and liberatory politics, however we interpret those terms, worked mainly within a framework that has two key parts. First, a universal and totalising theory and practice were sought. Second, the dichotomy between labour and capital, however defined or practised, gave content to the overall framework. Class was universally the framework that defined oppressions and inequalities and the working class were ultimately the bearers of the power to end these oppressions and inequalities: when that had been accomplished, the world would essentially be a fairer place. The existence of this framework has become even clearer with its failure, as outlined by Pakulski, to grasp some of the most politically potent post-1970s liberatory movements, and is true of both the extra-parliamentary and the parliamentary left.

For such a framework, the emergence of many universalities is a crisis. One path has been to try to integrate these new *loci* of oppression and liberation within the class framework. Lynne Segal recounts how socialist-feminists attending the fourth British socialist-feminist conference, held in 1974, were asked, 'Do we see the women's movement as some kind of vanguard movement or as a petty-bourgeois movement which may be ideologically useful but is essentially marginal to the main political struggle?'[6] Either irrelevant to or part of the real (class) struggle, is the meaning of this question. As with many of the attempts of the left to incorporate non-class based struggles, the basis of this question was rejected by feminists.

The failure of a simple theory and practice of incorporating all struggles into class politics returns the left to this moment of crisis. What can it mean to say that there are many universals of liberation and oppression?

WE GOT THE MANY

The emergence or recognition of many movements and of many liberatory universals is both a critical and a constructive moment. The old certainties may die joyfully or tearfully, but gone they are, and it is those of us who still wish to transform society from some sort of a left perspective who are left at the wake, wondering where to go.

The problem is sometimes misinterpreted as the end of political activism. We need only think of the nostalgia surrounding the student protests of the 1960s, almost invariably replayed at the beginning of every academic year to the tune of: 'why is modern youth so conformist? so little interested in changing the world?' But as the protests against the building of the Newbury Bypass, or those detailed in McKay, show this is a misguided understanding of present day radicalism.[7] The problem does not reside in a lack or failure of political activism. Confusion in the left is confusion about the meaning of present day political activism.

Left, or liberatory, politics is confused about which activities are liberatory and which are not. If we take one area of undoubtedly active politics during the 1980s and 1990s, animal liberation, we can see the problem. The left has traditionally been concerned with human oppression and its social sources. But where does the liberation of animals fit in? Where does the concern with the human oppression of non-humans fit into the left? This question is posed dramatically when such public demonstrations as those at Brightlingsea against the export of veal calves occur. Here are demonstrations from the grass roots that many on the left might instinctively think of as part of their larger project of social transformation, but the content of the demonstrations disturbs long buried left assumptions. Similar points could be made when we consider the politics of pleasure, for example in raving.[8]

The universalism of the left or of liberation in general has collapsed into many universal liberations. The result of this is a dislocation of the vision of political change that has – at deep and often unconscious levels – governed understandings of revolutionary social change. One expression of this dislocation is a challenge to our usual understanding of the term 'universal', as meaning 'all-encompassing'. We come across many universals, many different politics, each of which seems to be universal, but how can they all be universal forms of politics if a universal is all-encompassing? Shouldn't each universal politics incorporate all the others? We might think of these universals as particular or specific universals, but that generates a contradiction in terms: the universal that is particular. How can something be universal, and so all-encompassing, but simultaneously specific or particular, and so not all-encompassing? A brief example of this peculiar contradiction can be given by exploring two understandings of sexual violence, from a class and from a feminist perspective. Needless to say, this attempt is not meant to cover the full complexity of sexual violence but to function as an example for the present discussion.

The initial point is that the two frameworks, of class politics and feminism, are universal frameworks. Everyone is involved in the economic and sexual relations of these two overarching structures of inequality. How might these two frameworks differently understand sexual violence?

Class politics begins from the centrality of production and consumption in structuring society and our lives. Consumption includes the necessary reproduction of workers on a day-to-day basis, that is workers must be rejuvenated with food, sleep and play in order to be able to contribute to production each day. This reproduction is centrally carried out within the family. Part of reproduction can be seen to be sexual: a workforce with no outlet for sex will produce certain problems. Sex can then be understood as part of the necessary regeneration of workers. From this conclusion, it is not hard to understand sexual violence as part of this reproduction. Sexual violence can be theorised as a necessary result of workers demanding sex within familial bonds: women are expected as part of the family structure to provide sex and, when they don't, male sexual violence becomes somehow legitimate. This can then explain judicial structures that do not recognise rape within marriage. Sexual violence becomes in this way a result of the class system.[9]

Feminism might provide a different explanation of sexual violence. If we take Sylvia Walby's theory of patriarchy as one example, we find that it has six major structures: employment, household production, culture, sexuality, violence and the state.[10] Sexual violence here appears as a core concern for gender relations, playing a major role in at least two of the six categories that define unequal relations between men and women. She states: 'Male violence against women has all the characteristics one would expect from a social structure'.[11] Sexual violence here is an immediate and central component of a feminist framework for understanding oppression between men and women.

The contrast between these two (oversimplified) pictures of where sexual violence would appear in class and in feminist politics is that for class politics sexual violence can be explained as a result of core relations – sexual violence appears as the result of the need for the reproduction of the workforce – but within feminism sexual violence *is* a central component of understanding inequalities between men and women. The point is not that either of these understandings is wrong or that they are mutually exclusive, but that both are right from the perspective of the politics that they are articulated within. In one sexual violence is a result of certain central political processes; in the other, sexual violence is a central political process.

Class politics appears universal, as does feminist politics, and both organise all the components of the world according to their central political interests. If you begin by trying to grasp the class based inequalities of this world, then sexual violence can be integrated but may well not be a central component of your understanding. If you begin by trying to grasp the gender-based inequalities of this world, then sexual violence stands at the centre of your understanding.

The example of sexual violence suggests that different universals are not pieces in a jigsaw puzzle and neither are they mutually exclusive. Both feminist and class politics can see the same object in the world, but then understand that object's meaning in a different way. These two are different universal perspectives on the world, but neither is comprehensive. This point can now be generalised by recognising that all forms of politics mentioned so far, and examined in this book, can be expected to advance the same conclusions. Pollution examined from class, eco-activist, national or species-centred perspectives may well be understood in different ways; and many other examples could be given. The point is not only that from different political perspectives one might see different components in the world, but that from different political perspectives one might understand the same, or what appears to be the same, object differently. The current state of liberatory politics is characterised by the self-contradiction of many particular universals.

PARTICULAR UNIVERSALS

The self-contradiction of 'particular universals' appears to be a logical problem: what is meant by particular and what by universal? However, answering this question will show it to be a political question, and examining it will allow an alternative framework for liberatory politics to be developed, one built from the reality of a plurality of oppositional politics.

The recognition of many universals means that any one universal political theory and practice is not so much all-encompassing – organising all aspects of society, inequality and oppression within the one total and self-consistent theory – but that different forms of oppression may articulate a particular universal framework for its theories and practices. Each form of oppression or liberation can be articulated as a universal and can accordingly appear as if it should encompass all forms of liberation. However, the appearance that a universal should encompass all forms of oppression – rather than all facets of society relating to the form of oppression under discussion – is unjustified. It is possible that a movement can articulate an understanding that is universal in the sense that it encompasses all aspects of society understood in relation to the movement. It is further possible that this understanding makes no attempt to encompass all forms of oppression. One way of putting this is that the self-contradiction of a 'particular universal' is only a contradiction when viewed from within previous left and liberatory visions that demand a view that encompasses all oppressions within the one understanding of and movement against oppression. Here is the root of one of the left's recurrent problems: how to incorporate all the different forms of liberation into one universal framework? And how to do this in a way that meets the urgent need of each movement to grasp the specificity of its own oppression and liberation?

If we take the existence of many universals as a given, instead of being bound by the conviction of the necessity of one universal, our concept of a universal changes: theoretical understandings are now reoriented to the multiple struggles that are going on around us, instead of the struggles being reoriented to our theory. Universals become the expression of a perspective – an all-encompassing perspective and so universal – on a particular oppression. Many different universals can then co-exist as each expresses a viewpoint that is all-inclusive, but only in relation to a particular form of liberation or oppression. Each social or liberatory movement can be expected to articulate, in many different ways, these visions of social change. Each such vision may or may not include elements covered in other visions, but even if they do this does not mean they are viewing exactly the same object. Rather, each movement will articulate its own understanding of common elements, as these will be embedded in a particular perspective that will give each element a particular meaning for a particular movement.

To return to sexual violence: it can now be seen that each understanding of sexual violence, the feminist and the class, may be correct if viewed from within its particular framework. From a feminist perspective sexual violence is a key, central component of patriarchal societies, while from a class perspective sexual violence is an important result of the central needs of capitalism. Both capitalism and patriarchy can be condemned from these understandings and social change launched. But these two understandings will also be misunderstood when confronted from outside their perspectives. Class-based activists may see sexual violence as important but not really the heart of the struggle, while feminists might be angered at the removal of sexual violence from the centre of political activism. The understanding of sexual violence and its significance is coloured by the perspective of the particular movement that is viewing it.

If this picture is accepted, then the result seems to be many co-existing movements that constitute liberatory politics. It also seems that for this approach to be consistent, the only criticisms or understandings that can be given will have to come from within each movement. If each perspective is self-consistent but is misunderstood from outside, there is no external vantage point from which to criticise movements. The often mooted political problem of difference is raised here. If there are no principles outside of movements to appeal to, then how do we know which political movements might be considered liberatory? How do we judge exploitation and liberation? It might seem easy to reject neo-fascist social movements, but on what basis could this be done? Other movements, such as animal liberation, pose more complex problems.

Having grasped that there are a multiplicity of liberatory movements, each of which articulates and struggles against its own form of oppression, the problem emerges of how to tell if any particular movement is a liberatory one. The twin principles of difference and ethics (or values) re-emerge here.

The final piece of this particular puzzle is a value or set of ethics that does not subordinate the values of particular movements to its own values, and so does not seek to integrate all political movements into one political movement, but which gives some measure or standard by which to judge different movements. Each particular movement provides us with a new definition of liberation and oppression, its own, but we also need a general definition to guide us through each of the movements we might encounter or participate in.

Such a definition can only be achieved by recognising that the general definition of oppression is an abstraction based in no particular movement and can do no more than guide activists working in particular movements. Real struggle to change society occurs in specific movements, such as those discussed in Part 1 (of this book), and not in the attempt to construct an all-encompassing movement that integrates all struggles into the one struggle. Understood this way, new political forms offer not only many new definitions of oppression and liberation, beyond the specifically class-based nature of the Marxist definition of exploitation, but also a new definition of oppression. The general understanding is not about particular struggles but about grasping what is and is not liberatory in particular struggles. This is the first innovation of a new politics, different from the socialist-based understanding of exploitation.

The second component of this new understanding follows quickly from the first, as the unanswered question is: 'What is the content of this general definition of exploitation?'. The general definition needs to be discussed and argued about within the abstract space of theoretical discussion outside or between particular movements. The nature of specific definitions of already existing oppressions and liberations can only be generated from within particular movements. These definitions can only be generated through engagement with political struggles, while the general definition can only be generated by theoretical or abstract exploration of the dynamics of exploitation. There is not the space here to develop such a definition in the necessary detail, although the path to it can be noted.

A definition of oppression that fulfils the requirements which have been mentioned must be less substantial than many previous definitions of oppression. In effect, it must grasp all the different oppressions of our world. To fulfil its role as a guide or marker – and not as a definition of an already existing oppression – it must be, to an extent, vaguer than previous definitions such as Marx's of exploitation or de Beauvoir's of alienation. This does not mean that the definition is conjured out of thin air. Rather it must survey different definitions of oppression and liberation and condense what is common to them. One path to an understanding of the general nature of exploitation in new politics is a comparative study of the definitions of exploitation and oppression that already exist. This volume provides, in chapters 2-7, just such an exploration, with each chapter exploring a particular new political movement. In Patrick Field's and Rupa Huq's chapters we can see the gradual building up of definitions of what is to be fought and of what a movement wants in the anti-roads and anti-criminal justice act protests. Merl Storr's account of the bisexual movement is the most important for the present argument because it provides a direct challenge to it. Storr explicitly takes up the viewpoint being developed here in order to show that it does not work for understanding the bisexual movement. Examining Storr's account will allow an examination of what the content of an abstract and general definition of exploitation might look like.

Storr argues that what had been the usual axes through which activist movements had articulated their sense of subordination, notions of exploitation and oppression, are rejected within the bisexual movement in favour of more diffuse notions of power. This illustrates the way the definitions of particular movements have political primacy over the abstract, overarching definition of oppression. Here Storr's account of the bisexual movement supports what has been called the first conclusion from a new politics definition of exploitation: that the definitions of individual movements have primacy over general definitions.[12] Where Storr appears to undercut the theory of the general meaning of new politics is in her claim that the bisexual movement shifts from notions of oppression and exploitation to a diffuse multi-centered concept of power. She argues: 'An increasing focus on "visibility" and "alternative forms of life" suggests the development of an implicit understanding of power as diffuse and ubiquitous, rather than more traditional notions of power as formal or hierarchical.' Storr's point is that a general concept of exploitation must fall back on notions of power as a hierarchy rather than as distributed networks. She also notes that a redefinition of liberation and exploitation is one of the components of new politics, in the theory I propose. And if this were the case, then the present theory would be contradicted.

However there seems no reason why the abstract definition of oppression and exploitation cannot embrace the bisexual movement's understanding of power. Storr has too quickly placed the new definition of exploitation back into old understandings of exploitation. The part of the definition she focuses on is that exploitation is the transfer between two collectives of something that enriches one while simultaneously impoverishing the other. If this were all there were to it then Storr's analysis would be correct. But this is only part of a definition, which also argues that understandings of exploitation and liberation emerge from diffuse, decentred networks of activists, theories and organisations that make up a movement.

The understanding of a common exploitation is that which enables a movement to be a movement and not just a diffuse collection of events or individuals. This means that the definition explicitly encompasses diffused notions of power but argues that, when defining a movement, there must be something that brings its differential elements into relation with each other. And Storr's account of such factors as 'visibility' or 'alternative forms of life' are exactly the things that make a political movement out of bisexuals. These factors are, as Storr argues, diffused and not centralised. They also help create the sense that this is a subordinated community because its ability to be visible and to construct its own way of life is denied, in order that straight or gay and lesbian communities can be visible and can know that their way of life is validated. This does not mean that straights and gays and lesbians have to be constituted as the one oppressor community. It does mean that in this relationship of oppression several communities are constituted, but straights and gays and lesbians are seen by some bisexuals as benefiting (even if they benefit in different ways) because bisexuals are invisible. What is gained by the straight community or gay and lesbian communities is lost for bisexual communities. In this way, the definition I am proposing is able to encompass the bisexual movement and does not reduce it to formal notions of power.

The second innovation in this new political definition of exploitation is the content of an abstracted and general definition of oppression, exploitation and liberation. Summarising the two innovations I have outlined offers the following three-part definition of exploitation beyond the traditional ones. First, this definition conceives oppression at an abstract level while noting that manifestations of oppression only ever exist in particular material social relations. Second, it claims that oppression, or emancipation, is the unity around which emancipatory collectives or social movements coalesce their networks of activists, organisations and events. Third, there is a need to give content to this definition. (The content I have proposed elsewhere is the following: oppression is a non-essentialist relationship in which one collective enriches itself through a mechanism that simultaneously impoverishes another.) Whatever this content is, it will have to take account of definitions using theft, such as in the Marxist definition of exploitation, or of alienation of a collective's interests, as in de Beauvoir's definition of women as the Other to the male Subject, or Storr's account of visibility and ways of life.[14]

Liberation can be redefined from this basis, for it means the transgression of at least one mechanism of oppression. From this perspective, the left or liberatory politics must address many oppressions. This understanding drains the general struggle for liberation of all but intellectual content. The general definition of oppression does not describe something that can be fought by activists because it is a guide to oppressions rather than the articulation of an existing oppression. Political struggle occurs in the various networks and organisations that make up the collective action systems of particular social movements and not in one overarching movement. The new patterns of emancipatory politics consist of many movements each centred around a project of emancipation or experience of oppression. It is these movements that are politically primary because they can effect fundamental social change.

NOTES

1. F. Stern, *Gold and Iron: Bismark, Bleichroder and the building of the German Empire*, Penguin, Harmondsworth 1977, p81.

2. E. Laclau and C. Mouffe, *Hegemony and Socialist Strategy: towards a radical democratic politics*, Verso, London 1985, p2.

3. These 'fine distinctions' were forced by the interviewers' questions and it should be noted I was one of the interviewers.

4. See also T. Jordan, *Reinventing Revolution: value and difference in new social movements and the left*, Avebury, Aldershot, 1994, pp76-79; J. Pakulski, 'Social Movements and Class: the decline of the Marxist paradigm'; and K. Eder, 'Does Social Class Matter in the Study of Social Movements?: a theory of middle class radicalism', both in L. Maheu (ed), *Social Movements and Social Classes: the future of collective action*, Sage, London 1995.

5. J. Pakulski, *op. cit.*, p56.

6. L. Segal, *Is the Future Female ?: troubled thoughts on contemporary feminism*, Virago, London 1987, p50.

7. G. McKay, *Senseless Acts of Beauty: cultures of resistance since the sixties*, Verso, London 1996.

8. McKay, *ibid*. See also T. Jordan, 'Raving and the Future of Revolution: cultural and political social movements', paper given at the *Shouts from the Street* Conference, Manchester Metropolitan University Institute for Popular Culture, September 1995.

9. See M. Barrett, *Women's Oppression Today: the Marxist/Feminist encounter*; revised edition, Verso, London 1988, pp19-29, passim.

10. S. Walby, *Theorizing Patriarchy*, Blackwell, London 1990.

11. *Ibid.*, p128.

12. See T. Jordan, 1994, *op.cit.*

13. *Ibid.*

14. *Ibid*, chapter 7.

Appendix: UK Labour Party's aims and values (old and new Clause IV)

The old Clause IV: 1918-1995

Party objects
National

1. To organise and maintain in Parliament and in the country a Political Labour Party.

2. To co-operate with the General Council of the Trades Union Congress, or other Kindred Organisations, in joint political action in harmony with the Party Constitution and Standing Orders.
3. To give effect as far as may be practicable to the principles from time to time approved by the Party Conference.
4. To secure for the workers by hand or by brain the full fruits of their industry and the most equitable distribution thereof that may be possible, upon the basis of the common ownership of the means of production, (*distribution, and exchange*), and the best obtainable system of popular adminstration and control of each industry or service.
5. Generally to promote the Political, Social, and Economic Emancipation of the People and more particularly of those who depend directly upon their own exertions by hand or by brain for the means of life.

*Added 1929

The new Clause IV: 1995-on

Aims and values

1. The Labour Party is a democratic socialist party. It believes that by the strength of our common endeavour we achieve more than we achieve alone, so as to create for each of us the means to realise our true potential and for all of us a community in which power, wealth and opportunity are in the hands of the many not the few, where the rights we enjoy reflect the duties we owe, and where we live together freely, in a spirit of solidarity, tolerance and respect.
2. To these ends we work for:
   a dynamic economy, serving the public interest, in which the enterprise of the market and the rigour of competition are joined with forces of partnership and co-operation to produce the wealth the nation needs and the opportunity for all to work and prosper, with a thriving private sector and high quality public services, where those undertakings essential to the common good are either owned by the public or accountable to them;
   a just society, which judges its strength by the condition of the weak as much as the strong, provides security against fear, and justice at work; which nurtures families, promotes equality of opportunity and delivers people from the tyranny of poverty,

prejudice and the abuse of power;

an open democracy, in which government is held to account by the people; decisions are taken as far as practicable by the communities they affect; and where fundamental human rights are guaranteed;

a healthy environment, which we protect, enhance and hold in trust for future generations.

3. Labour is committed to the defence and security of the British people, and to co-operating in European institutions, the United Nations, the Commonwealth and other international bodies to secure peace, freedom, democracy, economic security and environmental protection for all.

4. Labour will work in pursuit of these aims with trade unions, co-operative societies and other affiliated organisations, and also with voluntary organisations, consumer groups and other representative bodies.

5. On the basis of these principles, Labour seeks the trust of the people to govern.

NEW WELFARE ASSOCIATIONS: AN ALTERNATIVE MODEL OF WELL-BEING

Tony Fitzpatrick

INTRODUCTION[1]

Students of social policy have long been aware of the contribution which non-state and non-market institutions make to social and individual well-being. Charities, churches, voluntary organisations and self-help groups of various kinds have often worked to relieve poverty and to satisfy basic human needs. In addition, feminist theorists have highlighted the extensive contribution which informal and domestic labour make to social welfare. As such, it has become common practice to term state, market, voluntary and informal types of provision as, respectively, the first, second, third and fourth sectors of welfare.[2]

Yet the actual social policies of successive governments have tended to pay little more than lip-service to both voluntary and informal welfare provision. Post-war governments emphasised the centralised, statist collectivism that they considered to be necessary if capitalism were to be given a human face. The value of the third and fourth sectors was acknowledged, but they were thought of as 'extras' by comparison to the leading role which only state welfare could play. More recent Conservative governments have insisted upon the necessity of market reforms if various economic and social problems, which they interpreted as being created by state welfare, were to be addressed.[3] The third and fourth sectors were invoked as part of such governments' anti-statist rhetoric. In practice, however, and with only a few exceptions, they have preferred to commercialise welfare provision while unloading many public responsibilities onto unpaid female carers, usually in the name of family values.

In short, it is the first and second welfare sectors that have dominated policy-making in Britain for most of the twentieth century. It is presently unclear as to whether or not Tony Blair's Labour government will challenge this dominance.

This chapter rejects the assumption of both academics and politicians that there are only four welfare sectors and aims to suggest that there are now welfare associations emerging within an additional fifth sector, to which all of those interested in a 'new politics' should pay attention. Increasingly, a variety of associations, groups, networks and affiliations are coming into being which are dedicated to the principles of mutuality and community, but which have relatively little faith in the ability of either the state or the market to secure such principles.

Up to a certain point, fifth sector welfare associations resemble the provision to be found in both the voluntary and the informal sectors: they are non-profit making, rooted in civil society and are dependent upon volunteers who work within a variety of mutual exchanges to raise the general level of welfare for themselves and/or for others. But welfare associations may be located 'beyond' either the third or fourth sectors for two reasons: firstly, because they are generally less dependent than the voluntary and informal sectors upon either state or market provision, and secondly, because they are intended to be less dependent. Welfare associations are 'political' alliances in that they offer motivations, methods of organisation and models of group alignment that are different, often radically so, from those to be found in the state and the market and which could, potentially, inspire reform, especially within the first and second sectors. Is this the case? Could the fifth sector inspire wider social and economic reform? These are questions I shall return to below.

The next section will outline the principal associations that have emerged in recent years. The final section will then clarify what is meant by the 'fifth sector', before explaining the significance of welfare associations and relating them to the goal of wider social and economic reform.

MAPPING THE UNMAPPABLE

It is not simply the sheer number of associations that impedes any attempt to assemble and classify them. Even if the numbers were more manageable, associations can emerge, evolve and dissolve with such rapidity that any attempt to take a snapshot of the existing scene is likely to be highly blurred by the time it is developed. In addition, it is in the nature of many of these associations to be elusive and indefinable, to resist being fossilised into history or, even worse, into a new orthodoxy. Many new social movements combine a variety of roles – welfarist, political, economic – so perhaps it is artificial to infer the existence of welfare associations out of this complex network. Since the chief rationale of this book is that the new politics is one of diversity, fragmentation and disorganisation, an attempt to discern and locate welfare associations under convenient headings seems perversely illogical. Despite these considerations, I propose to identify the following areas.

Local currency schemes

Also known as Local Employment and Trading Systems (LETS) these schemes are a non-profit making form of systematic barter, where goods and services are traded without the need for money.[4]

Originating in Canada in the early 1980s, a group of at least a dozen people form an association that has its own currency, or unit of exchange, in which goods and services will be traded. Each member compiles one list of the goods and services that they can offer, setting their own prices, and one list of those which they might want to purchase. A directory of members' offers and requests is then distributed, and updated periodically, and trading then begins. Each member has an account and the association keeps a record of all transactions by means of credit notes written in the local currency unit. These units may be used either as a complete alternative for, or in conjunction with, money issued by the national bank. LETS is therefore vastly superior to direct barter where whatever is exchanged between parties must be of equivalent value.

In 1996 there were about 400 LETS in Britain, ranging from groups of several dozen people right up to groups of several hundred; in total, approximately 20,000 members could be found in LETS organised throughout both urban and rural areas. Additionally, there were something like 100 LETS in Europe, 200 in Australia, 90 in New Zealand and several dozen large schemes throughout Canada and the USA. All of these systems share the essential features described above, but there are any number of variations to be found depending upon the wishes of members. For some, LETS is a way of simulating national economic exchange at a local level, whereas others are motivated by values that they see the formal economy as being unable to recognise. I shall discuss some of the main advantages of LETS in the last part of this essay.

Credit Unions

Credit Unions (CUs) are similar to LETS in that they are voluntary and non-profit making. They are, however, concerned exclusively with financial matters and are more likely to be run according to detailed procedures and codified rules. The first British CU was legally recognised in 1964 and, after an initial steady growth, their numbers have risen dramatically in the 1990s. There are over 500 CUs with upwards of 150,000 members.

The main purpose of a CU is to provide a cheap source of finance to those on low incomes. As such, they issue loans to their members at modest rates of interest, as well as offering financial advice and support. Another aim of CUs is to encourage their members to save and it is out of these savings that loans are subsidised. To join a CU, then, the main requirement is that members save regularly at whatever level can be afforded. After a specified time, usually several months, members can then borrow funds up to a maximum amount, currently about £5000. This loan is charged by the CU at a maximum rate of interest of 1 per cent per month and is to be repaid over an agreed period. Any surplus that is made by the CU is churned back to those members who are in credit as an interest on savings, the maximum dividend rate being 8 per cent per annum.

Their financial emphasis makes CUs the most 'conservative' of the associations dealt with here. Indeed, about one million people in Ireland belong to CUs, due largely to the ethos of the Catholic church with its familialist stress upon self-help. Furthermore, CUs are often set up with the assistance of local government. Nevertheless, CUs do not quite fit into the other four sectors of welfare. Their emphasis upon income security means that, given the right social circumstances, they may possess a radical potential that has long been abandoned by the building societies.[5] In a progressively ecologically-minded society, for instance, CUs could fund collective projects and programmes aimed at improving the quality of the urban and natural environments, with fewer risks of poverty and insolvency than at present.

Environmental co-operatives

CUs are a financial form of co-operative and co-ops *per se* date back at least to 1844. There have traditionally been just three forms of co-op: consumer, worker and producer. In essence, they are purely voluntary, and largely democratic, organisations that attempt to be entirely self-financing and where profits are distributed on an equitable basis to members. Control and ownership, therefore, are 'horizontal' rather than 'vertical' or hierarchical, belonging to members rather than to managers and shareholders. This means that co-ops combine an ethos of solidarity, on a small, local scale, with one of autonomy, without subordination to the imperatives of either the market or the state. Around this essential core an infinite number of variations is possible, many of which have been realised in practice. What seems certain, however, is that since the 1970s and 1980s we have seen the emergence of environmental co-operatives. These can be thought of as encompassing three forms of association.

Firstly there are housing co-ops, of which there seem to be several hundred in Britain at the present time and which attempt to be less hierarchical and élitist than the kind of housing associations that Conservative governments encouraged from the late 1980s onwards.

Recent years have seen an increase in homelessness, a decrease in quality, affordable housing – especially due to the decline in the public sector – and a deterioration in the existing public housing stock because of scarce resources and attendant social problems. It is against this background that there has been an upsurge of interest in co-operative housing unlike anything seen since before the Second World War. Some of those who are most in need of decent public housing have been trying to gain influence in the face of social policies that largely ignore them but upon which they are dependent.

In the main, housing co-ops range from those which are co-owned to those which are co-operatively managed but rented from landlords. Some public or semi-public financial support has been forthcoming, but since the Housing Act of 1988 such co-ops have increasingly had to look for private sector finance. Even so, there are many examples of co-operatives successfully implementing new approaches to Britain's housing problems. And some areas have seen the growth of broader community co-operatives that attempt to supply a demand, for shops and workspaces, which both the state and market sectors fail to supply.

Secondly there are what might be called 'caring co-operatives'. Some of these are run by and for those with disabilities and special needs. They may aim to provide job and training opportunities, or they may simply be concerned with home care. Other co-ops look to the health of the wider population. Many, though not all, Well Women Clinics attempt to provide non-hierarchical, decision-making structures within community clinics, in order that female patients may gain greater control over their bodies and the nature of their own health care.[6]

Finally there is an increasing proliferation of Green co-ops, whose purpose is to develop and implement ecologically sustainable ways of living. The number of such co-operatives is difficult to estimate. Many are not only concerned with ecological well-being but also with political action (as has been the case with protesters against road building or airport extensions) or with business matters (many workers' co-operatives have pursued ecological objectives). Others, of course, hark back to 1960s communes or to the Israeli-type Kibbutz. Some groups attempt to popularise and disseminate specific ecological agendas, such as the Centre for Alternative Technology; others are more inner-directed and disorganised: many Travellers have adopted lifestyles that are ecologically anarchistic and have formed what might be thought of as fluctuating groups of mobile, nomadic co-operatives.

Citizen Action Groups

Whereas voluntary organisations in the third sector usually focus their time, energy and resources on a single issue, Citizen Action Groups (CAGs) tend to perform a multiple number of roles and functions: mutual protection, political lobbying, democratic representation, advice and practical help. CAGs are, therefore, not only welfare associations but are closely related to the wider social and political movements dealt with elsewhere in this book.

Firstly, there are those housing groups that are more directly political than the housing co-ops mentioned above. There are, for instance, various housing movements that assist and advise squatters. We could also include the *Big Issue* which not only promotes self-help through the sale of its magazine but also offers assistance with training, interviews and re-location, as well as campaigning more generally on behalf of the homeless. We might also mention some of the more radical housing co-operatives that not only provide roofs over heads on the basis of communal, participative ownership, but which see themselves as the prototypes of a wide-scale urban regeneration that could be founded upon the principles of democratic management and ecological sustainability.

Secondly, there are numerous groups which campaign for an ecologically sensitive transport system and/or against the privatisation and commercialisation of public spaces. Some of these groups are advisory, umbrella organisations; others are concerned with confrontational, direct action, whether in opposition to things such as road-building programmes or as an attempt to reclaim roads and thoroughfares that have been remodelled almost as privately owned interiors.

Finally, there are those grass roots organisations that divide their time between support for member groups and campaigns directed towards the representative political system. For instance the Gypsy Council for Education, Culture, Welfare and Civil Rights not only gives concrete support to Travellers (not just Gypsies) but also lobbies central and local government, as well as liaising with schools, the police, the media and health authorities, in order to promote the rights and the image of Travellers. Similarly there are a variety of broad-based organisations contained within the Citizen Organising Foundation, through which thousands of the poorest in society are re-empowering themselves. These groups have taken on a diversity of tasks: job creation, anti-crime initiatives, health care, anti-pollution drives, renovations of houses and local facilities, and the representation of minority communities and immigrants.

THE FIFTH SECTOR: ECOLOGICAL VALUES, COMPLEMENTARY STRATEGIES, ASSOCIATIVE WELFARE

It can be seen, then, that welfare associations are not easy to categorise, quantify and assess. I firmly believe that the effort must be made, however, if we are not to lose sight of those small-scale, mutualist innovations in civil society whose large-scale implications may well be considerable. Empirical research and theoretical elaboration are therefore both badly needed. But what such an effort also requires is that we have a clearer idea of what is meant by the 'fifth sector'. Initially we face two problems.

Firstly there is the danger of regarding the fifth sector merely as a recent phenomenon. Our search for novelty and originality should not lead us to treat the past as something which lacked radical initiatives. Innovations designed to question and challenge the existing systems of welfare may be traced back throughout the period of the twentieth century, i.e. to the point at which social welfare began to assume its modern character. It should therefore be theoretically possible to write a history of the fifth sector and of how it has affected, and been affected by, mainstream forms of welfare provision. Welfare associations might be thought of simply as the most recent innovations in a social space that stretches back over a long period of time.[7] And whether such organisations and groups become influential, or just fade away, depends upon the political response that we make to them.

Secondly, however, we should not commit the antithetical mistake of denying the distinctness of the fifth sector. It would perhaps be possible to take welfare associations, and all of those groups that preceded them, and crowd them into the four welfare sectors traditionally emphasised by commentators. I have already noted similarities between welfare associations and both voluntary and informal provision. But, by and large, the welfare that is provided by voluntary organisations and by the household tends to be more immediate in its aims and practical in its content. The fifth sector has a long-term, idealistic emphasis that gives it a distinct significance. So, whereas the third and fourth sectors adapt themselves to the imperatives of the market and the state, perhaps challenging the particular efficacy but not the overall rationale of existing institutions and of market forces, the fifth sector implies a 'critical autonomy', i.e. some sort of reaction against both the state and the market, often in addition to a search for alternative models of well-being.

In any event, a history and general theory of the fifth sector will have to wait for another time. The basic point is this: welfare associations bear whatever significance we wish to give them. They may fade into history, or continue to be of marginal importance, or inspire wider reforms (especially to the welfare state); there is no a priori determination one way or another. Now, because I have a considerable sympathy with the aims, methods and accomplishments of welfare associations, I suggest that we think through their potential significance in a way illustrated by the following diagram:

Figure 1

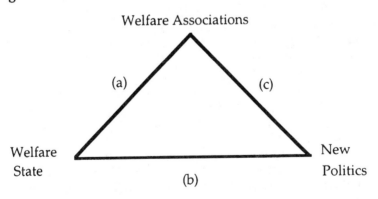

In the remainder of this chapter I shall concentrate upon (a), while dealing with (b) and (c) more briefly.

(a) An ecological model of welfare

What significance might welfare associations bear for the future of the welfare state? I propose that we conceive of welfare associations as embodying the embryo of an alternative model of welfare, one that encompasses both social justice and ecological values.[8] Of course this is not true of every association taken individually, but if we are to move into an era of 'associationalism', taking us beyond the tired debate between (state) collectivism and (market) pluralism, then something very much like the following model has to be taken on board.[9]

Traditionally, welfare states have had four objectives: to enhance individual liberty, to facilitate economic efficiency; to maintain national and cultural cohesion; to equalise social conditions. In practice, the means through which such objectives are to be realised conflict, so that some goals are given priority over others and differing welfare regimes have been formed as a result: social democratic, liberal collectivist, social market, liberal individualist.[10] And yet, underlying the differing emphases of these regimes, there has been a conformity to what I shall call a productivist model of welfare.[11] The productivist model implies three ingredients.

Firstly, it implies a considerable emphasis upon economic growth. In effect, growth has been seen as the 'motor' of all four welfare objectives, yet growth has been defined in an extremely indiscriminate fashion, with little reference to the kind of particular moral dimension that the goals of cohesion, equality and liberty might be thought to require. The 'creative destruction' of modern economies turns out to have had an ecological, as well as a socio-economic and symbolic, meaning: the production of waste is as valuable, to such blunt economic indicators as GNP and GDP, as the production of goods. Polluted rivers and air are signs of affluence, too.

Secondly the productivist model implies an 'employment ethic', where it is wage-earning activity in the formal labour market that is valued over all other forms of human activity.[12] As I said in the introduction, feminist theorists have long highlighted the extent to which the contribution made by domestic labour to social well-being is taken for granted by the bulk of public, economic and social policies. The employment ethic arises because of two widely held assumptions.

One assumption is that the nuclear, heterosexual family is the *sine qua non* of social cohesion. Despite wide-ranging changes to family types, attitudes and working patterns, families are still expected to conform to the 'male breadwinner' model. Gendered roles continue to be the 'symbolic solvents' of modern societies, so that the employment ethic might be regarded as the moral flip-side of the sexual division of labour. By emphasising this ethic, the bulk of public, economic and social policies continue to have a conservative effect in that they functionally reproduce existing relations, roles and identities.

The employment ethic also reflects the assumption that jobs should be the principal means by which income and status are distributed to the vast majority of people. Transfer incomes are regarded as second best, even when they are closely employment-related. In short, the employment ethic works against the suggestion that there should be multiple sources of income upon which individuals could draw. It expresses the common instinct that the business of government is to effect a limited redistribution of resources once individuals have fallen out of the labour market.

The third and final ingredient of the productivist model concerns what might be called 'acquisitive lifestyles', i.e. the notion that our personal worth can and should be measured against a materialistic yardstick. You are what you own, what you drive, what you do for a living, where you holiday. We certainly spend much of our lives valuing intangibles such as love and friendship, but those intangibles tend to be expressed in highly individualistic terms when it comes to making hard-headed political and economic decisions. The quality of life easily becomes confused with the standard of living. (There are often good reasons for this. A fear of poverty all too easily disciplines us into a narrow range of lifestyles and forces upon us myopic conceptions of the good.) The evidence of the last fifty years is that western society has become more, not less, materialistic; this is reflected in the electoral success of the political right and the post-socialist drift of the centre-left. Undoubtedly, post-materialist values are now more prevalent throughout the west, but such values do not necessarily translate into post-materialist practices. Whether as economic or as political consumers, there is little evidence of people abandoning either the desire for the benefits of economic growth or the reassuring constraints of the employment ethic.

Welfare associations do represent, to varying degrees, an attempt to break away from the seductive embrace of the productivist model and an attempt to point the way to a non-productivist, or ecological, model of welfare. I shall sketch this below, with particular reference to LETS.

Firstly, welfare associations tend to be more concerned with sustainability as opposed to growth.[13] The precise meaning, as well as the social implications, of sustainability are too complex to delve into here, yet there is a general feeling throughout the fifth sector that indiscriminate growth and social justice do not go together.

One of the advantages claimed for LETS is that, because local currencies encourage local trading and exchange, they put less pressure upon national and international infrastructures, and so place less strain upon the environment. And because LETS facilitates financial security and encourages a certain amount of risk-taking, they are conducive to investment in ecologically friendly projects (as are CUs). LETS are one way of rebuilding the local communities that have been hollowed out by our increasingly globalised and environmentally hostile economies, where the bottom line is always profit, competition and flexibility.

Secondly, the ecological model encourages a broader conception of work. It is not enough to praise informal, non-employment activity, still less to invoke such activity as a stick with which to beat so-called welfare dependency; rather, a more liberal, pluralistic definition of work must become a central plank of social policy. This might mean retrieving the Lockean notion of work as 'mixing one's labour with the fruits of the earth', perhaps for ends that may well contradict our contemporary obsession with production for consumption's sake.

Accordingly, social cohesion has little to do with an involuntary, unthinking adherence to tradition: what might be called the conservative instinct; nor is it automatically created through the volatility and impersonality of market forces – the individualist instinct. Instead, welfare associations seem to represent something else altogether: reflexive communities, continually undergoing a process of renewal and re-definition. So whereas the employment ethic seeks to preserve the mythologies of the patriarchal family and of the meritocratic market, the 'pluralistic work ethic' allows the formation of the new relations, roles and identities which welfare associations, as reflexive communities, embody.

It has been claimed that the local, informal economies of LETS are more sensitive than the formal labour market to the diversity of skills and abilities which people possess. Whereas 'normal' jobs and occupations tend to concentrate particular skills, and to exclude others, LETS provides the opportunity for people to perform a range of tasks that they might not have previously recognised as a source of value. Whereas in the formal labour market workers are paid exclusively to perform a particular occupational role, LETS encourages the expansion of informal economies within which there is more likely to be a demand for people to use skills and knowledge that might otherwise go unnoticed.

A pluralistic work ethic also undermines the idea that jobs should be the principal means through which income and status are distributed. It advances the idea that there ought to be multiple sources of income upon which people can draw. With LETS, because members' accounts are interest-free, and have no fixed repayment schedule, they are of most help to the unemployed and the low-paid since it is possible for one's account to go into debit without the daunting consequences created when debt occurs with banks and other lending institutions. What all of this seems to imply is that we should stop regarding wages as the superior form of income and begin to conceive of 'wage/non-wage combinations'. As well as local currencies, this might suggest support for a basic Citizen's Income and/or a Social Dividend, through which employment becomes merely one of a number of income sources.[14]

Finally, welfare associations seem far less attached to the notion that personal worth equals material standard of living. Research reveals that participants in LETS un-learn the tendency to measure the self in terms of socially acceptable criteria, i.e. that individual worth means observing and playing by the rules. Instead, welfare associations such as co-operatives provide the space and the opportunity for new criteria to emerge, for people to devise their own rules by which to live. On a basic level, LETS helps people to re-connect with those from whom our fractured, fragmented societies pull us away. In short, the fifth sector seems to represent a kind of 'second-order modernity': embodying the freedoms of the modern era while resisting the disruptive, atomising processes to which we have been brought by modernity.

The ecological model, then, retains an emphasis upon social justice, mutuality, redistribution and upon a 'particularistic universalism', but also revises the materialistic assumptions of existing welfare provision.[15] As such, the ecological model suggested by fifth sector welfare associations presents alternatives to the malign authoritarianism of the right, as well as to the benign authoritarianism to which some on the centre-left seem drawn.

(b) Between assimilation and separation

Of course there are those who would deride the exercise carried out above. For some, the new politics represents such a radical alternative to traditional forms of organisation and mobilisation that attempting to relate things such as LETS to broader social policy reform is a naive and probably futile activity. Perhaps, these people might suggest, welfare associations should simply be left alone to flourish, or not, as individuals see fit. This kind of 'separatist' approach is anarchist in its inspiration and is celebrated by many in the new social and political movements.

Then there are those, as I have acknowledged, who might allow for the existence of welfare associations but not as occupying a distinct sector, i.e. not as offering a different model of welfare. This 'assimilationist' approach is advocated by many social policy researchers. The debate with the assimilationists is too lengthy to reproduce here. I do, however, wish to mention two reasons why I believe the separatists to be mistaken.

Firstly, it is not possible to draw borders around associations and treat them as discrete, insulated entities disconnected from the rest of society, any more than it is possible to draw boundaries around individuals and families and insist that something else, society, does not exist. Secondly, associations should not be treated as separate. If, indeed, they represent new sources of well-being then social justice demands that we find ways of harnessing them for the greater good. Critics might say that this contradicts the voluntarist ethos of welfare associations where individuals are free to join without the state prodding them into doing so. But there is no inherent reason why such voluntarism should be compromised by the state encouraging, and perhaps even financing, their creation. The alternative is for a new politics based upon separatism and so threatening to reproduce the *laissez-faire*, do-your-own-thing attitude of the new right.

Essentially, then, I believe that we should think of welfare associations in terms of a 'complementary' strategy or approach, one that relates them to wider social issues and problems.

(c) Associative welfare

If we do this, then what significance do welfare associations bear for a new politics? Recent years have seen the emergence of a debate concerning 'associative democracy'.[16] This implies a pluralist form of social and economic federalism, the aim of which would be to rejuvenate democratic governance. Representative democracy has produced a wide gap between the polity and civil society. Repairing this rift through some form of participatory democracy might, in practice, risk subordinating civil society to the dictates of the state. But those who argue for an associative democracy envisage a strengthened role for secondary associations as mediators between the state and civil society.

This role consists of a double democratisation.[17] The state is 'pluralised', i.e. made more open and accountable to ordinary citizens through a range of forums, not just mass political parties and lobbying groups; civil society is 'publicised', i.e. control of, and responsibility for, a range of social and economic institutions is devolved across the board to citizens' groups. An associative democracy, it is argued, would improve the levels of political participation, while avoiding statism, and would decentralise without setting everything on a market-ised, commercial basis.

Such ideas can be applied to the subject of welfare reform. Associations could act both as agencies through which citizen involve-ment in service determination and delivery could be strengthened, and as 'media' through which state and market bureaucracies could be monitored and made more accountable.[18]

In short, we can identify a convergence between the ideas of some political theorists, and local innovations in social policy. If so, then it is a convergence to which all of those interested in a new politics should pay attention.[19]

CONCLUSION

The objective of this chapter has been to suggest that there is a fifth sector of welfare, that is usually ignored by social policy comment-ators, that welfare associations have, in recent years, begun to populate. These associations have a radical potential with, for the most part, an ecological bias.

Much work remains to be done. How can this potential be exploited? How can associations be encouraged to be inclusive and empowering? How can fifth sector innovations be made to work more effectively towards the goal of social justice? These are only a few of the questions that need to be asked. Time we started asking them.

NOTES

1. Many thanks to Hartley Dean for comments on an earlier version of this chapter.
2. P. Spicker, *Social Policy: Themes and Approaches*, Prentice Hall/Harvester Wheatsheaf, Hemel Hempstead 1995, pp109-21; P. Alcock, *Social Policy in Britain: Themes and Issues*, Macmillan, London 1996, pp44-116.
3. An approach corresponding to the ideas of various theorists: e.g. R. Hadley

& S. Hatch, *Social Welfare and the Failure of the State: Centralised Services and Participatory Alternatives*, Allen & Unwin, London 1981. Also, D. Green, *Reinventing Civil Society*, IEA, London 1993; and *Community Without Politics: A Market Approach to Welfare Reform*, IEA, London 1996.

4. G. Dauncey, *After the Crash*, Green Print, London 1988; C. Offe & R. Heinze, *Beyond Employment*, Polity, Cambridge 1992; R. Dobson, *Bringing the Economy Home from the Market*, Black Rose Books, Toronto 1993; P. Lang, *LETS Work: Rebuilding the Local Economy*, Grover Books, Bristol 1994; C. Williams, 'The New Barter Economy: An Appraisal of the Local Exchange and Trading Systems (LETS)', *Journal of Public Policy*, volume 16, part 1, January-April 1996, pp85-101.

5. C. Hird, 'Building Societies: Stakeholding in Practice and Under Threat', *New Left Review*, No. 218, July/August 1996, pp40-52.

6. P. Foster, 'Well Women Clinics – a serious challenge to mainstream health care?' in M. Maclean & D. Groves (eds), *Women's Issues in Social Policy*, Routledge, London 1991.

7. Preceded, as Hartley Dean pointed out to me, by claimants' unions, for instance.

8. I deal with this at greater length elsewhere: T. Fitzpatrick, 'The Implications of Ecological Thought for the Welfare State', *Critical Social Policy*, No. 54, February 1998.

9. However, as with the fifth sector, a theory of what is meant by Welfare Associationalism will have to wait for another time.

10. See N. Ginsburg, *Divisions of Welfare: A Critical Introduction to Comparative Social Policy*, Sage, London 1992.

11. This notion of the welfare state as being too productivist is derived from the work of Claus Offe. For example, see his most recent book: *Modernity and the State: East, West*, Polity, Cambridge 1996.

12. This idea that what is normally called a work ethic is, in fact, an employment ethic is one shared by B. Sherman & P. Judkins, *Licensed to Work*, Cassell, London 1995.

13. For an introduction to the concept of sustainability, see D. Reid, *Sustainable Development: An Introductory Guide*, Earthscan, London 1995.

14. See my forthcoming book, *Freedom and Security*, Macmillan, London.

15. For a discussion around the issues of what I here call 'particularistic universalism' see, S. Thompson & P. Hoggett, 'Universalism, Selectivism and Particularism: Towards a Postmodern Social Policy', *Critical Social Policy*, volume 16, number 1, 1996.

16. P. Hirst, *Associative Democracy*, Polity, Cambridge 1994; J. Cohen & J. Rogers, *Associations and Democracy*, Verso, London 1995.

17. An idea promoted in D. Held & C. Pollitt (eds), *New Forms of Democracy*, Open University Press, Milton Keynes 1986; J. Keane, *Democracy and Civil Society*, Verso, London 1988.

18. It is also worth mentioning the connections which some have made between mutual associations and the stakeholding principle: see, J. McCormick, 'Mapping the Stakeholder Society' in G. Kelly, D. Kelly & A. Gamble (eds), *Stakeholder Capitalism*, Macmillan, London 1997.

19. For example, Offe has proposed 'co-operative circles' as a means of enhancing self-sustainability. A co-operative circle would be an inter-household market, publicly subsidised and maintained through the circulation of service vouchers. He insists that this would be a way of improving the autonomy of households and such ideas would seem to converge with the kinds of ideas which I have touched upon here. See Offe, *op.cit.*, pp141-44.

INTERNAL DIVISION AND NEW POLITICAL MOVEMENTS

Adam Lent

THREE TENDENCIES IN MOVEMENTS OF CHANGE

Based on considerable historical evidence, one can state with confidence that most, possibly all, movements which seek to make substantial changes in existing conditions will divide over strategies for achieving that change.[1] Furthermore, based on the same evidence, it seems reasonable to assert that such divisions have formed and will continue to form around two main poles: the transformatory and the temperate. In addition, there is a third tendency which has played a less adversarial role until recently: the personal-local. This chapter will define each of these tendencies, examine the nature of their rivalry and argue that, despite the likelihood that such division is unavoidable, each is vital to the life and success of a movement.

The transformatory and the temperate

The transformatory is the more radical of the two main positions. It is a wide-ranging, ambitious and highly-fuelled response to existing conditions. Those aligned to this side of the division argue that there is a need for comprehensive and fundamental social, political, economic and cultural change if a movement is to achieve its goals. Sometimes this is because the goals sought by those of a transformatory persuasion are very different from existing conditions; sometimes it is because they feel the existing conditions to be highly resistant to meaningful change. But the transformatory is also defined as much by a general ethos of iconoclasm and radicalism, and by the personal attraction this ethos holds for various individuals, as by any rational assessment of conditions. Due to the ambition of the transformatory tendency's strategy and goals, it usually emphasises the need for mass mobilisation and/or extreme tactics involving actions outside the law.

The temperate is by definition the more moderate position. Those aligned to this side of the division feel that piecemeal reform is acceptable. This is either because their overall goals are not particularly ambitious or because they feel that significant change can gradually be wrung out of existing conditions. As with the transformatory, the temperate is defined by ethos and personal preference, but in this case there are more complex factors involved such as attraction to convention and existing power, fear of disorder and violence and, possibly, a liking for hard-headed realism. Due to these values, the temperate tendency emphasises working within the existing political and legislative system for change, usually employs legal tactics and only makes use of mass mobilisation or extreme tactics for short-term gain and when existing conditions are resistant even to the most limited change.

A highly-developed and complex division between transformatory and temperate can be seen in the socialist movement of the last hundred years. Not only did the division harden into highly distinct organisations aligning themselves with each strand, but the gradations between and articulations of different features became diverse and plural. Socialism also spawned the most elaborate justifications yet developed for these contrary positions. The transformatory tendency has been upheld by more than a century of Marxist and associated analysis, while millions of words have been dedicated to upholding the temperate approaches of social democracy and democratic socialism.

In most cases the division has not been as sophisticated as in the socialist movement, but then few (if any) movements have been as developed or sophisticated as socialism itself. Sometimes the division has been less pronounced, sometimes one tendency has managed to maintain a dominance over the other throughout the lifetime of the movement, but a division between transformatory and temperate has always existed in some significant form. Nationalist movements, continental liberalism, anti-colonialism, religious fundamentalism, first wave feminism, chartism, black civil rights – to name a few – all underwent divisions along these lines with refinements and variables in the detail of each division occurring by virtue of their specific characters and circumstances. In addition, movements of the right have undergone such a division: fascism, nazism, the New Right, anti-Soviet groups have all had their more temperate and more transformatory wings. Most recently, even anti-Castro exile groups in Miami have been vigorously divided along these very lines.

Of the deepest relevance to this volume though, we have seen this old division occurring again in the post-1960s movements. Second-wave feminism, peace campaigns, gay and lesbian rights and liberation, anti-racism, the green movement have all had, and continue to have, their ambitious transformatory exponents and their conciliatory temperate exponents. Sometimes the division has hardened into severe periods of organisational splits and hostile opposition. In the early 1970s the gay movement split into transformatory wings such as the Gay Liberation Front (arguing for a revolution of class and sexuality), and temperate groups such as the Campaign for Homosexual Equality (arguing for peaceful change in legislation and discriminatory practices).[2] The women's movement has for many years, but especially in the late 1970s, been divided between temperate liberal and socialist feminists and transformatory radical and Marxist feminists: each branch having its own journals, groups and issues of concern.[3] In addition green movements and parties have undergone considerable division between temperate 'realos' and transformatory 'fundis' with regard to tactics, and temperate 'light greens' and transformatory 'deep greens' with regard to broader ideological issues.[4]

Why this division keeps recurring is an interesting and important question. Although it is not the prime concern of this chapter, it is worth stating that the division may at its most basic reflect the obvious choice which confronts any human when faced with conditions (and other humans who uphold those conditions) which dissatisfy him or her: to compromise or to fight. (There is of course the option of surrender, but this is rarely chosen until at least one of the other two options has been tried and failed.) Which is chosen may depend upon a wide variety of circumstances: the assessment one makes of the power of those upholding the unsatisfactory conditions; one's assessment of the willingness of those upholding the conditions to reform; an assessment of one's own power, and the understanding one may have of how conditions need to change in order to end dissatisfaction. The divisions of the above movements do tend to reflect such calculations and, more importantly, disagreements over such calculations. A further important factor which may influence the tendency one associates with is one's personal inclinations: some people are simply more inclined to fight and some to compromise.

Integral and tactical
The transformatory and temperate strands as outlined above are ideal types but clearly most historical movements for change have divided at some point along the continuum between those two ideals. Indeed

there are times when movements or factions of movements seem to take a 'mix-and-match' approach, articulating aspects of the transformatory to temperate goals or aspects of the temperate to the transformatory. An example of the former may be the common use of mass mobilisation by temperate strands (peaceful and moderate in their demands, of course) to impress upon existing powers the degree of support for their cause, e.g. demonstrations demanding changes to laws relating to gay lifestyles. An example of the latter would be the support given by many different shades of a movement to significant changes in legislation, e.g. the broad support for reform of the law on domestic violence provided by the whole women's movement.

The key factor here though is the distinction between the 'integral' and the 'tactical'. 'Integral' indicates the view of one's own preferred tendency: i.e. that all its assertions, ideals and methods are collectively worthy and are the true route to success. 'Tactical' is taken to indicate the view of one tendency to specific aspects of another tendency, be they methods of change, analyses, even ideals; i.e. those aspects can be appropriated by one's favoured tendency and used for one's own aspirations. However, in the tactical view, that other tendency is not useful as a whole and may actually be counter-productive if treated as such.

So, for those of a predominantly temperate approach, any aspect or method borrowed from the transformatory will tend to be regarded in a largely tactical fashion. Mass mobilisation may be employed but only to provide support for the short-term or medium-term reforms to be carried out or bargained for by the leadership of a movement. Temperate activists would be just as horrified as those upholding existing power structures if mass mobilisation were to become an *integral* good-in-itself, sweeping away the political system and starting the process of radical change in a moment of transformatory uprising.[5]

Equally, transformatory activists have often played a significant part in campaigns for piecemeal reform, working closely, on occasion, with temperate activists. However these campaigns are usually regarded as transitionary demands: they may do some good in themselves but their real importance lies in their ability to raise consciousness and create the organisational foundations which will in time lead to 'real change' in the form of comprehensive transformation. For temperate activists, of course, such limited reforms are far from tactical: they are integral in that they alleviate suffering and/or enhance the standing of the movement, and thus are worth struggling for on those grounds alone.

This point is emphasised because it is necessary for my description of the personal-local.

The personal-local

While the division between the two main tendencies has historically been the most intense and has been the most likely to harden into organisational separation, a third response to existing conditions can be identified: the personal-local.[6] The personal-local is a completely different response to unsatisfactory conditions from that proposed by the transformatory and temperate alternatives. The personal-local approach is formed upon the notion that individuals who are dissatisfied with the existing conditions must change themselves and their immediate environment, thus bypassing the main concern of the other tendencies, i.e. how to relate to existing power structures. Usually the change involves enhancement of self-confidence, self-reliance and self-respect, improved understanding of one's own motivations, goals and place in the world; creation of a stronger ethical sense; and a re-organisation of one's everyday life. The strategies and tactics employed in pursuit of such personal-local change are varied. They may be meeting and forming bonds with those who are similarly dissatisfied; public declarations of pride in the personal-local characteristics that give rise to one's dissatisfaction; cultural activities based on those characteristics; religious activities; self-education; and radical changes in one's day-to-day relationships with others in one's own family and local community.

Concrete examples of the personal-local are provided below but first it is important to look briefly at the history of the personal-local. It was undoubtedly an important aspect of utopian socialism and anarchism and was most evident in the co-operative movement. However it was often seen as a means to grander ends, especially when contributing to either transformatory or temperate projects. In short, the personal-local has often taken a tactical rather than an integral form. Transformatory approaches in particular have urged personal-local change, but usually only as a stimulant or pre-condition for greater mass collective transformation based upon a more direct political challenge to existing power structures. The Marxist strands of new social movements, so influential in the late 1960s and early 1970s, have almost without exception taken such a view of the personal-local: openly attending gay clubs, challenging the gender relations in one's family, studying black history, may have been worthy, but they were only preparations for a more collective uprising against the whole oppressive system.

However, since the 1960s the personal-local has become more significant as a tendency in itself, increasingly taking on the characteristics of the integral. During the recent past the personal-local seems especially to have hardened as a tendency, with some of those involved in movements covered here rejecting all formally-organised collective action, whether it be transformatory or temperate, preferring instead to concentrate solely on local campaigns and personal development. A clear example of this is the environmental (dis)organisation Earth First!, which is hostile both to temperate groups such as Friends of the Earth and to formally-organised transformatory groups such as the far-left Socialist Workers Party, which tries to marry environmental security to orthodox Trotskyite politics and organisation.[7] Elements in rave culture have also focused upon the personal-local approach, as have (dis)organisations in the recent women's movement such as Riot Grrrls.[8]

As with so many aspects of post-1960s politics, it was the African-American movement of the 1950s and 1960s that first elevated the personal-local response. The non-violence of the civil rights movement was seen by Martin Luther King not simply as an effective tactic: it was regarded as a good which would enhance the pride and ethics of those involved in the struggle.[9] But it was the black power movement of the 1960s which took the personal-local tendency further. Although many black power groups and activists were wedded to a transformatory approach, it was the personal-local aspect that had the deepest influence by encouraging black Americans to develop an understanding of their history, to take pride in, and build, their unique culture, to have confidence in themselves as individuals, and to strengthen their local communities.[10] The Nation of Islam also contributed the qualities of self-discipline and religious devotion. In fact the Nation of Islam, in predating the civil rights movement and influencing black power in the late 1960s, may be seen as one of the earliest examples of the personal-local response.[11]

With an explosion of new movements in the late 1960s and early 1970s, enhancement of the personal-local continued. The extra confidence given to individual women and the changes brought about in their everyday relationships through their involvement in the women's movement is well-documented and was specifically encouraged by that movement.[12] Gay and lesbian politics recognised the importance of the personal-local response to the point where the most famous slogan of those movements – 'Pride' – was based largely on that aspect. Radical feminism of the mid-to-late 1970s elevated the personal-local response to an even higher level of importance, arguing that women could end unsatisfactory conditions in their immediate social and cultural environment through personal-local decisions (i.e. woman-centredness, political lesbianism) without worrying too greatly about grander liberatory schemes. (Some radical feminists however, clearly saw such decisions as the starting point for a mass of similar decisions which would lead to *de facto* liberation, thus giving the personal-local a more, though not entirely, tactical aspect).[13] The green movement, which has proved so influential in the recent flourishing of new politics, has also had a strong personal-local strand most clearly represented by the deep greens who emphasise the need for change in individual attitudes towards materialism and consumerism and who promote profounder ways of living linked to spiritual development and strong ethical behaviour.[14] This has of course continued in the recent growth of newer green movements which have built whole ways of life around spirituality involving religious practices, outright rejection of conventional Western lifestyles, and close identification with nature and the defence of nature.

More recently some feminists and post-feminists (most famously Camille Paglia) have emphasised and embodied the self-confidence and power of individual women specifically *against* transformatory and temperate strands of feminism both of which, they argue, reduce women to victim status. In addition the rise of the 'queer' movement has taken the logic of pride to new heights of self-confidence: rejecting both the straight world *and* the temperate or transformatory schemes which position themselves in relation to that world.[15] We have also seen the rise of economic personal-local responses in the form of Local Exchange and Trading Schemes and Credit Unions which aim to encourage self-confidence and dignity by actively involving individuals in the creation of personal and local wealth.[16]

There is a need here for qualification. It seems that the personal-local has more difficulty than the other tendencies in treating itself as completely integral. Even groups as determinedly disorganised as Earth First! implicitly base their action upon a transformatory *vision* of an ecocentric world, although they may have serious reservations about such organisational and state-oriented trappings as have gone hand-in-hand with that vision. Maybe only those wedded to personal spiritual change and change in a small group of associates can truly create a personal-local approach that is integrally good-in-itself.

This qualification should not be taken as a failure in the elegance of my typology. It points to the deeper truth about the relationship between the three tendencies. For those deeply involved in the day-to-day life of a movement the division between transformatory and temperate, and more recently the personal-local, may seem of vital significance. Indeed, the division often seems of such vital significance that most movements have at some point in their history dedicated as much time and energy to the battle between the tendencies as to the battle against existing power structures and conditions. In the terms presented in this chapter, we may say that the internal struggles within movements represent the practical outcome of the belief that one of the tendencies is integral and should not merely be reduced to a tactical aspect of the others. Or to put it another way: the temperate (or the transformatory or the personal-local) can survive alone and achieve all that the movement desires for itself, and the other tendencies are, if not used purely tactically, potentially destructive of the movement. The point, for which the rest of this chapter will argue, is that, in fact, none of the tendencies can achieve pure integrity for itself (and defeat for the others) and claim that the movement will succeed. Each tendency brings characteristics to a movement without which that movement would probably not survive (and would certainly not flourish) and thus not one of the tendencies could operate alone.

STRENGTHS AND WEAKNESSES OF EACH TENDENCY

Movements require certain fundamentals to be able to survive, to grow and to maintain progress towards their goals. There are many different factors which contribute to a movement's success or failure and I could not hope to cover them all here. I have, instead, chosen factors which are both highly significant and which, I feel, are most illustrative of the specific strengths and weaknesses one tendency may display in contrast to the others. These factors are:

a movement's ability to generate values
a movement's ability to mobilise support
its capacity to alleviate, relatively rapidly, some of the suffering of its constituency
its ability to create the necessary political space and freedom within which to operate and have an impact

its ability to provide the members of its constituency with a sense of empowerment

its ability to maintain the viability of its project in the face of crises.

These characteristics are vital to the life of a movement although others of less importance could be named and examined.

While one might argue that each of these vital factors is produced more effectively by one tendency as opposed to the others, the considerations presented below should not be taken to mean that each tendency serves a particular function of which the others are *completely* devoid. The relationship between a tendency and the necessary characteristics of a movement is complex but there are certain strengths and certain weaknesses that each tendency displays and which are broadly upheld by historical evidence. I apologise in advance therefore for what may seem a slightly schematic argument made for the sake of clarity and brevity.

THE POWER OF THE TRANSFORMATORY I: VALUES

All movements have values upon which they base their demands for change. Even movements based upon purely corporate interests do not make their claims on the grounds of self-interest alone. Principles of fairness, freedom, justice and many others will be employed in, and will shape, a struggle for improved conditions.

While each of the tendencies outlined above has been able to produce principles upon which to base action, the transformatory tendency has proved most successful at generating values which provide the framework around which a movement initially forms. Those values also produce basic principles for the whole movement, including all tendencies. In its struggle for comprehensive change, the transformatory seeks to identify universal oppressions against which a movement can revolt and thus bring about rapid improvement in the conditions of one large group and, often, the whole of humanity. Initially, during the late 1960s and early 1970s, this meant merging the specific demands of a new movement with the universal ambitions and analyses of Marxism. However, over time, significant transformatory sections of movements ditched the Marxist perspective but maintained its universalism. Thus radical feminists identified patriarchy as the key determinant of oppression and therefore the key focus for revolutionary change, for deep greens it was anthropocentrism, for the black power movement it was inherent white racism, and for sections of the gay movement it has become homophobia and dominant and rigid notions of sexuality. As a consequence, each transformatory tendency posited a universal state devoid of these universal oppressions. As each of these oppressions was so universal and so central to the fabric of politics, culture and society, only mass mobilisation and a commitment to radical change could bring about the desired state devoid of the oppression. Thus the desire for radical, comprehensive change requires and is motivated by, the observation of universal oppressions and the universal transformations that logically follow from their destruction.

The significance of these characteristics for any movement is that they provide that movement with its own principles of change. A movement can gain massively from such universalism in that it provides activists with a clear explanation of their dissatisfaction, allows the creation of their distinct, rational values and, maybe most importantly, provides the very reason for a movement's existence: that suffering is not individual and the result of personal failings, but is collective and the result of widely-imposed oppressions and thus is an adequate condition for joint action. This distinction is common in the genesis of movements. For example, the shift from regarding disability as a medical condition suffered by the individual to disability as a result of discrimination, prejudice and denial of rights was absolutely fundamental to the rise of the disabled movement thirty years ago.[17]

This contrasts with both the temperate and the personal-local. The temperate, without the value-generation of the transformatory tendency, has often been solely an extension of liberal rights. Prior to the late 1960s, gay, women's, and anti-racist movements were dominated by the belief that the prime goal of their activity must be to extend to their groups the rights enjoyed by heterosexuals, men or white people.[18] The problem with such a simple articulation between traditional liberalism and the new movements was an inability to address fundamental issues of identity, economic deprivation and difference. These movements were addressing oppressions which resided outside the public sphere so narrowly defined by liberalism and could not be understood or resolved purely in terms of the extension of political rights.

Logically, it is those factions of a movement which refuse to accept the terms of existing power structures that create the values most applicable to the situation of the oppressed group who have, as a matter of course, been denied recognition and explanation of their circumstances in a way that would alleviate their suffering.

As a result, temperate strands often eventually employ terms and ideas associated with transformatory analyses adapted to a more moderate project, i.e. they take a tactical rather than an integral approach to these principles. Notions of patriarchy, once the preserve of radical feminists, now inform the whole women's movement; the identification of 'homophobia' and the goal of 'pride' are mainstream within the gay movement where at one time they were key terms for transformatory tendencies; the once radical belief that racism is inherent in existing systems and dominant ideologies, and not simply the result of discrimination or ignorance has gained wide acceptance throughout anti-racist movements.

This process is not reserved solely for movements based on identity. Many movements have developed from a period of initial dominance by a temperate strand into their most vital and imaginative stage dominated by a transformatory strand, the ideas of which are then treated tactically by a newly-revived temperate strand. This has been the case for much of the socialist movement and the green movement throughout Western Europe. The only break from this pattern comes when the transformatory strand is in a position to take the first steps towards radical reform. However even in these circumstances a more temperate strand revives, but usually employs the rhetoric and structures established by the transformatory tendency.

The personal-local also faces problems with the generation of values for a movement. A movement, or even an analytical approach such as postmodernism, which is based upon the celebration of particularism and personal taste, will face great, maybe insuperable, difficulties in discovering the principles upon which its struggle is based: without universals it is very difficult to decide what is good and what is bad. If we accept that that which is particular to the person or the locality must be respected, we have no grounds upon which to choose between oppressive behaviour (which is clearly to the taste of many individuals and localities) and liberatory behaviour. Postmodernism has struggled with this issue for years and has only produced solutions of a partial and unsatisfactory nature.[19] Thus, in truth, even the most personal and local of political activities has in all likelihood drawn upon a grander universal and transformatory vision at some point for its inspiration and for its ongoing motivation. The most recent flowering of the personal-local in certain green campaigning still maintains a grander vision of a safer world plus the universal value of preserving areas of natural beauty and biodiversity. One would hardly be consistent in arguing for the preservation of Oxleas Wood while simultaneously supporting the destruction of Twyford Down. Even the most 'nimby' approach to the issue could not logically argue against the right of those who live near Twyford Down to campaign for its conservation in the same 'nimby' fashion. By declaring a *right* to 'nimbyism' there is an implicitly proclaimed universal. Any other approach is solipsistic – purely personal – and not relevant to the issue of identifying values upon which a battle against oppression can be waged.

Thus we can see that while the temperate and personal-local are able to produce values appropriate to a cause, they do not play the role that (at least, initially) transformatory values do in defining and promoting a flourishing movement.

THE POWER OF THE TRANSFORMATORY II: MOBILISATION

Logically, if they are to exist at all, movements must be able to mobilise people and resources. While temperate tendencies have mobilised large numbers around specific issues and, in recent years, the personal-local has spurred many to action, it is the transformatory tendency that has proved the most effective at mobilising very large numbers of people. The temperate can mobilise for a campaign but it is the transformatory which has the power to turn a campaign into a movement.

This benefit of the transformatory tendency is seen most clearly in the explosion of new social movements in the late 1960s and early 1970s. The women's, gay, green, anti-racist, and contemporary peace movements all have their most significant point of expansion in the high ideals and revolutionary aspirations that so inspired activists of that period. While all of these movements had existed for many years prior to the late 1960s, their predominantly temperate nature had ensured that they remained elitist affairs with low public profiles. The infectious utopias of their transformatory expressions after 1968 delivered a higher level of commitment and enthusiasm, from a larger and more diverse range of supporters than had previously existed. Part of this may be to do with the fact that transformatory visions are so much more inspirational (especially for the young) than the more limited goals of temperate tendencies. It is also true that the painstaking process of lobbying and political deal-making cannot compete with the sheer theatre, comradeship, adventure, and attention-grabbing capacity of mass mobilisation and street protest when it comes to encouraging those who may have had no previous involvement to support a movement. Furthermore, this successful mobilisation is also related to the previous points about transformatory values providing a more appropriate basis upon which to voice the oppression and the demands of a specific group.

In addition, many successful temperate campaigns and personal-local changes of the last thirty years have benefited enormously from the way in which the transformatory periods in their past shifted the political agenda to include issues such as gender, sexuality, race, peace and ecology; added a touch of romance and glory to what had otherwise been lacklustre campaigns; and provided an enormous pool of committed activists and supporters upon which they could draw.

THE POWER OF THE TEMPERATE I: SHORT-TERM ALLEVIATION OF SUFFERING

There is clearly a moral imperative which declares that a movement must alleviate as much suffering for its constituency as possible. We can also accept that movements require some immediate successes in bringing about change if they are to maintain adequate levels of support and activist commitment.

The temperate tendency, with its focus on influencing existing power structures, is a more effective short- to medium-term alleviator of the misery resulting from particular oppressions. Campaigns for limited legislative change have greatly reduced the suffering of oppressed groups. Legislation against forms of discrimination based upon race, sex, sexuality, disability and age has clearly been significant (if often limited) in providing legal recourse for certain groups and in expressing state disapproval of discrimination, thus making such actions less socially acceptable. The gay movement, for example, has made many important advances through its temperate wing. Decriminalisation of gay sex throughout the United Kingdom and Ireland between 1967 and 1993 has been a truly great achievement resulting from years of lobbying and political activity. In addition, reductions in the age of consent for gay sex will prevent a number of unjust prosecutions and will make counselling and advice for teenagers more easily available.

Of course, as mentioned above, transformatory factions have often played central roles in temperate campaigns. The success of such campaigns, though, often relies upon the political networking and 'respectability' of those more fully committed to a temperate approach, and there are examples of significant legislative or constitutional change with which transformatory wings would not get involved and might even oppose. A case in point is the intense disputes within the women's movement over the Sex Discrimination Act of 1976.

The personal-local has also proved a very effective way of alleviating suffering, sometimes very immediately. Decisions by individuals to change their everyday lives can be painful and difficult, but they are decisions which can be acted upon with speed and which can have immediate positive impact. However there are circumstances in which no amount of personal-local activity will alleviate suffering if there is intense political or social resistance to change. A woman's action designed to change her personal relationships in 1970s Britain, while difficult, was clearly possible and has become increasingly possible. A woman's action designed to change her personal relationships in a rigidly patriarchal society, where such action may lead to the severest social or legal sanction, is much less possible. Under the latter circumstances, methods other than the personal-local are required. Equally there are areas of life which are more susceptible to personal-local change (such as family, friendships and self-development), but there are other areas (the workplace, in particular) where the resistance to change is much greater and where temperate methods are realistically more likely to provide speedy relief than the personal-local.

THE POWER OF THE TEMPERATE II: POLITICAL SPACE

Equally important for a movement's success is political space and freedom within which a movement can operate and expand. Once again in this area temperate campaigns appear the most effective. For example, it is unlikely that the birth of gay liberation in the early 1970s would have occurred without the more sober campaigning and lobbying of the homophile movement in Europe and America throughout the 1950s and 1960s, which gradually extended legislative and social tolerance of homosexuality long before the Stonewall riot.[20] Could the Gay Liberation Front really have been as 'out and proud' as it proclaimed if the 1967 Sexual Offences Act, which decriminalised gay sex and had been lobbied for by homophile groups, were not already enshrined in law? Similarly, partial erosion of sexist attitudes – the liberation of women from utterly restrictive property law, and women's entry into the public sphere through voting and parliamentary representation – were all brought about by First-Wave Feminism and undoubtedly created an environment conducive to the far-reaching demands of Second Wave Feminism.

Of course on occasion temperate tactics and goals may be even more necessary. If there is legal restriction on association, expression and protest, limited lobbying and pressure for changes to such laws may be necessary before any group, transformatory or temperate, can act. At a less extreme level one could cite the First Past the Post electoral system, which has played such a significant part in maintaining the conservatism of the British electorate and which has prevented minority and radical causes from having much impact at election time. In this area, using a temperate approach to reform the electoral system might provide a political environment within which new movements would be able to flourish. A large number of transformatory tendencies might then gain a public platform – denied to them under the present system – despite the fact that some transformatory tendencies continue to see such temperate campaigning as a distraction.

THE POWER OF THE PERSONAL-LOCAL I: SENSE OF EMPOWERMENT

All movements have flourished by bringing a sense of empowerment to their activists. For many the simple act of 'doing something' about their situation provides, at least initially, this strong sense of empowerment. However that 'initially' is important because both transformatory and temperate strands tend to suffer, increasingly over time, from the problem of the 'deferral' of satisfactory change. In the case of the transformatory, substantial change and alleviation of suffering are often deferred to 'the future' when conditions are in place for a radical shift in social relations. Whether that transformatory tendency is of a socialist hue, black nationalist, Marxist feminist, radical feminist, gay liberationist or some other particular expression, none can hope to bring about real change until there is the required breakdown in existing social and political relations. In each of the above cases, we are still waiting for the *appropriate* breakdown.

The temperate also suffers from a different form of deferral. Decisions are deferred, as well as most of the important work needed to cause the political elite leading the movement to force existing powers to carry out necessary legislative reform. In temperate campaigning, the mass of those suffering under oppression must hope that their leadership is politically powerful and competent enough to persuade or blackmail the state into acting on their behalf and changing the law.

Although the forms of deferral are different, both have the effect of disempowering those who are actually suffering by demanding that they trust to the vagaries of social development or high politics; that they place their destiny in forces largely beyond their control.

The personal-local suffers from no such deferral. Its very nature is predicated upon the immediate seizing of the initiative of change by those dissatisfied with the conditions of their life. Others may help by providing support or advice but the decision to change and the details of that change are taken by the individual and sometimes his or her immediate or local network of associates. If the temperate defers change to *somewhere else* and the transformatory defers change to *later*, the personal-local initiates change *here* and *now*.

THE POWER OF THE PERSONAL-LOCAL II: MAINTAINING A MOVEMENT'S VIABILITY

There are many reasons why a movement loses its viability either as a united organisation or as bearer of certain values. Some movements, both temperate and transformatory, have faced the problem of having to compromise their founding principles. Some movements have simply collapsed as a result of the internal conflict between temperate and transformatory tendencies. Others have discovered a shortfall between their hopes for their constituency, following legislative or radical social change, and what that constituency could realistically do. In each case the viability of a movement's mission is severely damaged.

Compromise has taken the form of what can be called 'rational sell-out' in that the price for a certain degree of success is compromise of the movement's principles, usually in a context which makes such compromise the most reasonable choice.

In the case of the temperate approach, 'rational sell-out' usually arises when a movement is close to achieving change or becoming a significant political force. At such a time the movement's leaders are normally faced with an historic compromise with existing powers. As is the nature of high politics, little is achieved by influential interest groups without a deal being struck or a mutually-beneficial bargain being made.[21] Under such conditions movement leaders are often required to compromise (in order to avoid expense, lost votes or adverse reaction by other groups) in return for seeing some limited degree of change being sponsored by leading state actors. In short, temperate campaigners will usually face a grim choice: limited change or no change at all. Quite reasonably, following many long years of tireless campaigning, and having no certainty that the opportunity will present itself again, temperate leaders opt for the former. Thus the relative weakness of the

Equal Opportunities Commission; reduction in gay age of consent to eighteen years rather than sixteen in 1995; half-hearted commitment of Labour Party leadership to unilateral nuclear disarmament during the 1980s; very limited moves towards environmental security made by world governments; and any number of other compromise formulas delivered by existing power structures. Indeed, one could easily write a history of the temperate wing of the socialist movement as a series of such compromise formulas and rational sell-outs.

The choice is rarely quite so stark and rational sell-out may occur over a lengthy period during which groups discover that moderation of demands and a more conventional approach to campaigning wins them greater influence over state actors. Environmental groups in particular, such as Friends of the Earth, have increasingly responded to such pressures by taking a more piecemeal approach to reform and by employing conventional research and lobbying tactics.[22]

Occasionally transformatory wings have also been willing to make such compromises (the communist parties of Western Europe are prime examples), but usually they face a very different form of rational sell-out. If transformatory wings achieve enough support to present a serious threat to existing power structures, they will usually face the most extreme forms of suppression in the shape of police or military violence. In such circumstances transformatory groups often face the stark choice between seeing their organisation violently destroyed or re-forming in a fashion similar to existing power structures in order for there to be any chance of survival, let alone progress. Once again, many quite reasonably opt for the latter. Re-formation usually involves the establishment of strong hierarchies and militaristic culture and practice, plus an intense struggle for an immediate increase in material resources. Under such circumstances power becomes entrenched within the upper echelons of the movement and may lead to an oppression as bad as, and possibly worse than, that against which the group was revolting.

The clearest historical example of this is the Bolshevik Revolution of October 1917 in which such choices led to their most extreme conclusions (as has often been the case with the socialist movement) in the form of War Communism. In short, what is initially argued for as a necessity rapidly develops into a virtue.[23] None of the post-1960s transformatory groups has achieved a level of success demanding such a rational sell-out, although there is no reason to assume that similar problems would not confront such groups if they are successful in the future. There are already accounts of serious abuse of power within transformatory movements which have chosen to adopt militaristic and/or hierarchical structures. Some Trotskyite parties and black power groups have faced such accusations. Of course corruption and abuse of power can occur within temperate groups, but they have never reached the degree of systematic oppression present in transformatory bodies.

The personal-local is free of such problems because it offers change without the necessity of a vertical organisation directed primarily against existing powers. Hence it need face none of the organisational weaknesses inherent in managing large groups of people. If one 'sells-out' at a personal-local level, one chiefly harms oneself: major oppression or a 'cowardly' betrayal of a group's supporters do not enter into the decision.

Indeed it is possible for personal-local change to continue even after movements have collapsed as organised interests due to internal conflict or external pressures. Although the organised women's move-ment was severely damaged by ideological and strategic disputes in the late 1970s, this has not stopped the continuing growth in the number of individual women deciding to live their lives as free as possible from the restrictions their mothers and grandmothers faced. During the early to mid-1980s when the gay movement was still divided over a number of issues and traumatised by the spread of HIV, a growing stream of men and women decided to live individual lives buoyed by pride in their sexuality. Although the civil rights movement lost direc-tion, and black power organisations were as hostile to one another as they were to the state organisations systematically destroying them, black cultural activity and pride in colour continues to flourish in the US.[24] And while the green parties in Europe divided over electoral strategy or floundered in political obscurity as in Britain, the number of people deciding to become vegetarian, or who carry out local protests against destruction and cruelty, grows.

In short, when a movement, temperate or transformatory, faces fail-ure or compromise and sees the viability of its founding principles disappear, the struggle for change need not be over: the personal-local can prove an effective promoter of liberation from oppression, defend-ing such change against the inherent problems of the other tendencies.

Movements also prove more successful in their goals, and less likely to face a loss of viability, when they manage to integrate their demands for collective change with tangible change at the level of the individual. As movements have often found to their cost, freedoms provided for from above mean nothing if the constituency at which they are aimed still reside in the local conditions and mentality of oppression. This was the discovery of many who turned to black power and who were disappointed by the continuing problems facing black Americans after the passing of civil rights legislation in 1965; equal pay and sex discrimination legislation has made little difference to those women who do not have the confidence and local support networks to challenge employers in the UK; and many greens have recognised that national and international changes to environmental law is only effective or likely if there is a concomitant change in the mentality and behaviour of consumers and producers at local and regional level. The personal-local though, with its emphasis upon individual growth, clearly provides the most appropriate basis upon which to develop a programme of change that integrates the collective with the individual, allowing collective ideals to inform personal-local change and personal-local experience to indicate what is possible and what is desirable at a collective level.

CONTRADICTORY BUT NECESSARY
Thus each tendency provides a necessary factor in a movement's make-up, without which the movement would undoubtedly be the poorer. Over time, the lack of any one of these tendencies could cause a fatal flaw to develop and the movement to fracture and die. Despite each tendency's desire to be treated by all members as integral, the movement's success is, in fact, based upon every tendency being treated tactically with specific aspects contributing vital benefits to the movement as a whole.

Equally, however, none of the tendencies can escape the clear contradictions of approach, principle and imperative of action that exist between them. There seems to be a drive for each tendency to proclaim its integrity at the expense of the other tendencies and to demand absolute faith from everyone in a movement. Such a drive may actually be important, though, in that the full benefits of each tendency may not be felt by a movement if those allied to that tendency do not have the energy and commitment generated by complete faith in the sole value of their approach.

These contradictions which exist between the different strands are well-rehearsed throughout history and need not be dwelt upon at length. Clearly while transformatory and temperate strands may co-operate for periods of time, especially when contributing to campaigns on specific single issues, there will always come a point when the two strands cannot agree. Intense division will follow, and possibly a permanent split, and thereafter separate development. Some examples are: co-operation with black power movements in the case of the gay liberation in the US; woman-centredness in the case of the women's movement in Britain; electoral alliance with mainstream parties in the case of Die Grünen in Germany; and the use of violence in the case of the black civil rights movement.

The personal-local, as is made clear above, does not have a history of quite such intense contradictions with the other tendencies, but the recent intensification of a division along these lines suggests that emphasis upon the personal-local as a distinct tendency does bring contradictions to light. When the attempt is made to treat the personal-local as integral, rather than tactical as in the past, the contradictions become clearer.

If these tendencies are contradictory and if – in their contradiction and in the willingness of different wings of movements each to assert the superiority of its tendency over the other – a movement is likely to self-destruct either as an organisation or as a bearer of principles, how can any activist who recognises the necessity of each wing, *and* their contradictions, act upon this recognition? In the intense and consuming disputes which have always existed (and it seems likely always will exist) between transformatory, temperate and personal-local tendencies within a movement, where can the activist who sees their shared failings and shared benefits stand?

CONCLUSION: THE ACTIVIST-CYNIC

A good starting-point for consideration of these questions is the recognition that division within movements is a constant. Thus acceptance of the points made throughout this chapter will probably be a minority taste, because the great majority involved in any movement will always prefer to take sides, as displayed by sheer weight of historical evidence. So for the sake of realism we must resist the temptation, which always exists when a contradiction is identified, to construct some rosily optimistic synthesis of all three tendencies which will appeal to everyone. Indeed in combining the three tendencies we would only rob them of the characteristics which make them so beneficial to a movement and yet, simultaneously, so contradictory: the transformatory would be shorn of its radical vitality, the temperate of its realistic practicality, the personal-local of its disorganised, anti-political immediacy.

But in accepting the constancy of division alongside the benefits provided by each tendency, we may be creating (or simply acknowledging) a certain political creature. This is the activist-cynic: the individual who plays his or her part for the movement knowing its goals are honourable and just, but who simultaneously is aware that claims made by each tendency for itself against the others are hopelessly overblown. This is the activist who is aware that no strategy is perfect and that movements, in choosing to emphasise one tendency over another (as they must do considering the contradictions between the different tendencies), will face one or more of the destructive problems outlined above.

Thus the activist-cynic sits through heated meetings with a wry smile on his or her face and keeps his or her own counsel knowing that their point of view, if aired, would be met by the mute, slightly embarrassed response that always greets the *non sequitur*. The activist-cynic is engaged but distanced – sane enough to be involved in struggling against the cruelties and oppressions of the day but sane enough not to be so involved in the struggle that s/he loses him or herself in the fantasies of the factions.

The activist-cynic is not a figure any tendency is likely to encourage and this may be a good thing. If the activist-cynic were a majority occupation then a movement would lose the benefits each tendency brings to its life; for any of the above tendencies really to contribute to a movement's growth, it does not need cynicism, it needs unqualified commitment. And yet, if there is any truth in the above arguments, above, such cynicism may be the only rational response.

NOTES

1. 'Movement' here is employed in its broadest sense to mean groups of individuals sharing a commitment to seek alleviation of certain conditions which those individuals as a group find unsatisfactory. While, like most definitions, this raises as many questions as it answers, it performs a necessary function for this chapter: i.e. to distinguish 'movement' from individual organisations which might exist *within* the movement, some of which might not split over strategy but which, in all probability, will represent one or other side in the division.
2. B. Adam, *The Rise of a Gay and Lesbian Liberation Movement*, G.K.Hall, Boston 1987; M. Cruickshank, *The Gay and Lesbian Liberation Movement*, Routledge, London 1992; D. Fernbach, 'Ten Years of Gay Liberation', *Politics and Power 2*, Routledge, Kegan & Paul, London 1980.
3. D. Bouchier, *The Feminist Challenge*, Macmillan Press, London 1983; A.

Coote & B. Campbell, *Sweet Freedom*, Basil Blackwell, Oxford 1982; S. Rowbotham, *The Past is Before Us: Feminism in Action Since the 1960s*, Penguin, Harmondsworth 1989.

4. P. Byrne, *Social Movements in Britain*, Routledge, London 1997; R. Goodin, *Green Political Theory*, Polity Press, Cambridge 1995; W. Hulsberg, *The German Greens*, Verso, London 1988; E. Kolinsky (ed), *The Greens in West Germany*, Berg, Oxford 1989.

5. Some may argue that even transformatory wings see mass mobilisation as tactical in that it provides the foundation for comprehensive social and political change. Of course within the diversity of any movement there will be many differing perspectives on every part of the political process, but I think it is generally true that those of a transformatory leaning tend to see *more* integral good in the act of sudden transformation extant in mass uprising than those of a temperate tendency.

6. A similar, although not identical, typology has been proposed before. See D. Aberle, *The Peyote Religion Among the Navaho*, Aldine Press, Chicago 1966.

7. See: http://www.envirolink.org/orgs/ef/primer/index.html.

8. See Rupa Huq's chapter in this volume for tensions in the anti-Criminal Justice Bill campaign and rave culture in general; see also: http://www.theoroc.org/roc-mag/textarch/roc-14/roc14-3b.htm.

9. R. Cook, *Sweet Land of Liberty: The African-American Struggle for Civil Rights in the Twentieth Century*, Longman, London 1998; R. Weisbrot, *Freedom Bound: A History of America's Civil Rights Movement*, Plume, New York 1991.

10. S. Carmichael & C. Hamilton, *Black Power: The Politics of Liberation*, Penguin, Harmondsworth 1967; M. Marable, *Race, Reform and Rebellion: The Second Revolution in Black America*, Macmillan, London 1991.

11. Marable, *op.cit.*

12. Coote & Campbell, *op. cit.*

13. *Ibid.*; M. Daly, *Gyn/Ecology: The Metaethics of Radical Feminism*, The Women's Press, London 1978; J. Evans, *Feminist Thought Today: An Introduction to Second Wave Feminism*, Sage, London 1995; M.Humm, *Feminisms: A Reader*, Harvester Wheatsheaf, Brighton 1992; S. Firestone, *The Dialectic of Sex*, The Women's Press, London 1970.

14. A. Dobson, *Green Political Thought*, 2nd ed. Routledge, London 1995; T. Hayward, *Ecological Thought: An Introduction*, Polity, Cambridge 1995; G. Sessions (ed), *Deep Ecology for the 21st Century*, Shambala, London 1995.

15. S.Phelan (ed), *Playing with Fire: Queer Politics, Queer Theories*, Routledge, London 1993; M.Warner (ed), *Fear of a Queer Planet: Queer Politics and Social Theory*, University of Minnesota Press, Minneapolis 1993.

16. See, for example, Tony Fitzpatrick's chapter in this volume.

17. P. Abberley, 'The Concept of Oppression and the Development of a Social Theory of Disability', *Disability, Handicap and Society*, 2(1), 1987; L. Barton & M. Oliver (eds), *Disability Studies: Past, Present and Future*, The Disability Press, Leeds 1997.

18. V. Bryson, *Feminist Political Theory: An Introduction*, Routledge, London 1992; Cook, *op.cit.*; Cruickshank, *op.cit.*; J. D'Emilio, *Sexual Politics, Sexual Communities: The Making of a Homosexual Minority in the United States, 1940-1970*, University of Chicago Press, Chicago 1983; B. Friedan, *The Feminine Mystique*, Penguin [1963], Harmondsworth 1986.

19. J. Squires (ed), *Principled Positions: Postmodernism and the Rediscovery of Value*, Lawrence & Wishart, London 1993.

20. A. Jagose, *Queer Theory: An Introduction*, NYU Press, New York 1996; D. West, *Homosexuality Re-examined*, Duckworth, London 1977.

21. Much of the Political Science study of interest groups has been given over to the nature of such compromises: Policy Network Analysis, in particular, places such bargaining and compromise at the heart of its analysis. See, for example: K. Dowding 'Model or Metaphor? A Critical Review of the Policy Network Approach', *Political Studies*, 43(1) March 1995.

22. Byrne, *op.cit.*

23. See, for example, Rosa Luxemburg's critique of the Bolshevik Revolution: R. Luxemburg, 'The Russian Revolution', *Rosa Luxemburg Speaks* (M-A.Waters ed.), Pathfinder, New York 1970.

24. R. Cook, *Sweet Land of Liberty? The African-American Struggle for Civil Rights in the Twentieth Century*, Longman, London 1998; A. Shaw, *Black Popular Music in America*, London, Collier MacMillan, 1986.

SOUNDING OUT NEW SOCIAL MOVEMENTS AND THE LEFT: INTERVIEW WITH STUART HALL, DOREEN MASSEY AND MICHAEL RUSTIN

Tessa Bird and Tim Jordan

INTRODUCTION

Stuart Hall, Doreen Massey and Michael Rustin share a common history of involvement in the left and a common engagement with the significance of current politics. In 1995 they launched a new journal as co-editors, *Soundings*, a journal of culture and politics, that explores current political struggles and their meaning.[1] The journal is an expression of the editors' ongoing engagement with the left and with projects of social change, as it aims not at an academic audience but at a far broader one. All three are also key intellectuals in a number of academic disciplines: sociology, cultural studies, psychosocial studies, urban studies, geography.

The conjunction of activism, intellectual work and driving a key new resource for rethinking the left and oppositional politics makes them ideal people to discuss the general significance of new politics. They have attempted in *Soundings* to engage critically and constructively with new politics by running articles on these issues. However, though the emergence of the journal prompted this interview, each participant spoke from her or his own point of view. As Stuart Hall said at the beginning of the interview, to general laughter, 'I don't know about speaking as editors with a line, as there manifestly isn't "one"!' The first editorial of *Soundings* was used, in particular, as a beginning point for questions because it addressed 'new politics' and set out an overall analysis of current politics, but Stuart, Doreen and Michael all answered from their own perspectives.[2]

CLASS, THE LEFT AND NEW POLITICS

Tessa Bird and Tim Jordan (TBJ) As a starting point, we wanted to discuss what you see as the relationship between new politics or new social movements, the left and capitalism. In the first editorial of *Soundings* you discuss the importance of new social movements or new politics and call them 'politics beyond politics', that is a new politics beyond, especially, parliamentary politics. The editorial also discusses these forms of politics as something that emerges out of the transformation of Fordism into post-Fordism in post-war Britain. How do you see or understand the politics of new social movements in relation to the labour movement or class politics in general?

Michael Rustin (MR) One starting point is to note that the concept of new social movements has been itself constructed in opposition to the old social movements, namely the labour movement, and the concept wouldn't have much meaning without that contrasting reference. Therefore, built into the very concept of 'new' social movements is the idea that whatever the old political antagonisms may have been about, there is now something else. So I think it is almost definitionally true as part of the landscape of the new social movement discussion that a break is assumed. One can also say that the New Left, in its earliest days, anticipated many of the themes that have subsequently become defined as those of the new social movements, even before people recognised that's what they were. But in the work of the New Left, this was both an assertion of the new and an insistence on continuity: it called itself the New Left, after all. On the other hand the rise to a central role of gender politics and ecological politics, in particular, does seem to identify a 'post class' phase of radicalism.

Stuart Hall (SH) I agree with Michael, in the sense that the two things are always juxtaposed because it is difficult to make sense of them without thinking like that. It sometimes means that we forget that what are now called the old social movements had a new social movement phase. It was the early movements that gave rise to what later became the organised labour movement, the left and the trade unions; they too were social movements long before they were organised into parties. But, of course, speaking from where we are now and looking back, the labour movement seems to be the well-established form of politics. This also relates to, not quite a settlement between society, state, economy and capital, but some settled ways of conducting the contradictions of struggles between those elements. The outcome wasn't settled but the way struggles were conducted was, and that was what constituted the terrain of the political. What we now call the new social movements arise when that way of stabilising the terrain of the political is disrupted.

One of the questions which has arisen ever since the appearance of the new social movements has been how new and how total they are. That is to say, are we talking about the disturbance of and displacement of what came to be taken as the political, and a kind of relativising of politics so that there are many areas of contention and many kinds of social movement? It's almost as if the old social movements go back to their new social movement phase, the working class becomes another social movement alongside race and women and so on. There aren't any clean breaks, those old politics don't disappear, and so we're talking about the coming apart of a configuration and a reconfiguring of the terrain of politics. Always in that movement you have the dissolution of the old forms and the old language and the old ways of understanding and conducting politics, but of course not their disappearance. Perhaps questions of poverty or class are not so central, they don't dominate the whole terrain, but no one could say that they have disappeared from the terrain of the political today. It would be an absurd statement. So we have to be careful about counterposing it as a simple old/new, then/now, gone/emerging set of oppositions.

A second point is that the era of the new social movements has been going for quite a long time now and there are already some old new social movements: some people were involved in civil rights in 1964, the peace movement in 1959 – CND was at its first height at that time, race politics from the late 1950s onwards in this country. What I think you were calling the new social movements is the eruption of another wave within the terrain of the new social movements. I think we have to be careful when what we are really talking about is two sorts of shifts: one between the old social movements and the new, and a second in the evolution and variations occurring in the field of new social movements, where the new social movements count as significant equals to that which in the old days was dominated by class politics.

Doreen Massey (DM) I agree with that last point. There's considerable variation between the various movements which we all-too-easily lump together as 'new social movements'! What's more, these variations link back to the question you originally asked about the relation between the Fordist/post Fordist transition and the emergence of the early new social movements. We might include here race politics, CND and feminism. I think there is a relationship but I would cast it rather differently. Surely it's not a question of the capital-labour settlement breaking down *and then* the other movements taking off, to fill the space as it were. There are a number of issues here. First, I have to confess that I put less credence in any simple Fordist-post-Fordist transition than you are inferring. Clearly many changes of that order have been under way, but it is a complex process. Second, although 'regulation theory', and even post-Fordism in general, tried to be less economistic I don't think it fully succeeds. And the formulation 'first the breakdown of Fordism then the rise of feminism' reinforces that. I would in fact – third – see things the other way around, or certainly as more complexly intertwined. If we understand the move towards 'post Fordism' as being part of bigger shifts in society, including some of the things sometimes convened under the headings of post modernism/ post structuralism, then surely we can see the causality as being at least in part the other way around. Feminism, sexual politics and post-colonial struggles were part of what destabilised the old, all-too-comfortable, consensus. They were part of the *cause* of the breakdown, not simply its effect. Sometimes I think we have a bad habit of detecting big (i.e. economic/systemic) shifts and then adducing politics as their effect. 'Politics' can be more disruptive/productive than that.

TBJ Following from Doreen's point that new social movements were part of the cause of the collapse of the 'old political settlement', and taking up the point that new social movements are new in the sense that they are new since the 1960s but are not new *per se*, one consequence would be that new social movements have partly been reacting against a set of theories and practices which were, in a broad sense, class based and/or Marxist. To what extent do you see one of the left's problems, or one of the challenges with which the left is wrestling, as being the extent to which class frameworks are adequate for dealing with this post-1960s politics?

SH There may be more than one position in relation to these questions and maybe people from outside will tell us better than we can ourselves, one isn't always aware of the mindset within which one is operating. You can operate in frameworks that you thought you'd given up! We have to first talk about what the framework for left politics is. For me, it certainly wasn't and isn't a straightforward classical Marxist account, though it certainly was profoundly influenced by Marxist and socialist themes. From this point I would then say that there are different positions.

One position is that of a broadly Marxist or socialist framework, which still directs attention to absolutely central determining features of the political context, but is inadequate in the sense that there are all sorts of other things that it is not good at explaining. One can begin within that framework but then you have to modify or extend it in order to begin to take on, genuinely, those things which don't come from the same contradiction. We could expand it, modify it, maintain basically the same outlook, but add to it. Another position is that the challenges of new social movements, properly grasped, are so profound and distinctive that what you ought to fasten on to is the destructive theoretical and conceptual work which new social movements do to the original paradigm. They are so different in their origins from that of the original socialist framework – and are even difficult to make visible – because the other framework, that of class, prevents you from seeing them.

Different people take up different positions within those two broad frameworks. People who are still attached to the first 'older' left one but who are willing to go very far in modifying it, and people who think there is a radically new framework but want to retain some awareness of the old, are pretty close together and may not be very different. From my point of view it goes back to the point I made before. If it is true that the old political configuration breaks up and a new configuration forms, then that new configuration can be composed of dramatically new elements and still retain some of the old elements. Even if the terrain is completely novel, that doesn't mean that everything in it just dropped out of the sky yesterday. If that is so, then some of the insights of the past can't possibly have gone away. In addition, a broad definition of the first position and a worried definition of the second are very close together and both of them are far away from a simple economism or a simple sort of 'every- and anything goes'. The problem for me is that then I don't know at what level a debate between these two positions could be resolved. Trying to think it out in the abstract won't work because the different sides are so close that there wouldn't be any way of resolving it. I think it's probably better to hear what someone says about the public sector, or about new forms of politics or about environmental or ecological issues, than to try and work out at a very general, abstract level what left politics now really means.

I'm talking in very general terms, but in so far as there is economic inequality – and there is – in so far as there are still large numbers of people who are poor and small numbers of people who are rich, and in so far as that distribution of wealth comes from the market – I can't tell you that all we understood about the market is of no use simply because it's inadequate to explain all sorts of other things. I have to retain some of those insights into economic class, though I think now I would want to say that we can't retain them in the old form. We have to be careful about picking them up from the past and slotting them in, because when the relationships between different antagonisms from the past change, then the theories have to explain something different. This means that a great deal of theoretical and conceptual work has to be done, which is probably why anybody who is in this game is starting new journals!

DM There's another point, which relates to something Stuart said. Certainly questions of poverty and class have not disappeared from the political terrain – or, at least, they should not be allowed to do so. Moreover, issues of poverty and issues of class are not the same thing. The vast bulk of the world's poor, for instance, are poor also because they are women. The politics of anti-sexism and anti-racism are important in combating poverty too, not just the politics of class.

MR I want to take up your reference to post-Fordism because we do indeed make that a reference point and that requires some mention of one of our immediate predecessors, which was *Marxism Today*, and its 'New Times' analysis.[3] We were all involved in that in different ways. What was being developed in that analysis was a response to the view that the problem was simply that the Labour Party was not left-wing enough. This is the view that we hadn't tried maximalist programmes, as these were traditionally set out (public ownership etc), and that if only we did everything would be all right. This was one reading of the failures of the Labour government between 1974 and 1979. The *Marxism Today* analysis criticised the frame of thinking which assumed there was a waiting proletariat, a trade union movement, and a ready-made set of socialist programmes and practices, and the idea that all that was needed was one big heave. Basically the *Marxism Today* analysis said that this was wrong. The world had changed in substantial ways and we had to recognise this if we were to construct a radical programme that would have a chance against Thatcherism. To that extent there is in the background of *Soundings* a repudiation of certain anachronistic versions of what the left project had become, in regard to questions both of agency and programme.

I think that the nature of our antagonist has changed rather less than the nature of the resources of agency, culture and programme we might be able to mobilise against it. What I mean by our antagonist comes back to the nature of capital and property: capitalism itself. One can illustrate that by reference to the issues raised by almost any new social movement. In a newspaper yesterday there was a report on global warming. The World Health Organisation was quoted as saying that many of the private corporations now lobbying against energy conservation – including oil companies, motor car companies and so on – were behaving rather like cigarette companies which pretend that tobacco doesn't cause cancer. The reason why it is difficult to make progress, when it seems self-evident that action is necessary (that something must be done about motor cars, fossil fuels etc.), is not primarily because of the state of the scientific arguments, but because of the power of lobbies and interests. This ecological problem is right at the very heart of the new politics, but nevertheless the old contradictions still emerge as central ones. Confronting those economic interests becomes again quite crucial.

It's not just a question of saying the old issues continue. They don't just continue, but in some cases get larger and worse. Social polarisation, exclusion, impoverishment and insecurity have become galloping problems throughout the West. Not only do these tendencies continue with renewed force and vigour, but even the 'newest' political problems also turn out to have their roots in the operations of capitalism.

Gender questions may be different in some ways. Capitalism has been more friendly to the cause of gender equality than it has to other kinds of problems. This issue is not symmetrical with the ecological issue. I would just want to say that some of the antagonists which left politics has always constructed as the real problem, remain the problem. In terms of the definition of the problems, or their sources, or the fundamental structures that have to be addressed, capitalism does remain alive, well and powerful. It continues to need to be named and thought about. Now that doesn't mean that ready solutions or ideologies or agencies are all in place and just waiting to be woken up. They are not and that is our problem. But both sides of the argument need to be kept in mind: both the weakness and outflanking of the responses that used to exist, and the fact that the capitalist engine which has outflanked them remains capable of doing its work, a lot of which is damaging. So to that extent we continue to be socialists and *Soundings* continues to be a socialist magazine. Though it isn't necessarily very useful to go on banging on about that because the term is so easily rendered lifeless by its echoes of the past.

DM We have to also understand some aspects of this apparent dilemma ('class' or 'new social movements') in terms of the political history in which the questions themselves were formulated. On the one hand there are huge political issues which are also deeply *theoretical*, about how much an old formulation of Marxism can be stretched to encompass the new things we have learned and which we now face. But the problem is that these questions have been posed within a particular political conjuncture, most importantly 1989. And their consideration has been deeply affected by that context. Certainly in the UK many people who had for long been in the Communist Party were torn apart, not only by 1989 but by what, over the longer term, they learned they had been part of and party to. I think we have all suffered, and debate on the left has suffered very seriously, from the impact of what these folk were going through. It was through those channels that the first dualistic, antagonistic, and totally unhelpful distinctions were made between 'hard left' and 'new left'. You had to be one or the other. Each was defined in terms of a rejection of the other. *Marxism Today* operated a lot with such binary choices. Its (in)famous table of Fordism/post-Fordism dualisms was only one of the most notorious; either/or choices were the whole frame of its position (quite old fashioned when you come to think about it!). And so, by this means and others, we were faced with choices *between* class and 'new social movements'. I refuse to make that choice. But for quite a long period this left me (and many other people too) no place to speak from. It was also a false choice in the sense that it wasn't really what was on offer. While *Marxism Today*, for instance, used feminism to bash the old labour movement (for which, read 'class'), it never really took feminism or sexual politics seriously. The big stuff, the long articles at the front, were much more likely to be, say, one of the boys on economics.

SOCIALISM AND NEW POLITICS

TBJ It's interesting that you see socialist as an important allegiance. In the journal you discuss the importance of democracy in relation to socialism. Could you explore those two words and their meanings for us?

MR Just as the term new social movements is constructed in antithesis to old social movements, so the idea of socialism is constructed in opposition to capitalism, and gains meaning from the idea that capitalism does represent a rather large scale problem. Now one of the things that's plainly happened in the ongoing political discourse of New Labour is the expunging of that idea. The notion of capitalism as a problem in some fundamental deep structural way is being annihilated, and we're being taught to live with capitalism as part of the everyday furniture and fabric of life. Changes and reforms are now to be seen merely as tinkerings, humanisations, in a relatively small-scale way. The reason why there is some real point in asserting some continuity with socialism is that we don't think this acceptance of capitalism, as the natural or inevitable way of things, is a valid view of the world. It's an accommodation, a statement of defeat. It represents a failure of imagination and a loss of nerve. A political system in which ideology disappears as irrelevant, and in which it cannot be said that there are fundamental conflicts of interest, constitutes a serious probem for the left. The idea that there are structural conflicts of interest, which it is the job of radical parties to do something about, remains fundamental.

SH I agree and think that the term 'socialist' is unlikely to be used very widely or strongly because of its different determinations, and that is because it belongs to a very complicated discursive field. Radical politics has to recognise that capitalism is a problem. Something has to be done about capitalism for radical change of any kind to happen. This use of socialism I find unproblematic. But socialism is also identified with a range of political forms, of political programmes – nationalisation and state planning from the centre – and when the word awakens that set of connotations, rather than a set of connotations about the structure of economic life, then there's too much baggage. It also commits one in ways which I don't want to be committed – not that I necessarily have any alternative to it. It's when these two axes come together – when, if you say socialism versus capitalism, then that must also mean the forms of socialist politics in which they have existed before – then there's a real problem.

Socialism and democracy discursively is a rather different sort of game. It's always been understood that socialism is about championing the cause of the less powerful, but it also has something to do with the forms of representation of the largely excluded numbers of people. So there's a long history in which socialism is part of democracy, but they're not mutually co-terminous. There have been times when socialism has been deeply undemocratic and there are forms of democracy which are not socialist, so I think one needs the two terms. The unfortunate thing is all the terms that combine the two are also unusable: neither democratic socialism nor social democracy is tenable. This is a problem of coming at the end of a language rather than the beginning:

none of the words will work for you any longer! So one keeps playing socialist words to those democrats who forget about capital, and the democracy card to those who really think the party elite should do it on behalf of the poor, ordinary folks.

I think the earlier discussion we had about class is contained in this problem. It's quite deliberate. Democracy *cannot* have the exclusive class reference that socialism has, and when democracy gets used in the context of socialism it has often been a code-word for the working class. But democracy can not be a code-word, because all sorts of things have happened to class, and all sorts of people are involved in social movements that don't in any obvious way belong to the old classic working-class subject of socialist politics. By talking about the democratic element of radical politics, much wider social constituencies are invoked which are likely to be involved in various forms of change.

MR There is some difference of emphasis or, at any rate, some quite difficult choices to be made in relation to what Stuart has just said, about the worn qualities of the old discourse, and how far it remains useable. Clearly there is a point at which a discourse becomes so tarnished or lifeless that one is better off not using it at all, and starting again. But it is a matter of judgement about whether that position has been reached or whether there is something to be said for hanging on to such continuity as there could be.

SH I agree, but it's true that, certainly during the period when I was working closely with *Marxism Today*, we did think that most of those terms were unusable. It may be just a strategic question or just a question of ducking it. I imagine myself on the doorstep with a sympathetic person and the last thing I would say is, 'Would you like to join the socialist cause?' But that doesn't mean that what is represented by the term won't come into the conversation, and maybe that person might end up saying, 'Well I see what socialism was supposed to be about'. But it would come at the end of the conversation though, rather than at the beginning. These are delicate matters of tactics and strategy, there's no law about them.

But at the outer edge of the problem there is a question of whether it is just tactical or whether there isn't something deeper there. Just imagine that there weren't these immediate barriers or responses to socialism, in what sense would one want to call some of the new social movements, in any sense, socialist? What would one mean by that? This could mean two things. One is they're part of a continuing oppositional politics, which is where socialism has been, and they appeal to the excluded, the powerless, and this is something that socialism has spoken on behalf of. The question in relation to capitalism would be: to what extent does the analysis of the problem these movements are addressing require an understanding of capitalism? There we have some way to go. The second position is, for instance, what I understand that socialist-feminist might mean, but I would find it strange to call feminism a socialist movement, it doesn't make sense to me. I don't even think it would make political sense to me, because I see feminism as having to reconstruct what socialism means as well as having to take on some of the lessons of socialism. Such difficult alliances couldn't be worked by just calling the two sides by one name. I think there are deeper problems behind this question of when one will use 'socialism' and how one will use it, and I think it has to do not with whether questions of capital and capitalism are important, but how you introduce them into the analysis.

Take the question of feminism again. I would say that nothing about feminist politics could be understood without understanding their articulation to questions of economic capital, but certainly the economy and capital do not constitute the problem of feminism. Capitalism and the economic are absolutely central to understanding the whole terrain, but they aren't what started it off; you can't put feminism into that determinant. Capitalism may shape it very urgently and maybe you can't disentangle the two, but you are nevertheless talking about an articulation between two formations or two antagonists or two contradictions, not the same contradiction with two manifestations. I think that is the deeper and more difficult distinction and I suppose I am more committedly on the second of these two.

I think capitalism is profoundly important in shaping the articulation of any social contradiction, antagonism or movement, but I suspend judgement on whether capitalism is 'determining in the last instance', and that for me is a profound movement away from a certain kind of Marxism – with which, incidentally, I was never happy, never liked, but I did sort of know that it was what I was supposed to think! I could never quite get myself thinking it, but I was supposed to think that if you could solve that one contradiction then the others would sort of fall into place. A very simplistic notion, but one that also carried a very powerful political logic that gave you a handle on the political world, whereas what I've just said doesn't give you this. There is now *no metatheory*, no 'meta' way of understanding the political effects of all these things operating in social life. Relationships between man and woman pre-date capitalism. Slavery and race pre-date capitalism. Ecology probably pre-dates it too. The histories are different. What one is always looking at is the articulation of a complex field between different antagonisms, and therefore between different social constituencies associated with the different antagonisms. And all of that is a different kind of political problem from the one that you would have if you imagined it all came from one place, because if it all comes from one place then your politics is to blast that one place out of existence and everything else will change.

DM I also no longer suspend judgement. I do not think capitalism (or the economy) is 'determining in the last instance'. In fact it's difficult to know exactly what that would mean; let me be honest, it always *was* difficult to know, but for a while I used the formulation anyway.

I agree strongly that feminism is distinct from socialism in the way Stuart described: two 'contradictions' (there's a good old word for you) rather than one contradiction with two manifestations. How many hours have we spent in women's groups discussing this.

But if one follows this path then other considerations arise. Perhaps instead of saying socialist-feminist these days one says socialist *and* feminist. One thing which that formulation underlines is that socialist is not the hegemonic term, it is not being used with pretensions to being all-encompassing. On the other hand one would want the two strands of politics to influence each other, and at a deep level rather than simply cosmetically. (There is a lot to be said, or at least explored, about the masculinism of the whole project of capitalism, for instance.) But to influence each other, rather than for one to (pretend to) frame or encompass the other holds open the recognition of all the difficulties, theoretical and political, which lie between them and which must be addressed.

I think the relationship between the existence of a metatheory and the possibility of politics is fascinating. It is not all one-way. Certainly we no longer have 'the key to everything' which we once thought we had. But (quite apart from the fact that it wasn't true!) that view was also profoundly demobilising. Capitalism was so big, so all-encompassing, so able to recoup any small ('reformist') moves one might make that it was difficult to make any move at all. It is indeed more complicated now and we do know that we are not going to bring the whole thing tumbling down in one go, but – if we could get our heads around it – there must be more openings, more space for imagination. We must refuse to be discouraged by some of the residual insults: that a particular intervention is 'only local', that 'it's not attacking the main issue' (for which read global capitalism). The terms of the whole thing have changed, but perhaps we haven't yet really got to grips with how to think that; how to think 'strategically' in a situation which is so differentiated and complex. How to have the confidence, in our imaginations, to do something different, and, as I said earlier, how to move beyond the old terms of debate, the old dichotomies.

MR I do have just one further observation I might make on these issues of socialism and democracy. When you raised the question of finding the language of democracy a more available language to use than, say, the language of socialism and capitalism, I think in one way that's true and in another way it isn't. 'Democracy' does provide a language which is open to elaboration and radical extension. But the idea that a self-evident programme can be conjured up by calls for more 'democracy' is something of a fantasy. Inasmuch as leftists find themselves using it as a convenient catch-all term: 'oh well, we want everything to be more democratic', you have to say that sometimes this doesn't have much definite meaning. When you try to deconstruct what goes on in most so-called democratic processes – how a local council rules over its terrain, or how a union leadership manages its space, never mind the way a national government behaves – you find that the processes that go on fall short of anything that anyone would intuitively think of as democratic. If there is one thing that does need to be reinvented in a serious way it is the idea of democracy, as applied to complex, multi-interest, pluralistic societies with multiple identities.

ACTIVISM IN NEW SOCIAL MOVEMENTS
Tessa Bird (TB)[4] How do you then see yourselves in relation to particular social movements, or how do you see this discussion helping or being helped by these social movements? One thing I'm really struck by in the anti-roads movement is that these are people who have never seen an active left and have never seen the socialisms that you are referring to or experienced the histories you're referring to. Yet they are forwarding a radical anti-capitalist critique through environmentalism and ecologism.

DM One thing to say immediately is that the new social movements – I'm here thinking perhaps particularly of anti-roads protests or the demonstrations against the export of veal calves – make us think. Mike Waite takes up this question in Issue 3 of *Soundings*, arguing much the same point, that there really must be exchange. What we must *not* do is stand inside (what remains of) our old frameworks, see if the new movements fit, find they don't, and consequently dismiss them. On the one hand there are histories from which new movements can learn. On the other hand part of what the new movements are about (in fact, if not always in explicit intention) is reconstituting the field of politics. In our first editorial we speak of having a wide, and open, view of 'the political' and of wanting to think that through. That's part of the more experimental side of the project of *Soundings*. It's one of the reasons why we have science articles, poetry, a whole range of material that previously would not have found its way into a 'political' journal. Many of the new movements, as well as a host of other social changes, are really stimulating in the way they push me to think through that issue.

SH Two things come to mind. One is, I think it's true to different degrees of almost all active current social movements, that they wouldn't see themselves as part of the left, certainly not the majority and certainly not the younger people. The question of how we see ourselves in relation to them, that really belongs to a larger question about very complicated languages and political practices. There has been a difficult problem in all of the new social movements in that they've all tended to divide between an activist wing that's impatient about ideas, about talking shop and wanting to get on, and a more theoretical and analytical wing that's been interested in analysing the underlying causes. This is a very common political feature, a very damaging one. It's hard to break through and I don't know that it's likely to be bridged in any general way, it's only likely to be bridged in the context of each movement. There is also a kind of cycle here. There's a number of dramatic flashpoints which bring a movement into existence, attract a new constituency and constantly construct a new constituency, even construct a new political question – as I think some of the new social movements have. Questions that have never been thought of as political questions before become political. I think of hunt saboteurs. There's always been an anti-hunting lobby which used to be part of a humanitarian, liberal politics but it's only the connection with environmentalism and a whole new way of trying to think about the relationship between nature and culture or the economic, the social and the natural, that makes a movement like anti-hunting acquire a political edge that it didn't have before. I think that there is an initial phase like this. But my experience is that a distinction between activists and intellectuals occurs very often when that first wave of activism sort of crests and in order to take the activism on a lot of questions arise.

First of all, how do you deepen a movement's political life without institutionalising it, without setting up committees and so on? Think of green politics, think of the first wave of environmentalism and of the impact it had. Then think of the success in the early stages of institutionalisation where you had the Green Party beginning to make an impact on a European level. Then think of the stasis or the discrepancy between the party that lives on and environmentalism, which is now a much bigger question than the Green Party. This juncture has happened between the institutionalisation of the issue and its political vigour and vitality. It seems to me that it's quite often at *that moment* that some of the more analytic questions start to come to the front. People have to say to themselves: what is it that we are struggling about? and who has been involved in this? and how many? and why have certain people that we would have expected not been involved? and why have, very surprisingly, some people we would never have thought of been involved? I think of the export of veal calves and the astonishment at the kind of people, the ages and the classes, that that touched, which you would never have been able to predict before it happened.[5] We still don't understand why it touched a nerve, whether it was something to do with the moment that it happened or was something deeper.

I'm sympathetic to the critique that says 'we're sitting here analysing, thinking and not doing anything about it', but I also want to resist the notion that there is a simple relationship between theory and practice. Sometimes it's the case that the same people are not good at doing but are good at thinking. One of the important things about Gramsci's notion of the party, which is very different from the kind of political parties that become bureaucratic organisations or vote-getting organisations, is that he understood that parties are organisations that have the advantage of bringing very different people together, the purpose of which isn't to dissolve those differences but to create the possibility of them talking to one another. He didn't want everyone to be an activist or everybody to be a theoretician but to create some larger organisation in which the contribution of people could find a space; intellectuals alongside people who have the gift or genius of mobilisation or who are good at writing. He accepted a certain division of labour, without setting one against the other. This is exactly the opposite of modern political parties where the office that publishes the journal doesn't talk to the executive, who doesn't talk to the agent etc. Gramsci's notion was quite the opposite. He called it an educative notion of party: educating the non-intellectuals to the intellectuals, the activist to the non-activist, to create the conditions for them to come together. But I think it's a very, very difficult operation. I think that one has to resist the temptation to say 'why don't you scrap all that chatter and get to the practicalities' as much as one has to resist the opposite – 'why don't you not do anything for the next ten years until we've got the correct line'. Both of these are very powerful temptations at different moments of a movement's political development. Gramsci called them, exactly, the oscillation between optimism and pessimism. When there's a pessimistic moment everybody says: 'Back to the drawing board! Where are the theoreticians? Why haven't they been writing about this and telling us what to do?!' In a mood of optimism we say: 'We're about to take the bastards, who cares about the books!' There are always those different moments, those lows and highs, and one has to try to create a continuity that goes behind those changes. Don't take the edge off the activism, don't take the depth off the thinking, and allow some people to do both and those who can't or don't do both, to benefit from the fact that both are going on.

One of the worst things about new social movements is the way they use people up. One of the most profound mistakes is to imagine that the life cycle of the social movement is the same as the life cycle of the activist – to think 'because I'm dead tired, the movement must be at an end'. But one has to disassociate oneself from that. A movement has a longer life, it may be just that I'm worn out: 'I cannot go to another demonstration, but does that mean there's no role for me?' Or is it part of the movement to say 'Yes, OK there is something else you could do, you could contribute in another way'. I'm talking about what appear to be very mundane features about how movements manage their political life to remind you of the internal diversity of people's lives, different people's experiences, of different ages, which have to come together if a movement is to have any life beyond the immediate first surge. And to do that it does have to contain and draw on the best of a variety of different contributions.

TBJ To what extent are there critical points to be made about new politics? In some ways, what we have been doing so far is to use new social movements to pose critical points back to the left – implicitly putting the three of you in the position of almost 'answering' for the left – but to what extent does the left, or the New Left tradition, have something to critically reflect back onto the movements that are to an extent fragmented into different struggles?

DM One thing I find problematic at the moment is a kind of wilful ignorance of history, a rejection of the past and what people have gone through and fought for. It may be just that I'm getting old but I think there's more to it than that. 'History' is now all heritage in aspic. It's not seen as, certainly not valued as, a grounded process that people lived through and which might be learned from. The attitude may in part be a kind of reflection in popular consciousness and culture, and in the new social movements, of the more 'theoretical' rejection of any notion of historical progress. Maybe it's another element of the 'end of modernity' (if such it is) and its understanding of history. What is clear is that there seems to be a valuation of 'the new' just because it *is* new and a rejection of 'the old' in a similar knee-jerk reaction. We see it in the (supposedly new, young) politics surrounding the Labour leadership. And in part I find it tiresome because so much of what they say isn't in fact new, sometimes it even repeats old 'mistakes', and sometimes it could benefit from knowledge of what has previously been tried. Now from my experience and from what I learn from reading and talking to people, the new movements have some of these characteristics, though I have much more sympathy with their learning processes than with some of the New Labour newness. There are problems over forms of organisation, for instance, some of which seem to be very similar to experiences in the women's movement and in the more libertarian left of my day. But it also has to be said that there has been a massive effort, politically and in the media, to eradicate from popular consciousness some of our better moments (I think of the GLC, for instance).[6] And there *are* some meetings of the older forms of politics and the newer things. In 'Reclaim the Future' in September, for instance, DIY direct-action activists converged on Liverpool in support of the dockers. It seems to have generated some of the wonderful mixtures of recognition-of-connection on the one hand and surprise-at-the-differences on the other which went on during the miners' strike. But of course it got hardly any media attention, though *Red Pepper* covered it very well. So, yes, I think there should be more of a two-way conversation.

MR Let me put it this way: the first New Left was in its way very hopeful. This optimism was based on assumptions about the basic strength of social democracy in western capitalist society because of a possibly misplaced hope that communist systems were reformable (this was the late 1950s, remember). It believed that its old fashioned commitments were grounded in major agencies and institutions. Even though we were quite dissident in relation to those structures, and continued to be so, we felt that we were part of them, and that they had the potential power to make a difference. Indeed, they did.

Now, my problem with the new social movements is that I am not sure that they have ground for such hope. The question I want to pose, to people holding any of the specific sets of beliefs is: what do you think could possibly happen that would actually make a difference?

One way of putting it is to say that what you have here is a set of vigorous and life-changing forms of identity politics, both individual and collective, that make local differences to all the individuals who take part in them. But what can they do to affect the larger structures of power? One way of reading these new political formations is as themselves the product of a post-Fordist, differentiated system. They provide opportunities for differentiated activities of all kinds, including protest activities. But there is a risk these are never going to get to grips with, or even see clearly, what the main organising structures of society are. They may therefore amount to little more than political bubbles, even though sometimes quite large and visible ones. What theory is there about the articulation of different movements, and the structures to which they find themselves in opposition? There is a problem of finding a sufficient coherence in this variety of political forms and activities. These are questions one needs to ask. We should be honest about not necessarily having good enough answers at this point.

What I find most useful in trying to make sense of the new political situation is the idea of an 'incomplete democratic revolution' which has been put forward by Ulrich Beck in his book *Risk Society*, though it is not the aspect of his work which has been most taken up.[7] 'Incomplete democratic revolution' is the idea that here is a society which has created a kind of semi-democratic capitalism, a sort of sham-democracy which has gone only so far. For example, conceding trade union rights but not rights which extend to the dissemination of profit; a limited democracy within the scientific community which however excludes most people from informed access to the scientific debate; limited gains in regard to gender; and so on. Ulrich Beck claims that maybe this is a democratic revolution which is at a half-way stage. 'Industrial society' may be only half-way there and has the potential to continue. So around ideas of democracy and rights, which need much elaboration, one could produce a connected challenge to each of these centres of residual hierarchical power. For example, the monarchy and the governmental structures that still derive their top-down qualities from it; patriarchal authority in the family (Beck was writing in Germany); capital and so on. All the centres of semi-democratised power that survive remain in need of further challenge.

SH I would agree that the variation and diversity of political struggles and constituencies is really one of the places where the New Left began. It was certainly aware of its own origins in that kind of diversity. I do think it was the last attempt to harness all of those things, new and old, within the one framework. One piece of evidence of that is the *May Day Manifesto*.[8] The Manifesto is a very interesting document because, let me put it this way, all the elements of 1968 are in it but 1968 is not. It sort of misses it! If you look at the Manifesto, it is obviously talking about the widening of the political, it tries to talk about everything under the sun within the one common framework and these are somehow going to make a difference – of course they're going to make a difference, they're going to explode all over the world! But somehow when 1968 came, we had not foreseen anything like that as the form in which this diversity of things would explode. In coming into existence it exploded the frame.

MR It blew us away! [laughter]

SH It completely blew us away. We had taken up this advanced position and whoosh it came from behind and pushed us over. We looked immediately like tame old-fashioned stuff, although at the time it felt enormously bold to be saying all these issues really belonged to the one issue, and politics is everywhere, and then politics *was* everywhere! [laughter]

MR Students came along and said 'exams!, why should we do exams?' I'd only been a lecturer for two years! [laughter]

SH The question since then has been the question of linkages between these different movements. What could they be? How could you explain them politically? Around what wider political agenda or programme or set of demands, could you unify them or bring them together? How could you dovetail the constituencies so that they didn't feel like each was this identity attached to something else? Those linkages were only really created in people's personal lives in so far as they lived all of them, people carried around a lot of different hats and so within themselves they unified them! But they couldn't unify them in the sense of an organisation which built on them all, or a vision of society which would include them all, and so on.

It may be that some people in the new social movements today would say that this lingering desire for some formal articulation between the different movements is really a holdover of the old grand narrative, that we want to go back to the time when everything was in capital and labour, and this may be true, but I like to think about it in terms of effects. What does anyone who's involved in these things want to see as an outcome? They're talking about forms of social change which are so extensive or so deep, in the sense of digging into deep structures in society, that unless they can form alliances or linkages their hope of confronting structures one after another, in serial form, is simply not very realistic. So that is a question that one should ask, not because, as Mike said, we have the answers but because it just seems to be implicit in the politics. If you came to the end of any one of them, would that be enough? Would everybody say that's utopia? No they wouldn't, they'd go off and find another similar issue.

There are connections between different social movements, and what people have in their minds is not just fewer roads, or different forms of family relationship, etc. It still remains all of those things; and they don't think you can heave it into existence by one single revolutionary upsurge, but they do need the changes to have knock-on effects on one another. Feminism does think that if you made a change in the way men relate to women, you wouldn't have workplaces like you do and you wouldn't have families like you do. Each of those things is connected. We seem to feel there might be some way these connections can get political expression, conceptual expression, and also link people together to build a much bigger constituency. The forces you are trying to move are so embedded and full of resources, that unless you can get a bigger lever than just a couple of good demonstrations you are going to be blown away, and in a few months' or years' time people will have forgotten you. Connecting people and issues is really to prevent moving around the circle throwing off new problems, only to have the old ones come back on you.

That is one of the reasons why, in the forms of analysis that seem to be useful to a lot of people involved in social movements, curiously, the question of capital has less relevance than the question of power. I know power is a very abstract term – patriarchal power is very different from governmental power and very different from economic power – but 'power' is used as the way of naming the enemy, rather than capital (which isn't to say that there isn't capitalist power, capitalism is a form of power), 'power' is used as a way of naming, generally, exclusion from power, exclusion from the capacity to have access to power which could make a change or make a difference, exclusion from the dialogue which goes on which counts in how things turn out. All of those forms of exclusion have met in power, which is partly one of the reasons why Foucault is so important. It isn't necessarily that people believe every single word of Foucault's analysis, but he somehow names power in a very resonant way for its very generality and luminousness. This is somehow what will grip people, they do feel they are up against power, though they don't know exactly how or what its mechanisms, and the intricacies of its organisation, are. In some ways this is too general, on the other hand it's a useful way of thinking about why democracy – and why powerlessness or relative powerlessness – are common features of politics in a variety of movements.

NOTES

1. To contact *Soundings* for subscription or information write to *Soundings* c/o Lawrence and Wishart, 99a Wallis Road, London E9 5LN, UK.

2. Stuart Hall and Michael Rustin were interviewed together. Thanks to Steve Cowden for transcribing this interview. Doreen Massey added her comments to a transcript of that interview, which was then circulated to all participants for comment. The interviewers were Tim Jordan, co-editor of *Storming the Millennium*, and Tessa Bird, activist with the anti-roads organisation *Reclaim the Streets*.

3. The *Marxism Today* and *New Times* analysis is collected in S. Hall and M. Jacques (eds), *New Times: the changing face of politics in the 1990s*, Lawrence and Wishart, London 1989. *Marxism Today* was a monthly magazine in which this analysis was first developed.

4. Tessa asked this question specifically based on her experience as a current activist.

5. Reference is being made here to protests in a number of ports in the UK, particularly Brightlingsea, over the export of calves for rearing as veal calves. The protests attracted a range of constituencies, in particular what appeared to be a clearly conservative, middle-class constituency.

6. GLC stands for Greater London Council, the left-leaning authority for London that was abolished by the British Conservative Government in the mid-1980s.

7. U. Beck, *Risk Society*, Polity, Cambridge 1992.

8. R.Williams (ed), *May Day Manifesto 1968*, Penguin, Harmondsworth 1968.

INDEX